THE NEW
GLUCOSE
revolution

Jennie Brand-Miller is Professor of Human Nutrition in the Human Nutrition Unit, School of Molecular and Microbial Biosciences at the University of Sydney, and President of the Nutrition Society of Australia. She graduated BSc (1975) and PhD (1979) from the Department of Food Science and Technology at the University of New South Wales. She has taught postgraduate students of nutrition and dietetics at the University of Sydney for over 24 years and currently leads a team of 12 research scientists (including five PhD students) whose interests focus on all aspects of carbohydrates—diet and diabetes, the glycemic index of foods, insulin resistance, lactose intolerance, and oligosaccharides in infant nutrition. She holds a special interest in evolutionary nutrition and the diet of Australian Aborigines and has published 16 books and 140 journal articles.

Kaye Foster-Powell is an accredited practising dietitian with extensive experience in diabetes management. A graduate of the University of Sydney (B. Sc., 1987, Master of Nutrition & Dietetics, 1994), she has conducted research into the glycemic index of foods and its practical applications over the last 15 years. Currently she is a dietitian with Wentworth Area Diabetes Services in New South Wales and provides consultancy on all aspects of the glycemic index.

Associate Professor Stephen Colagiuri is the Director of the Diabetes Centre and Head of the Department of Endocrinology, Metabolism and Diabetes at the Prince of Wales Hospital in Randwick, New South Wales. He graduated from the University of Sydney in 1970 and received his Fellowship of the Royal Australasian College of Physicians in 1977. He has a conjoint academic appointment at the University of New South Wales. He has over 100 scientific papers to his name, many concerned with the importance of carbohydrate in the diet of people with diabetes.

Lisa Lintner graduated with a certificate of Home Economics in 1974, a Diploma of Advance Cordon Bleu in 1977 and a Diploma of Teaching in 1979. She then lectured for ten years with the School of Hospitality and Catering at East Sydney and North Sydney TAFE colleges. Later, she published her cookbook, *Vegetables—A Taste of the Country*, and more recently, she created the recipes for *The New Glucose Revolution Life Plan*. Writing has complemented her work with the Lisa Lintner Cooking School on Sydney's northern beaches, showcasing the best of Australian produce, with a strong emphasis on low GI menus.

THE GLYCEMIC INDEX
SOLUTION FOR
OPTIMUM HEALTH

THE NEW
GLUCOSE
revolution

Prof Jennie Brand–Miller
Kaye Foster-Powell
Assoc Prof Stephen Colagiuri

Recipes by Kaye Foster-Powell
and Lisa Lintner

HODDER

A Hodder Book

First published in Australia and New Zealand in 1996 as *The GI Factor*
by Hodder Headline Australia Pty Ltd
(A member of the Hodder Headline Group)
Level 22, 201 Kent Street, Sydney NSW 2000
Website: www.hha.com.au

Reprinted 1996 (three times), 1997 (twice), 1998

Revised edition published in 1998
Reprinted 1998, 1999 (four times), 2000 (three times),
2001 (five times), 2002 (twice)

This third edition published as *The New Glucose Revolution* in 2002

Reprinted 2002 (twice), 2003 (twice)

**National Library of Australia
Cataloguing-in-Publication data**

Brand-Miller, Jennie
  The new glucose revolution : the glycemic index solution
  for optimum health.

  3rd ed.
  Bibliography.
  Includes index.
  ISBN 0 7336 1500 7.

  1. Dietetics. 2. Glycemic index. 3. Carbohydrates. 4.
  Food - Carbohydrate content. 5. Low-carbohydrate diet
  Recipes. I. Lintner, Lisa, 1949- . II. Colagiuri, Stephen.
  III. Foster-Powell, Kaye. IV. Title.

613.283

Cover and internal design by Greendot Design
Cover image © Getty Images
Text design and typesetting by Bookhouse, Sydney
Printed in Australia by Griffin Press, Adelaide

ACKNOWLEDGEMENTS

Many people have contributed to *The New Glucose Revolution* and we are grateful to them all. Back in 1995, when the first edition of the book (then called *The GI Factor*) was conceived, it was Catherine Saxelby who got us off to a good start. Then Philippa Sandall, our editor at Hodder Headline and now our literary agent, took over and ensured that our style and content were appropriate to our readers, and in many other ways contributed to the success of all the books. For this edition, we have been expertly assisted by the meticulous Deonie Fiford at Hodder and by Lisa Lintner, food consultant, who created and tested many of the recipes. Dr Susanna Holt is largely responsible for the comprehensive GI tables at the back of the book and we thank her and all the students and volunteers who undertake GI testing at the Human Nutrition Unit at the University of Sydney. We are indebted to those who have supported the GI approach and recommended our books, particularly Diabetes Australia and the Juvenile Diabetes Research Foundation. Many dietitians, doctors and readers have given us feedback and played a large role in our success, some of whom deserve special mention: Shirley Crossman; Martina Chippendall; Helen O'Connor; Heather Gilbertson; Alan Barclay; Rudi Bartl; Kate Marsh; Toni Irwin; Rick Mendosa; Ted Arnold; Warren Kidson; Bob Moses; Ian Caterson; and Stewart Truswell. Lastly, we thank our long-suffering partners, John Miller, Jonathan Powell and Ruth Colagiuri, respectively, for all those nights and weekends when we were otherwise occupied.

CONTENTS

Part IV – THE GI TABLES

INTRODUCTION

The New Glucose Revolution is for everybody! People with diabetes, heart disease, the metabolic syndrome (Syndrome X) or an interest in weight control will gain most from putting *The New Glucose Revolution* approach into practice. But it's also for those who want to do the best they can to *prevent* those problems in the first place, and improve their overall health.

In 1996 we wrote *The G.I. Factor*, the first book about the glycemic index (which we abbreviate as GI), the health breakthrough that revolutionised the way people approach their diet. Six years later *The G.I. Factor, G.I. Plus* and a series of pocket guides are worldwide bestsellers with American, British and many other foreign editions.

In those intervening years, there has been a lot of new research on the GI, and we've received thousands of letters and useful feedback from readers all around the globe. In response we've put together *The New Glucose Revolution*, the most up-to-date book about the GI.

The glycemic index (GI) is a physiologically based measure of carbohydrate *quality*—a comparison of carbohydrates (gram for gram) based on their immediate effect on blood glucose levels.

- Carbohydrates that break down quickly during digestion have **high GI** values. Their blood glucose response is fast and high.
- Carbohydrates which break down slowly, releasing glucose gradually into the blood stream, have a **low GI.**

The GI is simply a measure of carbohydrate quality—the extent to which the carbohydrates in different foods will raise blood glucose levels. A knowledge and appreciation of the GI will help you choose the right amount of carbohydrate and the right sort of carbohydrate for your health and wellbeing. Once thought to be of relevance only to people with diabetes, the GI is now considered a useful way for *everybody* to optimise their health.

Most people have some notion of how blood 'sugars' (in truth, glucose) rise and fall throughout the day. However, much of the information currently in print about food and blood glucose is wrong. *The New Glucose Revolution* tells you the true story about the connection between carbohydrate and blood glucose.

Our research on the glycemic index (GI) began in the 1980s when

- The blood glucose response to a meal is primarily determined by its carbohydrate content.
- Both the quantity and quality of carbohydrate in the food influence the rise in blood glucose.
- Meals containing the same amount of carbohydrate can produce either high or low effects on blood glucose, depending on the type (or quality) of carbohydrate. In other words, its GI.

health authorities all over the world began to stress the importance of high carbohydrate diets. Until then dietary fat had grabbed all the public and scientific attention (and to some extent this is still true). But low fat diets are by their very nature *automatically* high in carbohydrate. Nutrition scientists started asking questions—are all carbohydrates the same, are all starches good for health, are all sugars bad? In particular, they began studies on the effects of carbohydrates on blood glucose levels. They wanted to know which carbohydrate foods were associated with the least fluctuation in blood glucose levels and the best overall health, including reduced risk of diabetes and heart disease.

An overwhelming amount of research on the glycemic index over the past 20 years shows that different carbohydrate foods have dramatically different effects on blood glucose levels. These differences have important implications. We have played a significant role in validating and testing the glycemic index in the context of diabetes management, weight and appetite control, as well as sport. We know from our own experience and letters from our readers that understanding the GI of foods makes an enormous difference to people's lives. For some it means a new lease of life.

Scientists around the world, including our laboratory, have now tested the GI of hundreds of foods, both singly and in mixed meals (meals that consist of a number of foods), and carried out long-term studies on its potential to improve diabetes control. Studies in the US have shown that consuming low GI foods is associated with a lower risk of both type 2 diabetes and coronary heart disease.

It is now obvious, not only to us, but to many expert committees and health authorities around the world, that the GI of foods has implications for *everybody*. It is indeed a 'Glucose Revolution' in that it has changed forever the way we think about carbohydrates.

The New Glucose Revolution gives people with diabetes a new lease of life, freeing them from hard-to-follow, misguided and often counterproductive dietary restrictions. Many people with diabetes find

THE GLUCOSE REVOLUTION HELPS PEOPLE:

- with type 1 (juvenile onset) diabetes
- with type 2 (adult onset) diabetes
- with gestational diabetes (diabetes during pregnancy)
- who are overweight
- who have a normal weight but too much fat around the middle (abdominal overweight)
- whose blood glucose levels are higher than desirable
- who have been told they have 'impaired glucose tolerance' or a 'touch of diabetes'
- with high levels of triglycerides and low levels of HDL-cholesterol
- with Syndrome X
- who suffer polycystic ovarian syndrome
- who want to prevent all of the above and live a healthier life!

In all these conditions, high blood glucose levels are a key feature. High blood glucose levels are undesirable and have both short and long-term adverse effects.

that, despite doing all the right things, their blood glucose levels remain too high. *The New Glucose Revolution* provides the knowledge and know-how to choose the right kind of carbohydrate for optimum blood glucose control.

The GI is part of the solution to high blood glucose.

We also provide advice on choosing the best carbohydrates for weight reduction, the ones that give you control over hunger pangs, those that minimise insulin levels and help you burn fat. By preventing weight gain as we age, we give our body the best chance of avoiding diseases such as diabetes and heart disease. In this connection, we discuss high protein diets and Mediterranean diets. We provide a clear scientific rationale for choosing between all the different types of diets that are described in the popular press.

The New Glucose Revolution also helps answer your questions about diet in pregnancy and childhood, in specific diseases such as polycystic ovarian syndrome (a form of infertility closely linked to insulin resistance) and coeliac disease.

We argue more strongly than ever that the glycemic index is for *everybody, every day, every meal*. The scientific evidence that the GI is important for health is now beyond dispute and goes much further than we ever imagined ourselves.

We give you all the details on the glucose revolution, plus new recipes, more meal plans and information on the glycemic load which helps you calculate the amount *and* type of carbohydrate you are consuming. We also include all the very latest findings including:

- recent studies on the GI
- information on the glycemic load
- new studies on heart disease and blood glucose levels
- the latest studies on the GI and diabetes, including type 1 diabetes in children
- recent studies on the GI and weight reduction
- new studies on the GI and cancer
- the latest on the GI and polycystic ovarian disease, weight gain in pregnancy and gestational diabetes
- the lowdown on high protein diets
- new GI figures for recently tested foods, including high protein bars, gluten-free foods, convenience meals, and many more

Lastly, we've included some real-life stories of how much the GI has changed the lives of people who have adopted the low GI approach.

BLOOD SUGAR OR BLOOD GLUCOSE?

Blood sugar and blood glucose mean the same thing, although the latter is technically more correct. We use the term blood glucose in this book as this is the term recognised and used by Diabetes Australia in their 'Be Well, Know Your BGL' campaign. 'Glycemic' refers to blood glucose.

How you can use this book

We've arranged the chapters to make it easy for those who want to get straight to the point—exactly what you need to do to adopt a low GI approach to eating. We recommend you read the introductory chapters as they will give you a complete overview and scientific update on the carbohydrate story. The facts we reveal about carbohydrate will surprise many people—facts that can make life a lot easier.

Part I contains the most recent information about what is considered a balanced diet and why—information based on scientific research, clinical trials and large scale studies in whole populations. It stresses what's wrong with today's diet and the proven value of diets high in fruit and vegetables. In this section, we explain the importance of being 'choosy' about the types of carbohydrates *and* fats you eat, no matter what the proportions of protein, fat or carbohydrate. Part I discusses high protein diets and new concepts such as glycemic load and answers some of the most commonly asked questions about the GI.

Part II is your guide to low GI eating. We show you how you can include more of the right sort of carbohydrate in your diet, give hints for meal preparation, and practical tips and food combinations to help you make the GI work for you throughout the day. This section includes fifty imaginative and delicious recipes and meal ideas for breakfast, lunch, dinner and in-between snacks along with their GI rating and nutritional analysis.

In Part III, there are separate chapters for specific applications of the GI, including its use for weight control, type 1 diabetes, type 2 diabetes, heart disease and the metabolic syndrome (Syndrome X), pregnancy and gestational diabetes, children, and sports performance.

If it's just the GI values you are after, you'll find them in the updated and much improved tables in Part IV. We've grouped them according to types of food (breads, fruits, etc) and included not only the GI and amount of carbohydrate per serve, we've also added their glycemic load per serve. We've added the foods that were often queried—meat, fish, cheese, broccoli, avocadoes etc—even though they don't contain carbohydrate and their glycemic load is zero. This is the most comprehensive list of GI values for different foods *ever* published. Finally there's a complete list of scientific references on pages 340 to 343 to back up all we say.

With *The New Glucose Revolution* you will discover that a new, healthier way of eating is both easy and delicious.

Professor Jennie Brand-Miller
Kaye Foster-Powell
Associate Professor Stephen Colagiuri
Sydney 2002

Dispelling some myths about food

This book dispels many myths about food and carbohydrates. We now know from scientific research that the following popular beliefs about food and carbohydrate are not true.

MYTH 1 **Starchy foods like bread and pasta are fattening.**

FACT Most starchy foods are bulky and rich in carbohydrate. They fill you up and stave off hunger pangs—they are among the best foods you can eat to help you lose weight.

MYTH 2 **Sugar is the worst thing for people with diabetes.**

FACT Sugar and sugary foods in normal serves have no greater effect on blood glucose levels than many starchy foods. Saturated fat is of greater concern for people with diabetes.

MYTH 3 **Sugar causes diabetes.**

FACT Sugar has no unique role in causing diabetes. Foods that produce high blood glucose levels may increase the risk of diabetes, but sugar has a more moderate effect than most starches.

MYTH 4 **All starches are slowly digested in the intestine.**

FACT Some starch, like that in potatoes, is digested in a flash, causing a greater rise in blood glucose than many sugar-containing foods.

MYTH 5 **Hunger pangs are inevitable if you want to lose weight.**

FACT High carbohydrate foods, especially those with a low GI (e.g. rolled oats and pasta), will sustain the feeling of fullness almost to the next meal.

MYTH 6 Foods high in fat are more filling.

FACT   Studies show that high fat foods are among the least fill-
        ing. It is extremely easy to 'passively overconsume' foods
        like potato chips and crisps.

MYTH 7 Sugar is fattening.

FACT   Sugar has no special fattening properties. It is no more likely
        to be turned into fat than any other carbohydrate. Sugar
        is often present in foods high in energy and fat (e.g. cakes
        and biscuits), but it's the total energy (kilojoules) rather than
        the sugar in those energy dense foods that may contribute
        to new stores of body fat.

MYTH 8 Starches are best for optimum sports performance.

FACT   In many instances starchy foods (e.g. potatoes) are too
        bulky to eat in the quantities needed for active sports
        people. Sugars can help increase carbohydrate intake.

MYTH 9 Diets high in sugar are less nutritious.

FACT   Studies have shown that diets high in sugar (from a range
        of sources including dairy food and fruit) often have higher
        levels of micronutrients such as calcium, riboflavin and vit-
        amin C than low sugar diets.

MYTH 10 Sugar goes hand in hand with dietary fat.

FACT   The reality is that high sugar diets are usually low in fat and
        vice versa. Most sources of fat in the diet are not sweet-
        ened (e.g. potato chips) and most sources of sugar contain
        no fat (e.g. soft drinks). Yes, there are many foods high in
        both fat and sugar (chocolate, ice-cream, cakes, biscuits) but
        there are equally many that are delicious combinations of
        starch and fat (potato chips, french fries, savoury biscuits).

PART I

What is the GI?

All the latest research, new concepts and answers to your FAQs about the GI

CHAPTER 1

WHAT'S WRONG WITH TODAY'S DIET?

Stone Age diets

During the Palaeolithic period, humans were hunter-gatherers, consuming the animals and plants that were part of their natural environment. How do we know this? Well, we left behind the remnants of our meals, the bones of animals, the shells of shellfish, the tools used to hunt and cut meat and extract the bone marrow. And we were fussy about which part of the animal we ate. We preferred the hind legs of the largest animals and the females over the males because they contained more fat and were therefore juicier and more flavoursome. We also enjoyed the organ meats—the liver, kidneys, brains—foods that are extremely rich sources of nutrients.

It is now clear that as humans evolved, they became more and more carnivorous, eating more animal food and less plant food. Indeed, the latest studies of modern hunter-gatherers who lived

100–200 years ago, showed they obtained about two-thirds of their energy intake from animal foods (including fish and shellfish) and only one-third from plant foods. Some anthropologists believe hunting played a major role in allowing humans to evolve a large brain and high intelligence. Controversially, some believe we were responsible for the extinction of many of the giant animals that roamed the earth for thousands of years.

Since we wrote *The G.I. Factor*, there have been new studies of the nutrient composition of hunter-gatherer diets. It now appears that humans ate more protein and less carbohydrate than we do now. Their fat intake was roughly the same as now, but the type of fat was vastly different. Carbohydrate intakes were lower because the main plant foods were fruit and vegetables, rather than cereals. Wheat, rice and other cereal grains were largely absent until after the agricultural revolution, beginning some 10 000 years ago. These findings have implications for current dietary recommendations. It doesn't mean that we all need to eat large amounts of meat to be healthy, but it does imply that the type and amount of protein, carbohydrate and fat need to be carefully reconsidered.

The agricultural revolution

The agricultural revolution dramatically changed our diet. For the first time, we started eating large amounts of carbohydrate in the form of wholegrain cereals like wheat, rye, barley, oats, corn and rice. Legumes (beans), starchy roots and tubers, and fruits and berries also contributed to the high carbohydrate intake. Back then, food preparation was a simple process: grinding food between stones and cooking it over the heat of an open fire. The result was that all the carbohydrates in food were digested and absorbed slowly and the blood glucose rise was gradual and relatively small.

This diet was ideal because it provided slow-release energy that helped to delay hunger pangs and provided fuel for working muscles long after the meal was eaten. It was also easy on the insulin-producing cells in the pancreas.

As time passed, the flours were ground more and more finely and the bran was separated completely from the white flour. With the advent of high-speed roller mills in the nineteenth century, it was possible to produce white flour so fine that it resembled talcum powder in appearance and texture. These fine white flours have always been highly prized because they make soft bread and delicious, airy cakes and pastries.

As incomes grew, the barley and oats, legumes and beans commonly eaten by our ancestors were cast aside and fatty meat consumption increased. As a consequence, the composition of the average diet changed again: we began to eat more saturated fat, less fibre and more easily digested carbohydrates. Something we didn't expect happened too. The blood glucose rise after a meal was higher and more prolonged, stimulating the pancreas to produce more insulin (see box).

So, not only did we have higher blood glucose levels after a meal, we had higher insulin responses as well. Insulin is a hormone that is needed for carbohydrate metabolism; but it has a profound effect on

THE PANCREAS PRODUCES INSULIN

The pancreas is a vital organ near the stomach. Its job is to produce the hormone insulin. Carbohydrate stimulates the secretion of insulin more than any other component of food. The slow absorption of the carbohydrate in our food means that the pancreas doesn't have to work so hard and produces less insulin. If the pancreas is overstimulated over a long period of time, it may become 'exhausted' and type 2 diabetes develops in genetically susceptible individuals. Even without diabetes, high insulin levels are undesirable because they increase the risk of heart disease.

FOOD PROVIDES MORE THAN JUST NUTRIENTS

Food is part of our culture and way of life. Our food choices are determined by many factors ranging from religious beliefs to the deliciously sensual role that food plays in our lives. For babies, food has a comforting role that goes well beyond meeting the immediate physical need. For adults, food reflects status—we prepare special meals for special occasions and for special guests to show respect or friendship.

It is no wonder that with so many factors influencing our food choices, we tend to overlook the very basic role food plays in the nourishment and growth of our bodies. With the busy lives many of us lead it's easy to see food simply as a solution to overcoming hunger. In other circumstances, we focus on the social aspects of food and eat too much.

the development of many diseases. Medical experts now believe that high glucose and insulin levels are one of the key factors responsible for heart disease and hypertension. Insulin influences the way we metabolise foods, determining whether we burn fat or carbohydrate to meet our energy needs and ultimately determining whether we store fat in our body.

Thus one of the most important ways in which our diet differs from that of our ancestors is the speed of carbohydrate digestion and the resulting effect on blood glucose and insulin levels. Traditional diets all around the world contained slowly digested and absorbed carbohydrate—foods that we now know have a low GI. In contrast, modern diets with their quickly digested carbohydrates are based on foods with a high GI.

What's wrong with modern diets?

Today's Western diet is the product of industrialisation based on many inventions—pasteurisation, sterilisation, refrigeration, freezing, roller drying, spray drying, just to name a few. In the cereal foods world, there's high-speed roller milling, high temperature and high pressure extrusion, puffing guns, short-time fermentation—you name it, they've invented it.

The benefits are many. We have a plentiful, relatively cheap, palatable (some would say too palatable) and reasonably safe food supply. Gone are the days of monotonous fare, gaps in the food supply, weevil-infested and adulterated food. Long gone are widespread vitamin deficiencies such as scurvy and pellagra. Today's food manufacturers work hard to bring us irresistible and safe products that meet the demands of both gourmands and health conscious consumers.

Many of the new foods are still based on our staple cereals—wheat, maize, oats—but the original grain has been ground down to produce fine flours with small particle size that produces fine quality breads, cakes, biscuits, breakfast cereals and snack foods. Cereal chemists and bakers know that the finest particle size flour produces the most palatable and shelf-stable end product.

Unfortunately this striving for excellence in one area has resulted in unforeseen problems in another. Our bodies quickly digest and absorb today's staple carbohydrate foods, including ordinary bread. The resulting effect on blood glucose levels has created a problem of epidemic proportions.

All about fat

One of the most undesirable aspects of the modern diet is the *type* of fat we eat. Food manufacturers, bakers and chefs know we love to eat fat. We love its creaminess and mouth feel and find it easy to consume in excess. It makes our meat more tender, our vegetables and salads more palatable and our sweet foods even more desirable. We prefer potatoes as French fries or potato chips, our fish battered and fried and our pastas in rich creamy sauces.

With a wave of the fat wand, bland high carbohydrate foods like rice and oats are magically transformed into highly palatable, kilojoule-laden foods such as fried rice and toasted muesli. In fact, when you analyse it, much of our diet today is an undesirable but delicious combination of fat and quickly digested carbohydrate.

It's not just the amount of fat we eat, but the *type* of fat that can make us unhealthy. The problem is that most of the fat we now eat comes in the form of saturated fat.

Saturated fat is hard and tends to clog up our arteries, unlike the unsaturated oils that are liquid at room temperature. The fats used for baking and frying are usually saturated fats. The fat in *fatty* meats and dairy products is saturated fat. But the fat in lean meat, fish, olive oil, canola oil and other seeds like safflower and sunflower is unsaturated.

Hunter-gatherers, even though they ate a large amount of animal fat, did not eat vast quantities of saturated fat. This is because the fat of wild animals, including the fat in the brain and other organs, has much higher proportions of unsaturated fat.

In Australia and New Zealand we are lucky that our cattle and sheep are still mainly pasture-fed, rather than grain-fed, and are closer in composition to wild meat. As long as we remove the selvedge fat (most people do), our meat has a good ratio of unsaturated to saturated fat.

In our desire to reduce saturated fat, health authorities lumped all fats together as bad—the message 'reduce fat' was easier than 'reduce saturated fat'; but in many ways, we can see that this simplified message was counter-productive. People avoided even the most essential of fats, the highly polyunsaturated, long chain fats, that are fundamental to human health. Secondly, we avoided fat because of its high energy content and propensity to be overeaten, only to replace it with large quantities of fast-release carbohydrates that have the same properties. We fooled ourselves into thinking that *any* low fat diet, especially one formulated with the help of a sophisticated food industry, was automatically a healthy diet. *But it's not.*

In Part II of this book, we guide you to the best sources of carbohydrate for your health and wellbeing.

What is a balanced diet?

It makes sense to balance our food intake with the rate our bodies use it. This way, we maintain a steady weight. These days, however, this balance is difficult to achieve. It is very easy to overeat. Refined foods, convenience foods and fast foods frequently lack fibre and conceal fat so that even before we feel full, we have overdosed on kilojoules. It is even easier not to exercise. It takes longer to walk somewhere than it does to drive (except, perhaps, in peak hour). With intake exceeding output on a regular basis, the result is weight gain.

We need to adapt our lifestyle to our kilojoule-laden diet and fewer physical demands. Don't make the mistake of thinking that the best option is to just 'diet' most of the time—i.e. reduce food intake to a low level which matches a low level of energy expenditure. That's a recipe for failure. It's become very important to find ways of increasing our energy output, to catch bursts of physical activity wherever we can, to increase our energy needs. It means using the stairs instead of the lift, taking a 10-minute walk at lunch time, coasting on a treadmill while you watch the news, reading on the exercise bike, making more effort in the garden, walking to the shops, parking 200 metres from the office, or taking the dog for a walk each night. Whatever suits you, do it. Even housework burns kilojoules. All these seemingly small bursts of activity accumulate to increase our kilojoule output. You don't have to take exercise seriously, just regularly.

While you work on increasing your kilojoule output, *The New Glucose Revolution* can help you select the best foods to balance input and output. But what's a balanced diet, you ask? Is there just one healthy diet that all of us should be following, with a set proportion of fat, carbohydrate and protein? In other words, does one size fit all? To be honest, we don't know, but it's highly likely that we can be flexible. After all, there were many different hunter-gatherer diets, some very high in protein and some very high in carbohydrate or fat. Nutritionists are beginning to appreciate that a healthy diet comes in many different forms—traditional Mediterranean, Asian, Eskimo, Australian Aboriginal diets were all commensurate with good health, even though they differed greatly in terms of proportions of fat, protein and carbohydrate.

But there are two fundamental principles in *all* the traditional healthy diets—any carbohydrates were slow-release and any fat was relatively unsaturated (even if fat intake was high). So, our first message is to choose the type of diet that suits your lifestyle, cultural and ethnic origins best. This is the one you are most likely to stick to lifelong. But there are important principles to follow in all cases (see box: Six dietary guidelines).

Six dietary guidelines

1 Eat seven or more servings of fruit and vegetables every day
2 Eat wholegrain breads and cereals with a low glycemic index
3 Eat more pulses—beans, peas and lentils—and use nuts more frequently
4 Eat more fish and seafoods
5 Eat lean meats and low fat dairy foods
6 Use high omega-3 and monounsaturated oils such as olive oil and canola oil

The following chapters tell you how you can eat a balanced and healthy diet which is tailored for you. No diet will work long term if it eliminates your favourite foods, whether these are bread or potatoes, ice-cream or pasta. *The New Glucose Revolution* goes a *huge* step further than most nutrition books because the GI of carbohydrates plays such an important, but still underrecognised role, in determining health and wellbeing.

A balanced diet can still include your favourite high GI foods

CHAPTER 2

WHY WE NEED CARBOHYDRATE

Nature's primary fuel

Did you know that carbohydrate is the most widely consumed substance in the world after water? In fact, carbohydrates hold a special place in human nutrition. Glucose, the simplest carbohydrate, is *essential* fuel for the brain, red blood cells and growing foetus, and the main source of energy for the muscles during strenuous exercise. Carbohydrate is a vital energy source and you can't afford to leave it out. Carbohydrates, however, were not created equal—you must choose the right kind of carbohydrate for your lifestyle.

Our bodies run on fuel, just like a car runs on petrol. The fuels our bodies burn are derived from a mixture of the protein, fat, carbohydrate and alcohol that we consume. Every day we need to top up our fuel tanks with the right amount and the right kind of fuel for

What is carbohydrate?

Carbohydrate is a part of food. Starch is a carbohydrate, so too are sugars and certain types of fibre. Starches and sugars are nature's reserves created by energy from the sun, carbon dioxide and water. The building block of starch is glucose.

The simplest form of carbohydrate is a single sugar molecule called a **monosaccharide** (**mono** meaning one, **saccharide** meaning sweet). Glucose is a monosaccharide that occurs in food (as glucose itself and as the building block of starch) and is the most common source of fuel for the cells of the human body.

If two monosaccharides are joined together, the result is a **di-saccharide** (**di** meaning two). Sucrose, or common table sugar, is a disaccharide, as is lactose, the sugar in milk.

As the number of monosaccharides in the chain increases, the carbohydrate becomes less sweet. Maltodextrins are **oligosaccharides** (**oligo** meaning a few) that are five or six glucose residues long and commonly used as a food ingredient. They taste only faintly sweet.

Starches are long chains of sugar molecules joined together like the beads in a string of pearls. They are called **polysaccharides** (**poly** meaning many). Starches are not sweet to taste.

Dietary fibres are large carbohydrate molecules containing many different sorts of monosaccharides. They are different from starches and sugars in that they are not broken down by human digestive enzymes. Fibre reaches the large intestine without change. Once there, bacteria begin to ferment and break down the fibres.

Different fibres have different physical and chemical properties. Soluble fibres are those that can be dissolved in water. Some soluble fibres are very viscous when in solution and therefore slow the speed of digestion. On the other hand, many fibres, including cellulose, are not soluble in water and do not directly affect the speed of digestion.

Sugars found in food

Monosaccharides (single sugar molecules)	Disaccharides (two single sugar molecules)
glucose	maltose = glucose + glucose
fructose	sucrose = glucose + fructose
galactose	lactose = glucose + galactose

health, energy and wellbeing. The actual proportions in our fuel mix will vary from hour to hour and are determined to a large extent by the last meal we ate.

There is a fuel 'hierarchy', that is, an order of priority for burning the fuels in food. Alcohol is first off the rank because our bodies have no place to store unused alcohol. Protein comes second, followed by carbohydrate, while fat comes off last. In practice, the fuel mix is usually a combination of carbohydrate and fat in varying proportions. After meals the mix is predominantly carbohydrate and between meals it is mainly fat.

Our ability to burn all the fat we eat is vitally important to weight control. If fat burning is inhibited, fat stores gradually accumulate. The relative proportions of fat to carbohydrate in the fuel mix are therefore critical and are dictated *by the prevailing levels of insulin* in our blood. If insulin levels are low, as they are when we wake up in the morning, then the fuel mix is mainly fat. If our insulin levels are high, as they are when we consume a high carbohydrate meal, then the fuel mix we burn is mainly carbohydrate. But if insulin is always high, as in insulin resistant and overweight people, then the cells are constantly forced to burn carbohydrate and have trouble burning the fat we eat and using it as a source of fuel. When this happens, fat stores mount up. Scientists now believe that subtle abnormalities in the ability to burn fat are behind most states of overweight and obesity.

Sources of carbohydrate

Carbohydrate is the starchy part of foods like rice, bread, potatoes and pasta. It is also the essential ingredient that makes foods taste sweet: the sugars in fruit and honey are carbohydrates, as are the refined sugars in soft drinks and confectionery.

Carbohydrate mainly comes from plant foods, such as cereal grains, fruits, vegetables and legumes (peas and beans). Milk products also contain carbohydrate in the form of milk sugar or lactose. Lactose is the first carbohydrate we encounter as infants and human milk lactose is higher than any other mammal milk. It accounts for almost half the energy available to the infant. Some foods contain a large amount of carbohydrate (such as cereals, potatoes and legumes) while other foods are very dilute sources such as carrots, broccoli and salad vegetables.

Foods that are high in carbohydrate include:

Cereal grains including rice, wheat, oats, barley, rye and anything made from them (bread, pasta, noodles, flour, breakfast cereal).

Fruits such as apples, bananas, grapes, peaches, melons.

Vegetables such as potatoes, yams, sweet corn, taro and sweet potato.

Legumes including baked beans, lentils, kidney beans and chickpeas.

Dairy products such as yoghurt and ice-cream.

Sources of carbohydrate

Percentage of carbohydrate (grams per 100 grams of food) in food as eaten

apple	12%	milk	5%	split peas	45%
baked beans	11%	oats	61%	sugar	100%
banana	21%	orange	8%	sultanas	75%
barley	61%	pasta	70%	sweet corn	16%
bread	47%	peas	8%	sweet potato	17%
cornflakes	85%	pear	12%	tapioca	85%
flour	73%	plum	6%	water cracker	71%
grapes	15%	potato	15%	wheat biscuit	62%
ice-cream	22%	rice	79%		

Digestion of carbohydrates

To make use of the sugars and starches in foods, our bodies first have to break them down into a form that we can absorb and which our cells can use. This process is called digestion.

Digestion starts in the mouth where amylase, the starch-digesting enzyme in saliva, is incorporated into our food as we chew. Amylase chops up long chain, starch molecules into short chain molecules such as maltose and maltodextrins. Its activity is halted by the acids secreted into the stomach and most digestion continues only when the carbohydrate leaves the stomach and reaches the small intestine.

The rate at which food enters the small intestine from the stomach is called the rate of stomach (gastric) emptying. Some food components—such as viscous fibre, acidity and highly osmotic solutions—help to slow down stomach emptying and therefore the overall speed of carbohydrate digestion.

In the small intestine, starch digestion continues. Huge amounts of amylase are secreted in pancreatic juice into the small intestine, so much so that the biochemists call it amylase 'overkill'. The speed of digestion now depends on the nature of the starch itself—how resistant it is in a physical and chemical sense to being attacked by enzymes. Many starches in food are rapidly digested while others are more resistant and the process is slower.

Other food factors may influence the speed of digestion. If the mixture of food and enzymes is highly viscous, owing to the presence of viscous fibre, mixing slows down and the enzymes and starch take longer to make contact. The products of starch digestion will also take longer to move towards the wall of the intestine where the last steps in digestion take place. At the intestinal wall, the short chain starch products, together with the sugars in foods, are broken down by specific enzymes. The monosaccharides that finally result from starch and sugar digestion include glucose, fructose and galactose. They are absorbed from the small intestine into the blood stream where they are available as a source of energy to the cells.

Brain food

Except during starvation, carbohydrate is the only source of fuel which our brains can use. The brain is the most energy demanding of all the organs in our body—responsible for over half our obligatory energy requirements. Unlike muscle cells, that can burn either fat or carbohydrate, the brain does not have the metabolic machinery to burn fat. If you fast for 24 hours or decide to skip the carbohydrate in foods, the brain relies initially on small stores of carbohydrate in the liver, but within hours these are depleted and the liver begins synthesising glucose from non-carbohydrate sources (including your muscle tissue!). It has only a limited ability to do this and it's now clear that any shortfall in glucose availability has consequences for brain function.

The recent medical literature shows that intellectual performance is improved following the intake of a glucose load or carbohydrate-rich food. Demanding mental tasks are most improved, while easy tasks are not affected. Furthermore, blood glucose levels decline more during a period of intense cognitive processing. The tests included various measures of 'intelligence' including word recall, maze learning, arithmetic, short-term memory, rapid information processing and reasoning. The improved mental ability following a carbohydrate meal was demonstrated in all types of people—young people, university students, people with diabetes, healthy elderly people and those with Alzheimer's disease. These new studies give us all the more reason to avoid a low carbohydrate intake.

At all times, our bodies need to maintain a minimum threshold level of glucose in the blood to serve the brain and central nervous system. If for some reason glucose levels fall below this threshold (a state called 'hypoglycemia' that can occur in people who take insulin), the consequences are severe, including trembling, dizziness, nausea, incoherent rambling speech and lack of coordination. If not rectified quickly, coma and death may ensue.

What's wrong with a low carbohydrate diet?

There is little scientific evidence to back up or refute low carbohydrate diets. One reason for the popularity of low carbohydrate diets for weight loss is that initial loss is rapid. Within the first few days, the scales will be reading two to three kilograms lower. That's a really encouraging sign to anyone trying to lose weight. The trouble is that most of that weight loss isn't body fat, but muscle glycogen and water.

When carbohydrate is no longer being supplied in sufficient amounts by your diet, the body uses its small carbohydrate reserves to fuel muscle contraction. One gram of carbohydrate in the form of muscle and liver glycogen binds four grams of water. So when you use up your total reserves of 500 grams of glycogen within the first few days, you also lose two kilograms of water, for a total loss of 2.5 kilograms, none of it fat. Conversely, when you return to normal eating, the carbohydrate reserves will be rapidly replenished along with the water.

People who have followed low carbohydrate diets for any length of time observe that the rate of weight loss plateaus off and they begin to feel rather tired and lethargic. That's not surprising because the muscles have little in the way of glycogen stores. Strenuous exercise requires both fat and carbohydrate in the fuel mix. So, long-term, these low carbohydrate diets may discourage people from the physical exercise patterns that will help them keep their weight under control.

Our advice is that the best diet for weight control is one you can stick to for life—one that includes your favourite foods and which accommodates your cultural and ethnic heritage. This diet can vary somewhat in total carbohydrate, protein and fat. At the present time, there is more scientific evidence supporting the use of bulky, higher carbohydrate, low GI, low fat diets for weight loss. But the bottom line is that the type of carbohydrate and the type of fat are critical. Choosing low GI foods will not only promote weight control, it will reduce postprandial glycemia, increase satiety, provide bulk and a rich supply of micronutrients.

Only low GI diets have the weight of scientific evidence in their favour.

To ensure blood glucose levels can be maintained between meals, our bodies draw on the glucose stored in the liver. The storage form of glucose is called glycogen but supplies of this are strictly limited and must be replenished from meal to meal. If your diet is low in carbohydrate, your glycogen stores will be low too and easily depleted.

Once the body has used your glycogen stores up (within 12 to 24 hours of beginning a fast), it will start breaking down muscle protein to synthesise glucose for the brain and nervous system. But remember, this process can't supply all of the brain's needs. When absolutely necessary, the brain will make use of ketones, a by-product of the breakdown of fat. The level of ketones in the blood rises as the fast continues and you can smell the ketones on the breath (a little like apple cider!).

The brain is not at its best using ketones, however, and mental judgment has been shown to be impaired. In all likelihood, you'll have a headache and feel mentally sluggish. Since your muscle stores of glycogen will have been depleted, you'll also find strenuous exercise almost impossible and be easily fatigued. All this leads us to an important question.

How much carbohydrate do you really need?

As we have shown, there are good reasons to avoid a low carbohydrate diet, but what then is the optimal level of carbohydrate in the diet? Should it be high (50 or 55 per cent of energy), as most nutritionists are recommending, or more moderate (about 40 per cent of energy), as the Harvard Medical School and the Zone diet suggest?

If we look carefully at diets all around the world, it's clear that both high and moderate intakes of carbohydrate are commensurate with good health. We believe your carbohydrate intake can be *either* as long as you give due consideration to the type of foods you eat.

Is a high carbohydrate diet for you?

In many countries, official dietary recommendations state that the average adult should ingest about 55 per cent of energy as carbohydrate and less than 30 per cent as fat (the remaining 15 per cent or more should come from protein). Will you find this easy? That depends. If you have always been health conscious and avoided high fat foods, or you're of Asian origin or have followed an Asian food pattern, then chances are you're already eating a high carbohydrate diet.

This means you'll be consuming 35 grams of carbohydrate (equivalent to about two slices of bread) for every 1000 kilojoules/239 calories ingested. Of course, the number of kilojoules/calories and hence the amount of carbohydrate varies with your weight and activity levels. If you are an active person with average energy requirements who is not trying to lose weight (i.e. average eater on 8500 kilojoules / 2000 calories per day) you will require 300 grams of carbohydrate (equivalent to about 20 slices of bread). If you are trying to lose weight and are consuming a low-energy diet (i.e. a small eater on 5000 kilojoules / 1200 calories per day) it means eating about 175 grams of carbohydrate a day (equivalent to about 12 slices of bread). As an example of what these diets look like, see pages 28 to 31.

Is a moderate carbohydrate intake for you?

If you are a typical Australian or New Zealander, or you or your family have Mediterranean origins, you'll be accustomed to more fat in your diet and only 40 to 45 per cent of your energy as carbohydrate. In the past, most nutritionists would have frowned upon this, but that's no longer the case. As long as you carefully consider the types of fats and the types of carbohydrate, then this level of carbohydrate intake is perfectly commensurate with good health. At this level, you need to consume at least 125 grams of carbohydrate a day if you are a small eater and 225 grams if you are an average eater. If bread were the only source of carbohydrate that you ate, this would mean eating between nine and 15 slices each day.

> **HOW TO FIND A DIETITIAN**
>
> For specific information about your own kilojoule and exact carbo-hydrate needs, you can consult an accredited practising dietitian (APD). Look in the *Yellow Pages* under Dietitians. Make sure that the person you choose has the letters APD after their name.

What we emphasise is that the *type* or *source* of the carbohydrate and fat are more important than the amount. In the end the choice of how much carbohydrate (moderate or high) is yours. The diet that you'll enjoy and stick to over the long term is the one that is clos-est to your usual diet and to your cultural and ethnic origins. Unlike socks, we believe that one size does not fit all. Our approach has built in flexibility when it comes to the amount of carbohydrate you need to eat.

Most of the world's population eat a high-carbohydrate diet based on staples such as rice, maize (corn), millet and wheat-based foods like bread or noodles. In some African and Asian countries, carbo-hydrate may form as much as 70 to 80 per cent of a person's kilojoule intake (this is probably too high for optimum health). In contrast, industrialised nations such as Australia and the United States eat only half of this. Our diets typically contain about 40 to 45 per cent as carbohydrate and 33 to 40 per cent as fat.

The carbohydrate–fat seesaw

Carbohydrate and fat are not only the two primary fuels for the tis-sues, they are the two main components of food, displaying a reciprocal relationship to each other. The reason protein isn't one of the body's primary fuels is because it usually contributes less than 20 per cent of the energy in food, while fats and carbohydrates make up the other 80 per cent or more. In a high carbohydrate diet, at least 50 per cent of the total energy comes from carbohydrate and less than 30 per cent from fat. In a high fat diet, typically 40 per cent of energy comes from fat and only 40 per cent from carbohydrate.

This reciprocal or seesaw relationship means that carbohydrate displaces fat from our diet. When we make an effort to eat more carbohydrates, fat intake decreases, and vice-versa. Foods high in carbohydrates are often bulky and filling (think fruit and vegetables) and rich in micronutrients. The problem with fats on the other hand is that they are highly palatable—a lot of the flavour in food is actually dissolved in the fat (think chocolate and cheese). Fats are also very concentrated sources of energy, and gram for gram pure fat contains more than double the energy of pure carbohydrate or protein.

Today's health recommendations are more about the *type* of fat and the *nature* of the carbohydrate and less about the total amounts.

The upshot of this is that many foods that are high in fat are exceptionally palatable, low in bulk, high in energy and very easy to overconsume. If your diet is dominated by these foods and you're not very active, it's all too easy to put on excess weight. Saturated fat also plays a role in the development of heart disease. This is why many nutritionists have promoted high carbohydrate diets in which 50 to 60 per cent of daily kilojoule intake comes from carbohydrate.

There have been, however, unforeseen consequences to this universal low fat, high carbohydrate approach. For one, many people succeeded in reducing total fat intake to 30 per cent or less but still had an undesirably high intake of saturated fat. Consumers also demanded more palatable low fat foods and in the end they were eating foods that were just as energy dense and easy to overeat as the original high fat product (think low fat yoghurts and ice-creams). Nutritionists have had to rethink and fine-tune the health message.

Simple versus complex carbohydrate

So far, we've emphasised the *amount* of carbohydrate in the diet. What about the type or *nature* of the carbohydrate?

Traditionally, the nature of carbohydrates was described by their chemical structure: simple or complex. Sugars were simple and starches were complex, simply because sugars were small molecules and starches were big. By virtue of their large size, it was automatically assumed that complex carbohydrates like starches would be slowly digested and absorbed and would cause only a small and gradual rise in blood glucose levels. Simple sugars, on the other hand, were assumed to be digested and absorbed quickly, producing a rapid rise in blood glucose.

A few simplistic experiments on raw starches and pure sugars supported these assumptions and for 50 years they were taught to every medical and biochemistry student as 'fact'.

We now know that the whole concept of 'simple' versus 'complex' carbohydrate does not tell us anything about how the carbohydrates in food affect blood glucose levels. Twenty years of scientific research have shown that the assumptions about the speed of digestion were all wrong.

The rise in blood glucose after meals could not be predicted simply on the basis of a simple versus complex chemical structure. Another system of describing the nature of carbohydrates and classifying them according to their effects on blood glucose was needed: the glycemic index.

The nature of carbohydrate: the GI

Surprisingly, scientists did not study the actual blood glucose responses to common foods until the early 1980s. Prior to that, they'd tested solutions of pure sugars and raw starches and drew conclusions that did not apply to realistic meals.

Since 1981, hundreds of different foods have been tested as single foods and in mixed meals with both healthy people and people with diabetes. Professors David Jenkins and Tom Wolever at the University of Toronto were the first to introduce the term 'glycemic index' to compare the ability of different carbohydrates to raise blood glucose levels.

The GI is simply a scientifically valid way of describing how the carbohydrates in individual foods affect blood glucose levels. Foods with a high GI contain carbohydrates that have a dramatic effect on blood glucose levels, while foods with a low GI contain carbohydrates with much less impact.

The *GI* describes the type of carbohydrate in foods. It indicates their ability to raise your *blood glucose* levels.

This research has turned some widely held beliefs upside down (it truly is a revolution) and in the process, quite understandably, caused a lot of controversy.

The first surprise was that the starch in foods like bread, potatoes and many types of rice, is digested and absorbed very quickly, not slowly as had always been assumed.

Secondly, scientists found that the sugar in foods (like fruit, con-fectionery and ice-cream) did not produce dramatic or prolonged

Let's talk glycemic load

Our blood glucose levels are determined by both the quality, or GI, of the carbohydrate and the quantity of carbohydrate. We can predict the effect of a food on our blood glucose level by calculating the glycemic load which is the GI x the amount of carbohydrate, divided by 100. For example, the glycemic load of a $\frac{1}{2}$ cup serve of pumpkin is $(75 \times 4) \div 100 = 3$. The glycemic load of a teaspoon of jam is $(51 \times 5) \div 100 = 2.5$. For both these foods the glycemic load is very low, either as a consequence of low carbohydrate content of the food or the small serving size chosen.

The glycemic load is greatest for those foods which provide the most carbohydrate, particularly those we tend to eat in large quantities. Compare the glycemic load of the following foods to see how the serving size as well as the GI are significant in determining the glycemic response:

- Rice—1 cup of boiled Calrose rice (150 g) contains 43 g carbohydrate and has a GI of 83. The glycemic load is $(83 \times 43) \div 100 = 36$.
- Spaghetti—1 serve (150 g) of cooked spaghetti contains 48 g carbohydrate and has a GI of 44. The glycemic load is $(44 \times 48) \div 100 = 21$.

rises in blood glucose as had always been thought. The truth was that most of the sugars in foods, regardless of source, actually produced quite moderate blood glucose responses, lower than most starches.

We need to forget the old distinctions that have been made between starchy foods and sugary foods, or simple versus complex carbohydrates. They have no useful application at all when it comes to blood glucose levels. Even an experienced scientist with a detailed knowledge of a food's chemical composition finds it difficult to predict a food's GI.

Forget about the words *simple* and *complex* carbohydrate.
Think in terms of *low GI* and *high GI.*

Eating carbohydrates

To ensure that you are eating enough carbohydrate and the right kind you should eat:

- fruits and/or vegetables at every meal
- at least one food with a low GI at each meal
- at least the minimum quantity of carbohydrate foods suggested for small eaters (see pages 28–29)
- lots of bulk (foods with low energy density or fewer kilojoules per gram)

You will find that when you are choosy about your carbohydrate, your insulin levels will be lower and you will automatically burn more fat. Eating bulky foods will also help fill you up and prevent you overeating.

If you are looking at ways to improve your own diet there are two important things to remember.

1. Identify the sources of carbohydrate in your diet and reduce high GI foods. Don't go to extremes; there is room for your favourite high GI foods.

2. Identify the sources of fat and look at ways you can reduce saturated fat. Choose monounsaturated and polyunsaturated fats, such as olive oil and sunflower oil, instead of saturated fats. Again, don't

HOW COULD YOU CHANGE YOUR DIET?

Some of the most common foods that people tell us they have started eating to achieve a low GI diet are:

- grainy breads
- low GI breakfast cereals
- more fruit
- yoghurt
- lots of pasta, beans and vegetables

go overboard—the body needs some fat and there's room for your favourite fatty foods on occasions.

The right kind of carbohydrate diet

Both high and moderate carbohydrate intake can be healthy; the choice is simply up to you. Both types of diets, however, need to emphasise low GI carbohydrates and healthy fats.

A high carbohydrate diet

Here we show you an example of what's involved in eating a high carbohydrate diet (55 per cent of energy from carbohydrate) for small or average eaters.

For small eaters

Even the smallest eater needs these carbohydrate foods every day:

- around 4 slices of bread or the equivalent (crackers, rolls, English-style muffins)
- at least 2 pieces of fruit or the equivalent (juice, dried fruit)

Small eaters may:
- be small-framed females
- have small appetites
- do very little physical activity
- be trying to lose weight

- about 1 cup of high carbohydrate cooked vegetables (corn, legumes, potato, sweet potato)
- about 1 cup of cereal or grain food (breakfast cereal, cooked rice or pasta, or other grains)
- at least 1½ cups of low fat milk or the equivalent (yoghurt, ice-cream), including milk in your tea and coffee and with your cereal

If this amount of food sounds right for you, try it as a minimum amount of carbohydrate. This supplies 175 grams of carbohydrate, suitable for a 5000 kilojoule (1200 calorie) diet. Listen to your appetite if it demands more.

For average eaters

Average eaters need to eat:

Average eaters:
- do regular physical activity (but not strenuous exercise)
- are adults of average frame size

- around 6 slices of bread or the equivalent (crackers, rolls, muffins)
- about 3 pieces of fruit or the equivalent (juice, dried fruit)
- 1 cup of high carbohydrate vegetables (corn, legumes, potato, sweet potato)
- at least 2 cups of cereal or grain food (breakfast cereal, cooked rice or pasta, or other grains)
- 2 cups of low fat milk or the equivalent (yoghurt, ice-cream)

This provides 260 grams of carbohydrate, which is suitable for a 7500 kilojoule (1800 calorie) diet.

Overconsumption of food is highly unlikely on the high-fibre, high carbohydrate, low fat diet described above. So, base your diet on high-fibre carbohydrate foods like wholegrain breads, cereals, fruit, vegetables and legumes and let your appetite dictate how much you need to eat.

A moderate carbohydrate diet

If you think you'd prefer a more moderate carbohydrate intake (40 per cent of total energy) and more fat, then here's an example of how much carbohydrate food small and average eaters would need each day.

For small eaters

For a balanced intake of nutrients on a moderate carbohydrate diet, even a small eater needs these carbohydrate foods every day:

- around 4 slices of bread or the equivalent (crackers, rolls, English-style muffins)
- at least 2 pieces of fruit or the equivalent (juice, dried fruit)
- about ½ cup of high carbo-hydrate vegetables (corn, legumes, potato, sweet potato)
- about ½ cup of cereal or grain food (breakfast cereal, cooked rice or pasta, or other grains)
- at least 1½ cups of low fat milk or the equivalent (yoghurt, ice-cream)

Small eaters may:
- be small-framed females
- have small appetites
- do very little physical activity
- be trying to lose weight

These carbohydrate foods supply 130 grams of carbohydrate, which is about 40 per cent of energy from carbohydrate in a 5000 kilojoule (1200 calorie) diet.

For average eaters

Even on a moderate carbohydrate diet, the average person needs to eat:

- around 6 slices of bread or the equivalent (crackers, rolls, muffins)

Average eaters:
- do regular physical activity (but not strenuous exercise)
- are adults of average frame size

- about 2 pieces of fruit or the equivalent (juice, dried fruit)
- about ½ cup of high carbohydrate vegetables (corn, legumes, potato, sweet potato)
- at least 1½ cups of cereal or grain food (breakfast cereal, cooked rice or pasta, or other grain)
- 2 cups of low fat milk or the equivalent (yoghurt, ice-cream)

This provides 195 grams of carbohydrate which is 40 per cent of the energy in a 7500 kilojoule (1800 calorie) diet.

To work out the percentage of kilojoules supplied by carbohydrate, multiply the grams of carbohydrate by 16 (the number of kilojoules supplied per gram of carbohydrate) and then divide by the total number of kilojoules

Thus: (195 x 16 x 100)/7500 = 40 per cent

NB: 1 calorie = 4 kilojoules (approximately)

CHAPTER 3

ALL ABOUT THE GI

The glycemic index was first developed in 1981 by Dr David Jenkins, a professor of nutrition at the University of Toronto, Canada, to help determine which foods were best for people with diabetes. At that time, the diet for people with diabetes was based on a system of carbohydrate exchanges. Each exchange (or portion of food) contained the same amount of carbohydrate. In some countries, an exchange was equivalent to 15 grams of carbohydrate, while in others it was only 10 or 12 grams. The exchange system assumed that all starchy foods produced the same effect on blood glucose levels even though some earlier studies had already proven this was not correct. Jenkins was one of the first researchers to challenge the use of exchanges and investigate how real foods behave in the bodies of real people.

Jenkins' approach attracted a great deal of attention because it was so logical and systematic. He and his colleagues tested a large number of common foods with some surprising results. An exchange of ice-cream, for example, despite its sugar content, had less effect on blood glucose than an exchange of ordinary bread. Over the next 15 years, medical researchers and scientists around the world, including the authors of this book, tested the effect of many foods on blood glucose levels and helped develop this new concept of classifying carbohydrates based on the glycemic index.

For some years the glycemic index was a very controversial topic. There were avid proponents and opponents of this new approach to classifying carbohydrate. The two sides almost came to blows at conferences aimed at reaching a consensus.

Initially, there was some justified criticism. In the early days there was no evidence that the GI of single foods could be applied to mixed meals, or that the approach brought long-term benefits. There were no studies of the GI's reproducibility or the consistency of GI values from one country to another. Many of the early studies used healthy volunteers and there was no evidence that the results could be applied to people with diabetes.

Now, however, the evidence is in and we know that it is reproducible and a clinically proven tool in its application to diabetes, appetite and coronary health. To date, studies in the United Kingdom, France, Italy, Sweden, Australia and Canada have proven without doubt the value of the glycemic index. Notably, the United States remains officially opposed. Harvard School of Public Health and the Children's Hospital in Boston, however, recommend the glycemic index even for healthy people.

The glycemic index of foods is simply a ranking of carbohydrate exchanges in foods according to their immediate impact on blood glucose levels. To make a fair comparison, all foods are compared with a reference food such as pure glucose in equivalent carbohydrate amounts.

Today we know the GI of hundreds of different food items that have been tested following the standardised method. The detailed tables in Part IV give the GI of a range of common foods, including many tested by the University of Sydney.

The GI measures the rate of digestion

Foods containing carbohydrates that break down quickly during digestion have the highest GI. The blood glucose response is fast and high. In other words, the glucose (or sugar) in the bloodstream increases rapidly. Conversely, foods that contain carbohydrates which break down slowly, releasing glucose gradually into the bloodstream, have a low GI.

An analogy is the popular fable of the tortoise and the hare. The hare, just like high GI foods, speeds away but loses the race to the tortoise with his slow and steady pace. Similarly, the slow and steady low GI foods produce a smooth blood glucose curve without wild fluctuations. The graph on page 36 shows the effect of slow and fast carbohydrates on blood glucose levels.

For most people, the foods with a low GI have advantages over those with a high GI. But there are some athletes who can benefit from the use of high GI foods during and after competition. This is covered in chapter 13. High GI foods are also useful in the treatment of hypoglycemia (covered in chapter 10).

The GI is a clinically proven tool in its applications to diabetes, appetite and coronary health.

The substance which produces one of the greatest effects on blood glucose levels is pure glucose itself. *Most* foods have less effect than

How scientists measure the GI

1. An amount of food containing a standard amount of carbohydrate (usually 25 or 50 grams) is given to a volunteer to eat. For example, to test boiled spaghetti, the volunteer will be given 200 grams of spaghetti which supplies 50 grams of carbohydrate (determined from food composition tables).

2. Over the next two hours (or three hours if the volunteer has diabetes), we take a sample of their blood every 15 minutes during the first hour and thereafter every 30 minutes. The blood glucose level of these blood samples is measured in the laboratory and recorded.

3. The blood glucose level is plotted on a graph and the area under the curve is calculated using a computer program (Figure 1).

Figure 1. Measuring the GI of a food.

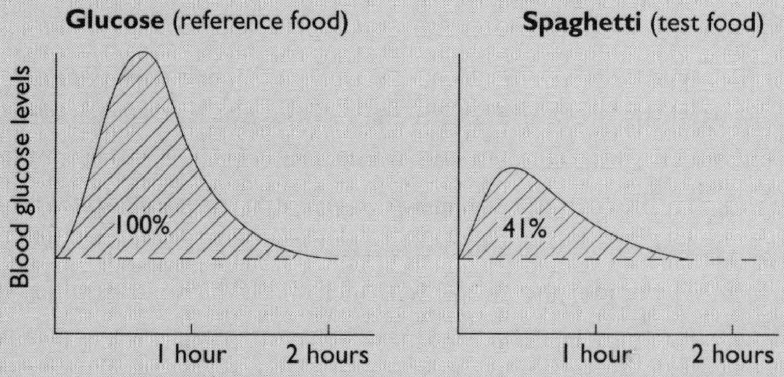

Glucose (reference food)   **Spaghetti** (test food)

(Blood glucose levels plotted against time; Glucose curve marked 100%, Spaghetti curve marked 41%; x-axis: 1 hour, 2 hours)

The test food and the reference food must contain the same amount of carbohydrate. The usual dose is 50 grams but sometimes 25 grams is used when the portion size would be otherwise too large. Even smaller doses such as 15 grams have been used. The GI result is much the same whatever the dose because the GI is simply a relative measure of carbohydrate quality.

4. The volunteer's response to spaghetti (or whatever food is being tested) is compared with his or her blood glucose response to 50 grams of pure glucose (the reference food).

5. The reference food is tested on two or three separate occasions and an average value is calculated. This is done to reduce the effect of day-to-day variation in blood glucose responses.

6. The average GI found in 8–10 people is the GI of that food.

glucose when fed in equal amounts of carbohydrate. The GI of pure glucose is set at 100 and every other food is ranked on a scale from 0 to 100 according to the actual effect on blood glucose levels. (Note: There are a few foods that have GI values over 100, e.g. Jasmine rice. While this seems extraordinary, there's a simple explanation. Glucose is a highly concentrated solution that tends to be held up briefly in the stomach. On the other hand, Jasmine rice contains starch that leaves the stomach without delay and is then digested at lightning speed.)

A *high GI* value is 70 or more. A *medium GI* value is 56 to 69 inclusive. A *low GI* value is 55 or less.

The GI of a food cannot be predicted from its composition or the GI of related foods. To test the GI, you need real people and real

GLUCOSE OR WHITE BREAD?

In the past, some scientists used a 50 grams carbohydrate portion of white bread as the reference food because it was more physiological—typical of what we actually eat. On this scale, where the GI of white bread is set as 100, some foods will have a GI over 100 because their effect on blood glucose levels is higher than that of bread.

The use of two standards has caused some confusion and the glucose = 100 scale is now recommended. It is possible to convert from the bread scale to the glucose scale using the factor 0.7 (70/100). This factor is derived from the fact that the GI of white bread is 70 on the glucose = 100 scale.

To avoid confusion throughout this book, we refer to all foods according to a standard where glucose equals 100.

foods. We describe how the GI of a food is measured on page 36. There is no easy, inexpensive substitute test. Standardised methods are always followed so that results from one group of people can be directly compared with those of another group.

In total, eight to ten people need to be tested and the GI of the food is the average value of the group. We know this average figure is reproducible and that a different group of volunteers will produce a similar result. Results obtained in a group of people with diabetes are comparable to those without diabetes.

The higher the GI, the higher the blood glucose levels after consumption of the food. Foods with a high GI usually reach a higher peak, i.e. the 'glycemic spike' is higher but sometimes blood glucose levels remain moderately high over the whole two hours—white bread is a good example of this.

Rice Bubbles (GI of 87) and baked potatoes (GI of 85) have very high GI values, meaning their effect on blood glucose levels is almost as high as that of an equal amount of pure glucose (yes, you read it correctly). Figure 2 shows the blood glucose response to white bread compared with pure glucose. Foods with a low GI (like lentils at 29) show a flatter blood glucose response when eaten, as shown in

Figure 2. The effect of pure glucose (50 grams) and white bread (50 grams carbohydrate portion) on blood glucose levels.

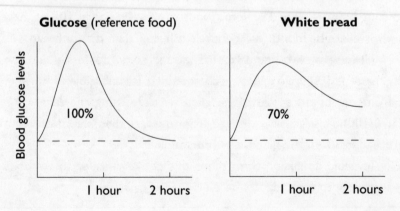

Figure 3. The effect of pure glucose (50 grams) and lentils (50 grams carbohydrate portion) on blood glucose levels.

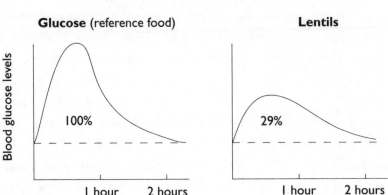

Figure 3. The peak blood glucose level is lower and the return to baseline levels is slower than with a high GI food.

Why the glycemic index is so important

The slow digestion and gradual rise and fall in blood glucose responses after a low GI food helps control blood glucose levels in people with diabetes or glucose intolerance. This effect may benefit healthy people as well because it reduces the secretion of the hormone insulin over the course of the day. (This is discussed in greater detail in chapters 1 and 9.) Slower digestion helps to delay hunger pangs and thereby promote weight loss in overweight people.

Lower glucose levels over the course of the day also improve coronary health by reducing the oxidative stress associated with glycemic spikes. Keeping blood glucose levels on an even keel helps ensure that the blood vessels remain elastic and supple, reducing the formation of fatty streaks and plaques that cause 'stiffening' of the arteries (atherosclerosis). Lastly, good blood glucose control means there's less tendency to form a blood clot, the final event that precipitates a heart attack.

These facts are not an exaggeration. They are not just preliminary findings. They are confirmed results of many studies published in prestigious scientific journals around the world.

Can the GI be applied to real meals?

Normally, real meals consist of a variety of foods. We can still apply the GI to these real meals, even though the GI values are originally derived from testing single foods in isolation. Scientists have found that it is possible to predict the blood glucose rise for a meal based on several foods with different GI values. The total carbohydrate content of the meal and the contribution of each food to the total carbohydrate must be known. Data like this can be found in food composition tables.

For example, say you have a breakfast based on orange juice, Weet-Bix™ with milk and a slice of toast with a little margarine. In the following table, you can see how the GI of the total meal has been calculated. This may look complicated. In practice, people don't need to make these sorts of calculations at all; but dietitians and nutrition

How we calculate the overall GI of a meal

Food	Carb. (g)	% total carb.	GI	Contribution to meal GI
Orange juice (150 ml)	13	24	46	24% x 46 = 11
2 Weet-Bix™ 30 g	21	38	69	38% x 69 = 26
Milk 150 ml	7	13	27	13% x 27 = 4
1 slice of toast (30 g)	13	24	70	24% x 70 = 17
Total	**54**			**Meal GI = 58***

* All calculations have been rounded off to the nearest whole number. These calculations provide a reasonably accurate assessment of the GI of mixed meals, as long as the single components have been tested in the physical state in which they are finally eaten. However, in recipes that incorporate ingredients such as raw wheat flour and sugar that are subsequently cooked (e.g. cakes and biscuits), the final GI is not predictable.

researchers sometimes have to. Many studies have shown a very close relationship between the predicted blood glucose response (based on published GI values of the relative effects of different foods and meals) and the actual observed blood glucose response.

Glycemic load

When we eat a meal containing carbohydrate, the blood glucose rises and falls. The extent to which it rises and remains high is critically important to health and depends on two things: the amount of carbohydrate in the meal and the nature (GI) of that carbohydrate. Both are equally important determinants of changes in blood glucose levels. Unfortunately, the amount of carbohydrate still gets the lion's share of the attention.

It's easy to determine the amount of carbohydrate in a food by looking at the food label or consulting food composition tables. What you can't yet determine from the food label or table of food composition is the GI of the carbohydrate. That's where the GI tables in the back of this book come in. They allow you to look up the GI of nearly 600 individual foods. It's the largest, most comprehensive and reliable list of GI values in the world.

Because both the amount and type of carbohydrate are needed to predict blood glucose responses to a meal, we need a way to combine and describe the two. Researchers at Harvard did this by coming up with the term 'glycemic load'. Glycemic load is calculated simply by multiplying the GI of a food by the amount of carbohydrate per serving and dividing by 100.

$$\text{Glycemic load} = (\text{GI} \times \text{carbohydrate per serving}) \div 100$$

For example, an apple has a GI of 40 and contains 15 grams of carbohydrate per serve. Its glycemic load is (40 × 15) ÷ 100 = 6. A potato has a GI of 90 and 20 grams of carbohydrate per serve. It has a glycemic load of (90 × 20) ÷ 100 = 18. This is not to say that the glycemic response will be exactly three times higher for a potato compared with an apple, but the total metabolic effect including overall insulin demand might be three times higher.

What determines a food's GI?

Scientists have been studying what makes one food high GI and another one low GI. There is a wealth of information which can easily confuse. We have summarised the results of their research in the following table which looks at the factors that influence the GI of a food.

The key message is that the physical state of the starch in the food is by far the most important factor influencing the GI value. That's why the advances in food processing over the past two hundred years have had such a profound effect on the overall GI of the food we eat.

Factors that influence the GI of a food

Factor	Mechanism	Examples of food where the effect is seen
Starch gelatinisation	The less gelatinised (swollen) the starch, the slower the rate of digestion.	Spaghetti, porridge, biscuits have less gelatinised starch.
Physical entrapment	The fibrous coat around beans and seeds and plant cell walls acts as a physical barrier, slowing down access of enzymes to the starch inside.	Pumpernickel and grainy bread, legumes and barley.

Factor	Mechanism	Examples of food where the effect is seen
High amylose to amylopectin ratio*	The more amylose a food contains, the less easily the starch is gelatinised and the slower its rate of digestion.	Basmati rice, legumes, Hi-Maize™ starch contain more amylose than other cereals.
Particle size	The smaller the particle size, the easier it is for water and enzymes to penetrate (the surface area is relatively higher).	Finely milled flours have high GIs. Stone-ground flours have larger particles and lower GIs.
Viscosity of fibre	Viscous, soluble fibres increase the viscosity of the intestinal contents and this slows down the interaction between the starch and the enzymes. Finely milled wholemeal wheat and rye flours have *fast* rates of digestion and absorption because the fibre is not viscous.	Rolled oats, beans and lentils, apples, Metamucil®.
Sugar	The digestion of sugar produces only half as many glucose molecules as the same amount of starch (the other half is fructose). The presence of sugar also restricts gelatinisation of the starch by binding water and reducing the amount of 'available' water.	Some biscuits, some breakfast cereals that are high in sugar have relatively low GI values.
Acidity	Acids in foods slow down stomach emptying, thereby slowing the rate at which the starch can be digested.	Vinegar, lemon juice, lime juice, salad dressings, pickled vegetables, sourdough bread.
Fat	Fat slows down the rate of stomach emptying, thereby slowing the digestion of the starch.	Potato crisps have a lower GI than boiled potatoes.

* Amylose and amylopectin are two different types of starch. Both are found in foods, but the ratio varies (see pages 46–47).

The effect of starch gelatinisation on GI

The starch in raw food is stored in hard compact granules that make it difficult to digest. This is why potatoes might give you a stomach-ache if you eat them raw. Most starchy foods need to be cooked for this reason. During cooking, water and heat expand the starch granules to different degrees, some granules actually burst and free the individual starch molecules. This is what happens when you make a gravy by heating flour and water until the starch granules burst and the gravy thickens.

If most of the starch granules have swollen and burst during cooking, the starch is said to be fully gelatinised. Figure 4 (page 45) shows the difference between raw and cooked starch in potatoes.

The swollen granules and free starch molecules are very easy to digest because the starch-digesting enzymes in the small intestine have a greater surface area to attack. The quick action of the enzymes results in a rapid, high blood glucose rise after consumption of the food (remember that starch is a string of glucose molecules). A food containing starch which is fully gelatinised will therefore have a very high GI.

In foods such as biscuits, the presence of sugar and fat and very little water makes starch gelatinisation more difficult, and only about half of the granules will be fully gelatinised. For this reason, biscuits tend to have intermediate GI values.

Figure 4. The difference between raw (compact granules, left) and cooked (swollen granules, right) starch in potatoes.

The effect of particle size on GI

Another factor that influences starch gelatinisation, and GI, is the particle size of the food. Grinding or milling of cereals reduces the particle size and makes it easier for water to be absorbed and enzymes to attack. That is why cereal foods made from fine flours tend to have a high GI. The larger the particle size, the lower the GI, as shown in Figure 5 (page 46).

One of the most significant alterations to our food supply came with the introduction of steel roller mills in the mid-nineteenth century. Not only did they make it easier to remove the fibre from cereal grains, the particle size of the starch became smaller than ever before. Prior to the nineteenth century, stone grinding produced quite coarse flours that resulted in slower rates of digestion and absorption.

When starch is consumed in 'nature's packaging'—whole intact grains that have been softened by soaking and cooking—the food will have a low GI. For example, cooked barley has a GI of only 25. Most cooked legumes have a GI between 30 and 40. Cooked wholewheat has a GI of 41.

The only whole (intact) grain food with a high GI is rice, specifically low amylose rice, such as Calrose rice (GI of 83). These varieties of rice have starch which is very easily gelatinised during cooking and therefore easily broken down by digestive enzymes. This may help explain why we sometimes feel hungry not long after

Enjoy lean meat, fish and low fat dairy products

Figure 5. The larger the particle size, the lower the GI.

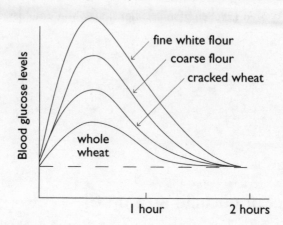

rice-based meals. However, some varieties of rice (Basmati, a long-grain fragrant rice, and Doongara) have lower GI values because they have a higher amylose content (see below) than normal rice. Their GI values are in the range of 50–58.

The effect of amylose and amylopectin on GI

There are two sorts of starch in food—amylose and amylopectin—and researchers have discovered that the ratio of one to the other has a powerful effect on a food's GI.

Amylose is a straight chain molecule, like a string of beads. These tend to line up in rows and form tight compact clumps that are harder to gelatinise and therefore digest (see Figure 6, page 47).

On the other hand, amylopectin is a string of glucose molecules with lots of branching points, such as you see in some types of sea-weed. Amylopectin molecules are therefore larger and more open and the starch is easier to gelatinise and digest.

Thus foods that have little amylose and plenty of amylopectin in their starch have higher GI values, for example, Calrose rice and

Figure 6. Amylose is a straight chain molecule which is harder to digest than amylopectin which has many branching points.

Amylose slowly digested

Amylopectin quickly digested

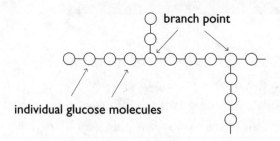

wheat flour. Foods with a higher ratio of amylose to amylopectin have lower GI values, for examples, Basmati rice and all sorts of legumes.

The effect of sugar on GI

Table sugar or refined sugar (sucrose) has a GI value of only 60-65. This is because it is a disaccharide (double sugar) composed of one glucose molecule coupled to one fructose molecule. Fructose is absorbed and taken directly to the liver where it is immediately oxidised (burnt as the source of energy). The blood glucose response to pure fructose is very small (GI of 19). Consequently, when we consume sucrose, in effect we have consumed only half as much glucose. This explains why the blood glucose response to 50 grams of sucrose

Glycemic load incorporates both the amount and type of carbohydrate

WHY DOES PASTA HAVE A LOW GI?

In the beginning, we thought that pasta had a low GI because the main ingredient was semolina (cracked wheat) and not finely ground wheat flour. Scientists have now shown, however, that even pasta made with flour has a low GI and that the reason for the slow digestion rate is the physical entrapment of ungelatinised starch granules in a sponge-like network of protein (gluten) molecules in the pasta dough. Pasta is unique in this regard. Pastas of any shape and size have a fairly low GI (30 to 60). Asian noodles such as hokkein, udon and rice vermicelli also have a low to intermediate GI values.

is approximately half that of 50 grams of corn syrup or maltodextrins (where the molecules are all glucose).

Many foods containing large amounts of refined sugar have a GI close to 60. This is the average of glucose (GI of 100) and fructose (GI of 19). It is lower than that of ordinary white bread with a GI averaging around 70. Kellogg's Coco Pops™ which contains 39 per cent sugar has a GI of 77, lower than that of Rice Bubbles™ (GI of 87) which contains little sugar.

So, contrary to popular opinion, most foods containing simple sugars do not raise blood glucose values any more than most complex starchy foods like bread.

Sugars that naturally occur in food include lactose, sucrose, glucose and fructose in variable proportions, depending on the food. The overall blood glucose response to a food is very hard to predict on theoretical grounds because stomach emptying is slowed by increasing concentration of the sugars, whatever their structure.

Some fruits for example have a low GI (grapefruit has a GI of only 25) while others are relatively high (watermelon has a GI of 72). It seems the higher the acidity and osmotic strength (number of molecules per ml) of the fruit, the lower the GI. Consequently, it is not possible to lump all fruits together and say that they will have a low GI because they are high in fibre. They are not all equal. See the tables in Part IV to compare fruits.

Many foods containing sugars are a mixture of refined and naturally occurring sugars. The overall effect on the blood glucose response is too hard to predict. This is why we need to test the GI of sugary foods in real people before we make generalisations about their GI value.

The effect of fibre on GI

The effect of fibre on the GI of a food depends on the type of fibre and its viscosity. Finely ground wheat fibre, such as in wholemeal bread, has no effect whatsoever on the rate of starch digestion and subsequent blood glucose response. Similarly, any product made with wholemeal flour will have a GI similar to that of its white counterpart. Breakfast cereals made with wholemeal flours will also tend to have high GI values, unless there are other confounding factors. Puffed wheat (GI of 80) which is made from well-cooked whole wheat grains has a high GI value, *despite* its high fibre content.

If the fibre is still intact it can act as a physical barrier to digestion and then the GI will be lower. This is one of the reasons why All-Bran™ has a low GI. It is also one of the reasons why whole (intact) grains usually have low GI values.

Viscous fibre thickens the viscosity or thickness of the mixture in the digestive tract. This slows the passage of food and restricts the movement of enzymes, thereby slowing digestion. The end result is a lower blood glucose response. Legumes contain high levels of viscous fibre, as do oats and psyllium (a seed which is a major ingredient in some breakfast cereals and laxatives such as Metamucil®). These foods all have low GI values.

The effect of acid on GI

Within the last few years, several reports in the scientific literature have indicated that a realistic amount of vinegar or lemon juice in the form of a salad dressing consumed with a mixed meal has significant blood glucose lowering effects.

As little as 20 ml of vinegar in a vinaigrette dressing (20 ml vinegar and 10 ml oil) taken with an average meal lowered blood glucose by as much as 30 per cent.

These findings have important implications for people with diabetes or individuals at risk of diabetes, coronary heart disease or the metabolic syndrome (see chapters 9–11).

The effect appears to be related to the acidity because other organic acids (such as lactic acid and propionic acid) also have a blood glucose lowering effect, but the degree of reduction varies with the type of acid. Our findings show that lemon juice is just as powerful.

It is well known that acidity in food puts the brake on stomach emptying, slowing the delivery of food to the small intestine. Digestion of the carbohydrate in the food is therefore slowed and the final result is that blood glucose levels are significantly lower. Good news for people with diabetes!

A side salad with your meal, especially a high GI meal, will help to keep blood glucose levels under control.

Sourdough breads in which lactic acid and propionic acid are produced by the natural fermentation of starch and sugars by the yeast starter culture, also produce reduced levels of blood glucose and insulin compared with normal bread. The area under the plasma insulin curve was 22 per cent lower with the sourdough product. In addition, there was higher satiety associated with breads having decreased rates of digestion and absorption. Thus there is significant potential to lower blood glucose and insulin and increase satiety with sourdough bread formulations.

THE GI WAS NEVER MEANT TO BE USED IN ISOLATION!

At first glance it might appear that some high fat foods such as chocolate might seem a good choice simply because they have a low GI. But don't be fooled! The GI value was never meant to be the sole determinant when choosing what food to eat. Large amounts of fat (and protein) in food tend to slow the rate of stomach emptying and therefore the rate at which foods are digested in the small intestine. High fat foods will therefore tend to have lower GI values than their low fat equivalents. For example, potato crisps have a lower GI (54) than potatoes baked without fat (85). Many biscuits have a lower GI (55–65) than bread (70). In these instances, a lower GI doesn't mean an automatically better choice from a nutritional standpoint. Saturated fat in these foods will have adverse effects on coronary health, far greater than the benefit of lower blood glucose levels. These foods should be treated as 'indulgences', or for special occasions.

This is not to say that all fats in foods should be avoided. One of the reasons why legumes have such a low GI is their relatively high fat content compared to cereal grains. But just as there are differences in the nature of carbohydrates in foods, there are differences in the quality of fats. We need to be choosy about fats too. Good fats, such as the omega-3 polyunsaturated fats are not only good for us, they help to lower the blood glucose response to meals.

The glycemic index and glycemic load of some popular foods

(GLUCOSE = 100)

	GI	GL
BREAKFAST CEREALS		
Kellogg's All-Bran™	30	4
Kellogg's Coco Pops™	77	20
Kellogg's Cornflakes™	77	20
Mini Wheats™	58	12
Muesli, toasted	43	7
Muesli, untoasted	49	10
Kellogg's Nutrigrain™	66	10
Porridge	42	9
Sanitarium Puffed Wheat™	80	17
Kellogg's Rice Bubbles™	87	22
Kellogg's Special K™	54	11
Kellogg's Sultana Bran™	73	14
Kellogg's Sustain™	68	15
Uncle Toby's Vita-Brits™	68	13
Sanitarium Weet-Bix™	69	12
Kellogg's Guardian™	37	5
GRAINS/PASTAS		
Buckwheat	54	16
Bulghur (burghul)	48	12
Rice—Calrose	83	36
—Doongara	56	22
—Basmati	58	22
—Instant	87	36
—Sunbrown Quick™	80	31
Noodles—instant	47	19
Pasta—egg fettuccine	32	15
—spaghetti (av)	38	18
—vermicelli	35	16
BREAD		
Bagel	72	25
Croissant*	67	17
Crumpet	69	13
Fruit Loaf (Burgen™)	44	6

	GI	GL
'Grainy' breads (av)	49	6
Pita bread	57	10
Pumpernickel	41	5
Rye bread (av)	58	8
White bread (av)	70	10
Wholemeal bread (av)	77	9
CRACKERS/CRISPBREAD		
Jatz™	55	10
Kavli™	71	12
Puffed crispbread	81	15
Ryvita™	69	11
Sao™	70	12
Water cracker	78	14
SWEET BISCUITS		
Highland Oatmeal™	55	10
Milk Arrowroot™	69	12
Morning Coffee™	79	15
Shredded Wheatmeal™	62	11
Shortbread (commercial)*	64	10
CAKES		
Apple muffin*	44	13
Banana cake*	47	18
Sponge cake	46	17
Waffles	76	10
VEGETABLES		
Beetroot, canned	64	5
Carrots	49	2
Parsnip	97	12
Peas (green, av)	48	3
Potato—baked (av)	85	26
—boiled	88	16
—French fries	75	22
—mashed	91	18

* Foods containing fat in excess of National Heart Foundation guidelines

	GI	GL
Pumpkin	75	3
Sweet corn	54	13
Sweet potato	44	11
Swede	72	7
Yam (av)	37	13

LEGUMES

	GI	GL
Baked beans (av)	48	7
Broad beans	79	9
Butter beans	31	6
Chickpeas, dried (av)	28	8
Haricot beans (av)	38	12
Kidney beans (av)	28	7
Lentils (av)	29	5
Soya beans, dried	20	1

FRUIT

	GI	GL
Apple (av)	38	6
Apricot (dried)	30	8
Banana (av)	52	12
Cherries	22	3
Grapefruit	25	3
Grapes (av)	46	8
Kiwi fruit	58	7
Mango	51	8
Orange (av)	42	5
Pawpaw	56	5
Peach—canned	58	9
—fresh (av)	42	5
Pear (av)	38	4
Pineapple	66	6
Plum	39	5
Raisins	64	28
Rockmelon	65	4
Sultanas	56	25
Watermelon	72	4

DAIRY FOODS

	GI	GL
Milk—full fat	27	3
—skim	32	4
—chocolate flavoured	42	13
—condensed	61	83

	GI	GL
Custard	43	7
Ice-cream—regular (av)	61	8
—low fat	50	3
Yoghurt, low fat	33	10

BEVERAGES

	GI	GL
Apple juice	40	11
Coca Cola,	53	14
Cordial	66	13
Fanta	68	23
Lucozade	95	40
Orange juice	52	12

SNACK AND CONVENIENCE FOODS

	GI	GL
Corn chips*	42	11
Fish fingers	38	7
Peanuts* (av)	14	1
Popcorn	72	8
Potato crisps*	57	10
Sausages*	28	1
Soup—lentil	44	9
—pea, green	66	27
—tomato	38	6
Sushi	48	17

CONFECTIONERY

	GI	GL
Chocolate*	44	13
Jelly beans (av)	78	22
Life Savers	70	21
Mars Bar®*	62	25
Muesli Bar*	61	13

SUGARS

	GI	GL
Honey (av)	55	10
Fructose (av)	19	2
Glucose	100	10
Lactose (av)	46	5
Sucrose (av)	68	7

* Foods containing fat in excess of National Heart Foundation guidelines

CHAPTER 4

FAQ

Everybody can benefit from adopting the GI approach to eating. It is the way nature intended us to eat. All the nutrients in nature's original packaging are in a slow-release form. Since the Industrial Revolution, however, we have taken natural carbohydrate foods and manufactured them into fast-release or instant food as part of our quest for a more palatable, eye-catching and less perishable food supply. Unfortunately, the effect of all those instant foods is catching up on us in the form of diseases of affluence such as obesity, heart disease and diabetes.

There is, however, no need to turn our backs on progress. We have sufficient knowledge of food and nutrition to let the pendulum swing back just enough to suit our needs. But we need the facts. We need answers. In this section we answer the most frequently asked questions about carbohydrates, diet and GI.

Can you tell me the GI of beef, chicken, fish, eggs, nuts and avocadoes? Why don't these foods appear in GI lists?

These foods contain no carbohydrate, or so little that their GI can't be tested according to the standard methodology. Bear in mind that the GI is a measure of carbohydrate quality, not quantity. Essentially, these types of foods, eaten alone, won't have much effect on your blood glucose levels. We've included these foods in the tables and given them a GI value of [0] for the convenience of our readers.

Can you tell me the GI of alcoholic beverages?

Alcoholic beverages contain very little carbohydrate. In fact, most wines and spirits contain virtually none, although beer contains some (3 or 4 grams per 100 ml). A middy of beer contains about 10 grams carbohydrate compared with 36 grams in the same volume of soft drink. For this reason, a beer will raise glucose levels a little. If you drink beer in large volumes (not a good idea really) then you could expect it to have a significant effect on blood glucose. The tables contain alcoholic beverages with an assigned GI value of [0].

Does the GI increase with the serving size? If I eat twice as much, does the GI double?

The GI *always* remains the same, even if you double the amount of carbohydrate in your meal. This is because the GI is a relative ranking of foods containing the *same amount* of carbohydrate (whether it's 15 grams or 50 grams). But if you double the amount of food you eat, you should expect to see a higher blood glucose response, i.e. your glucose levels will reach a higher peak and take longer to return to baseline compared with a normal serve.

The rise and fall in blood glucose after eating is determined by both the quantity and quality of the carbohydrate. Even if you eat twice as much, the blood glucose level (BGL) won't quite double because the body tries to limit the rise as much as it can. The area under the curve might be 50 per cent greater, instead of 100 per cent more.

If my BGL is determined by both the quantity and quality of the carbohydrate in a meal, how can I predict what I'll see? How can I compare two meals containing different foods with different amounts of carbohydrate and varying GI?

To do this, we calculate the glycemic load of each meal.

Let's say one meal contains 150 grams apple (15 grams of carbohydrate) with a GI of 40. The glycemic load is $(15 \times 40) \div 100 = 6$. Let's say the other meal contains 150 gram potato (20 grams of carbohydrate) with a GI of 90. The glycemic load is $(20 \times 90) \div 100 = 18$. So the glycemic load is about three times higher with a potato than an apple (18 versus 6). While the glycemic response might not be three times higher, the demand for insulin will be.

What is the effect of extra protein and fat on the GI and blood glucose response?

Eaten alone, protein and fat have little effect on blood glucose levels. So a steak or a piece of cheese won't produce a rise in blood glucose. It's the carbohydrates in foods that are primarily responsible for the rise and fall in glucose after meals. But that's not to say that protein and fat won't affect the blood glucose response when eaten together with carbohydrate. Both tend to cause a delay in stomach emptying, thereby slowing the rate at which carbohydrate can be digested and absorbed. So a high fat meal will have a lower glycemic effect than a low fat meal, even if they both contain the same amount and type of carbohydrate. However, you can still count on the fact that a high GI carbohydrate food will produce a higher response than a low GI food, even if there's extra fat and protein added to the meal.

If additional fat and protein cause lower glycemic responses, shouldn't we advocate higher protein or higher fat diets for people with diabetes?

The difficulty with both suggestions is that *very* high fat or high protein diets have been associated with insulin resistance. This means that, over the long term, the consumption of any carbohydrate, regardless of GI, will tend to greatly increase blood glucose and insulin levels and cause deterioration in overall blood glucose control.

More moderate increases in protein and fat (particularly monounsaturated fat) may be possible, but there is relatively little research to guide us. Diets high in monounsaturated fat may improve blood lipids, but they have not been shown to improve overall glycemic control as judged by glycated haemoglobin levels.

Does the GI predict the glycemic effect of a normal serving of food?

On the whole yes. Critics of the GI approach often argue that foods contain different amounts of carbohydrate (both per serve and per 100 grams), while the GI is based on a comparison of the same amount of carbohydrate. On the whole (there are some exceptions), the ranking of foods from high to low, however, turns out to be roughly the same when compared per serve, per 1000 kilojoule or per 100 gram food.

Can you use the GI to predict the effect of a meal containing a mixture of foods with very different GI values?

Yes, the GI can predict the relative effects of different mixed meals containing foods with very different GI values. Over 15 studies have looked at the GI values of mixed meals. Twelve of these studies showed an excellent correlation between what was expected and what was actually found. You can predict the GI of a mixed meal by making a few simple calculations (see page 40). If half the carbohydrate in the mixed meal comes from a food with a GI of 30 (e.g. a legume dhal) and the other half comes from a rice with a GI of 80, then the mixed meal will have a GI of (50% × 30) + (50% × 80) = 55. This is a good example, showing that you don't have to avoid all high GI foods to eat a low GI diet. Inclusion of one low GI food per meal is all that's needed.

What about low carbohydrate diets? If carbohydrates increase my BGL, wouldn't a low carbohydrate intake make sense?

The difficulty with this proposition is that there is hardly a shred of scientific evidence that very low carbohydrate intake benefits anyone. Some popular diets are based on the concept of avoiding carbohydrate foods—even fruit and vegetables are restricted, while meat and dairy foods laden with saturated fat form the basis of the diet. This is a recipe for sudden heart attack—there's a wealth of evidence that diets high in saturated fat are unhealthy.

Low carbohydrate diets come in many forms, however. Some are not so extreme as that described above. The Zone diet recommends less carbohydrate (about 40 per cent instead of 55 per cent) and more protein (30 per cent instead of 15 per cent) but keeps fats less than 30 per cent. It includes advice about quality of carbohydrate (low versus high GI) and type of fat (saturated versus unsaturated). To keep within the recommended limits, many specially prepared and packaged foods are often necessary. If you like this type of diet and can stick to it long term, then there's nothing really wrong with it. But you may find yourself yearning for high carbohydrate foods like bread and potatoes.

One recent study from the Netherlands gave support to a moderate increase in protein (from 15 to 25 per cent) and moderate decrease in carbohydrate (from 55 to 45 per cent). Fat intake was the same in both the control group and the high protein group—30 per cent of energy. Volunteers in the study were permitted to eat as much food as they wished but all were trying to lose weight. At the end of the 12-week study, both weight loss and body fat loss were higher on the high protein diet. The investigators suggested that the higher protein intake had increased the metabolic rate and also increased satiety. It is well known that protein stimulates more thermogenesis (heat production) than any other nutrient and is also the most satiating nutrient. There was no advice about GI on either diet.

You don't have to avoid all high GI foods to eat a low GI diet. Inclusion of one low GI food per meal is all that's needed.

The GI has been criticised because of variability in blood glucose responses between people and in the same person from day to day. How much variation should we expect? How much is acceptable?

When we measure the GI of a food in a group of individuals, not everyone produces the same GI (see Figure 7, page 61). For example, if we test apples (average GI of 40), then one individual might give 20 and another 60. This variation is a natural biological variation that has been traced back to day-to-day variability in glucose tolerance. One of the reasons we test the reference food three times in any one person is to obtain a reliable indication of their normal glucose tolerance. If we tested apples three times, we would also find that each person moved closer to the average result for the whole group. The bottom line is that foods classed as high, medium or low GI, will show the same ranking in different individuals (as shown in Figure 7 overleaf).

This natural variability in blood glucose response has been a major source of criticism of the whole GI approach. But it is illogical to criticise the GI on these grounds because the variability applies to all dietary

approaches, whether it be carbohydrate exchanges, carbohydrate count-
ing or a lower carbohydrate diet. You can rely on the published GI value
as a reliable ranking of foods, reflecting how you as an individual will
respond to different foods most of the time.

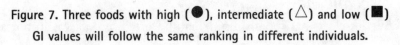

Figure 7. Three foods with high (●), intermediate (△) and low (■)
GI values will follow the same ranking in different individuals.

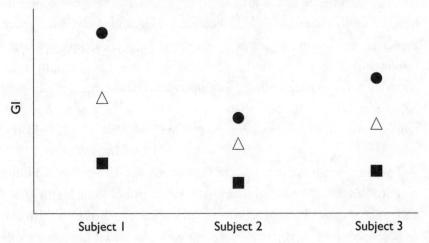

I've read that dairy products cause an increase in insulin secretion. Their GI is around 30–50 but their insulin index is three times higher.

Scientists don't know the reason why dairy products do this. Our guess
is that milk proteins are 'insulinogenic' because they are meant to stimulate the growth of young mammals. Insulin is an anabolic hormone
designed to drive nutrients into cells—not just glucose but also fatty
acids and amino acids, the building blocks of new tissue. Milk may contain a unique combination of amino acids that together are more insulin
stimulating than any alone. This disparity between glucose and insulin
response is not unique to dairy products. We've found that certain

confectionery and baked products also do this. Chocolate may also contain insulinogenic amino acids.

Isn't the insulin response more important? Wouldn't it be better to have an insulin index of foods, rather than a glycemic index?

While it's clear that the insulin demand exerted by foods is important for long-term health, it doesn't necessarily follow that we need an insulin index of foods instead of a glycemic index. When both have been tested together, the glycemic index is extremely good at predicting the food's insulin index. In other words, a low GI food has a low insulin index and a high GI food has a high insulin index. Furthermore, the level of glucose in the blood is directly related to adverse reactions such as protein glycosylation (linkages between glucose and protein) and oxidative molecules.

There are some instances, however, where a food has a low GI but a high insulin index. This applies to dairy foods and to some highly palatable, energy dense 'indulgence foods'. Some foods such as meat, fish and eggs that contain no carbohydrate, just protein and fat (and essentially have a GI of zero), still stimulate significant rises in blood insulin.

At the present time, we don't know how to interpret this type of response (low glycemia, high insulinemia) for long-term health. It may be a good outcome because the rise in insulin has contributed towards the low level of glycemia. On the other hand, it may be not-so-good because the increased demand for insulin contributes to beta-cell 'exhaustion' and the development of type 2 diabetes. Until studies are carried out to answer these types of questions, the GI remains a proven tool for predicting the effects of food on health.

Why do most varieties of rice have such a high GI?

In Australia and New Zealand most varieties of rice have a high GI—Calrose rice (GI of 83) is typical. Imported varieties from Thailand are also high and even brown rice usually has a high GI. The reason can be traced back to the state of gelatinisation of the starch in the cooked grains.

Despite the 'whole grain' nature of rice, complete gelatinisation takes place during cooking. This is because millions of microscopic cracks and fissures in the grains allow water to penetrate right to the middle of the grain during cooking, allowing the starch granules to swell and the starch to hydrate. Some varieties of white rice, such as Basmati and Doongara (CleverRice™) are substantially lower in GI. This is because they have more amylose starch which resists gelatinisation. If you are a big rice eater, we recommend choosing Basmati or Doongara, or alternatively rice noodles (rice vermicelli has a low GI). If you are fond of sushi, you are also in luck! The vinegar used in making sushi as well as the nori (seaweed) helps to lower the GI of sushi to only 48.

Why do GI values sometimes change? For example, one bread used to have a GI of 19, but now it is 36.

These changes worry a lot of people! But you should not be overly concerned. In the case of the bread above, the manufacturer changed the formulation because consumers were concerned that there was too much fat in the bread. Reducing the fat increased the GI but both types of bread were still classified as low GI. Both were the best choices for people who wanted to lower their BGL.

The issue is, however, important from a food labelling perspective. Manufacturers need to have their products retested if they make significant changes to the formulation of a product, or source ingredients from different suppliers.

Another example of a change in GI was the case of a breakfast cereal that increased from 54 to 73. This was a substantial change taking it from a low GI to a high GI food. In this instance, it turned out that the first value had been obtained incorrectly, using a 50 gram carbohydrate portion that inadvertently included the fibre. Since this particular food was a very high fibre product, fibre accounted for over a quarter of the weight. When the product was retested using the larger corrected weight (i.e. a 50 gram portion of 'available' carbohydrate), the GI was, of course, much higher.

This was a good lesson for all laboratories involved in GI testing. Reliable food composition data are needed and, in some instances, direct testing of carbohydrate content is required.

Why has the GI value of carrots changed from 92 to 47?

When carrots were first tested in 1981, the result was 92 but only five people were included in the study and the variation among them was huge. This was in the early days of GI testing and the reference food was tested only once. When carrots were assessed more recently, 10 people were included, the reference food was tested twice and an average value of 47 was obtained with narrow variation. It was clear that this result was more accurate and the other value should be ignored.

Unfortunately, one of the most repeated criticisms of the GI approach was the fact that carrots were being excluded from diets simply because of their high GI. This is a good example of the need for reliable, standardised methodology for GI testing. It is also another case for *not* using GI in isolation.

Does the area under the curve give a true picture of the blood glucose response? What about the shape of the curve and the size of the glycemic spike?

The area under the curve may not be perfect but it is thought to give the best summary measure of the overall degree of hyperglycemia experienced after eating. In research studies, the postprandial (after eating) area under the curve has correlated strongly with measures such as glycated haemoglobin (HbA1c) that are related to risk of complications. In fact, recent studies have surprised even the experts because the findings show that postprandial glycemia influences overall control much more than fasting or pre-meal blood glucose levels. Glycemic spikes appear to be important too but there is a close relationship between the area under the curve and the peak response. If one is high, the other is high and if one is low, the other is low.

If testing were continued long enough, wouldn't you expect the areas under the curve to become equal, even for very high and very low GI foods?

Many people make the assumption that since the amount of carbo-hydrate in the foods is the same, then the areas under the curve will finally be the same. This is not the case, however, because the body is not only absorbing glucose from the gut into the bloodstream, it is also *extracting* glucose from the blood. Just as gentle rain can be utilised better by the garden than a sudden deluge, the body can metabolise slowly digested food better than quickly digested carbohydrate. Fast-release carbohydrate causes 'flooding' of the system and the body cannot extract the glucose from the blood fast enough. Just as water levels rise quickly after torrential rain, so do glucose levels in the blood. But the same amount of rain falling over a longer period can be absorbed into the ground and water levels do not rise.

My doctor has recommended 'SugarBusters™'. Their advice is the opposite to yours and I'm a little perplexed.

SugarBusters™ uses the GI in their advice. The big difference is how they view sugar—they see it as a high GI food and recommend strict avoidance. Americans eat more sugar than Australians and New Zealanders and much of it in the form of corn syrup solids which have a GI of 100. So perhaps their advice is warranted in North America, but not here where sucrose is the main sweetening agent (GI of 68).

Is there a difference between naturally occurring sugars and refined sugar?

Naturally occurring sugars are those found in foods like milk, dairy products, and fruit and vegetables, including their juices. Refined sugar means added sugar, table sugar, honey, maple syrup or corn syrup. Both sources include varying amounts of sucrose, glucose, fructose and lactose. Some nutritionists made a distinction between them because natural sugars are usually accompanied by micronutrients like vitamin C.

The rate of digestion and absorption of naturally occurring sugars is no different, on average, from that of refined sugars. There is, however, wide variation within both food groups, depending on the food. The GI value of fruits varies from 22 for cherries to 72 for watermelon. Similarly, among the foods containing refined sugar, some have a low GI and some a high one. The GI of sweetened yoghurt is only 33, while a Mars Bar™ has a GI of 62 (lower than bread).

People who eat three or four serves of fruit a day (particularly apples and oranges) have the lowest overall GI and the best blood glucose control

Does sugar cause diabetes?

No. There is absolute consensus that sugar in food does not cause diabetes. Type 1 diabetes (insulin-dependent diabetes) is an autoimmune condition triggered by unknown environmental factors such as viruses. Type 2 diabetes (non-insulin-dependent diabetes) is strongly inherited, but lifestyle factors, such as lack of exercise and being overweight, increase the risk of developing it. Because the dietary treatment of diabetes in the past involved strict avoidance of sugar, many people wrongly believed that sugar was in some way implicated as a cause of the disease. While sugar is off the hook, high GI foods are not. Studies from Harvard indicate that high GI diets increase the risk of developing both diabetes and heart disease.

Why are people with diabetes now allowed some sugar in their diet?

For a long time, strict avoidance of sugar was the mainstay of diabetic diets. Healthcare professionals were taught that simple sugars were uniquely responsible for high blood glucose levels. But research has proven that people with diabetes can eat the same amount of sugar as the average person, without compromising diabetes control. It is important, however, to remember that 'empty calories'—whatever the source: sugar, starch, fat or alcohol—won't keep the engine running smoothly. 'Moderation in all things' is a good motto. On average, diets containing moderate amounts of refined sugars (i.e. 50–60 grams a day) contain more micronutrients than diets with more or less sugar.

Why do nutritionists still recommend starchy foods over sugary foods?

Sugar has an image problem stemming largely from research with rodents using unrealistic amounts of pure sugar. It's also seen as a source of 'empty calories' (energy without vitamins or minerals) and concentrated energy. But much of the criticism doesn't stand up in the cold, hard light of scientific fact.

Most starchy foods have the same energy density as sugary foods and even a soft drink has the same energy content per gram as an apple. Starchy foods, such as wholegrain cereals, can be excellent sources of micronutrients but there are many starchy foods that need to be fortified to bring them up to par. Furthermore, there are many pure forms of starch and modified starches being added to foods that are 'empty calories'. So there is really no big distinction between sugars and starches in either nutritional terms or in the GI sense. Our advice is to use sugar to your advantage, as a means of increasing the palatability of nutritious foods (such as brown sugar on porridge or honey on Weetbix™, or jam on bread).

A high fat food may have a low GI value. Doesn't this give a falsely favourable impression of that food?

Yes it does, especially if the fat is saturated fat. The GI value of potato crisps or French fries is lower than baked potatoes. The GI of corn chips is lower than sweet corn. Large amounts of fat in food tends to slow the rate of stomach emptying and therefore the rate at which foods are digested. Yet the saturated fat in these foods will contribute to a much increased risk of heart disease.

If we were to weigh up the health benefits of a high GI but low fat food (e.g. mashed potato) versus one high in saturated fat with a low GI (e.g. biscuits), then the prize goes to the potatoes. The GI was never meant to be the sole determinant when choosing what food to eat. It is essential to base your food choices on the overall nutrient content of a food, including fibre, fat and salt.

It is more important to look at the type of fat in foods rather than avoid it altogether. Foods that contain good fats such as avocadoes, nuts and legumes, are excellent foods. Foods that contain saturated fats, even if their GI is low, such as full fat dairy products, cakes and biscuits, are not as healthy. We'd all be better off if they were saved for special occasions.

Why do many high fibre foods still have a high GI value?

Dietary fibre is not one chemical constituent like fat and protein. It is composed of many different sorts of molecules. Fibre can be divided into soluble and insoluble types.

Soluble fibre is often viscous (thick and jelly-like) in solution and remains viscous even in the small intestine. For this reason it will slow down digestion, making it harder for enzymes to attack their substrate. Foods with more soluble fibre, like apples, oats and legumes, therefore have low GI values.

Insoluble fibre, on the other hand, is not viscous and doesn't slow digestion, especially if it's finely milled. Wholemeal bread and white bread have similar GI values. Brown pasta and brown rice have similar values to their white counterparts. In some instances insoluble fibre is present in a form which acts as a physical barrier delaying access of the enzymes and water to the starch. This applies to intact grains of wheat, rye and barley and to products like All-Bran™.

Can GI values obtained from tests on healthy people be applied to people with diabetes?

Yes, several studies show a good correlation between values obtained in healthy people and people with diabetes (type 1 and type 2). By its very nature, GI testing takes into account differences in glucose tolerance Although people with diabetes have defects in glucose metabolism, there is nothing wrong with their gastrointestinal digestion. High GI foods are still digested quickly and low GI foods are still digested slowly. People with diabetes may have faster stomach emptying early in the disease but, later on, this slows down. The ranking of foods according to their GI is still applicable.

Do low GI foods need to be eaten at every meal in order for people to see a benefit?

No, because the effect of a low GI food carries over to the next meal, reducing its glycemic impact. This applies to breakfast eaten after a low GI dinner the previous evening. It also applies to lunch eaten after a low GI breakfast. This unexpected beneficial effect of low GI meals is called 'the second meal' effect. Don't take this too far, however. On the whole, we recommend that you aim for at least one low GI food per meal.

Some vegetables, like pumpkin, appear to have a high GI. Does this mean that a person with diabetes shouldn't eat them?

Most definitely not, because, unlike potatoes and cereal products, these vegetables are very low in carbohydrate. So, despite their high GI, their glycemic load (GI × carbohydrate per serve divided by 100) is low. Carrots, broccoli, tomatoes, onions, salad vegetables etc that contain only a small amount of carbohydrate but loads of micronutrients should be seen as 'free' foods for everyone. Eat them to your heart's content!

Most breads and potatoes have high GI values (70 to 80). Does this mean I have to avoid my favourite foods?

Potatoes and bread, despite their high GI, can play a major role in a high carbohydrate and low fat diet, even if your goal is to reduce the overall GI. Only about half the carbohydrate needs to be exchanged from high GI to low GI to derive health benefits. So, there is still room for bread and potatoes. Of course, some types of bread and potatoes have a lower GI than others and these should be preferred if the goal is to lower the GI as much as possible.

Opponents of the GI approach say that low GI diets are too restrictive, narrowing the range of foods that can be eaten. Is there any truth in this?

It is a myth that you have to narrow the range of foods you eat on a low GI diet. In fact, some people have told us the opposite. They have found that the advent of the glycemic index has expanded their range of foods because they have been encouraged to try foods they have never eaten before (e.g. Indian dahls, Asian noodles, lentil soups). They also say that there is considerable relief that they now have 'permission' to consume foods containing sugar such as jams and ice-cream. In children with diabetes, studies have shown that those following flexible low GI diets ate the same number of different carbohydrate foods per day (i.e. there was no hint of restricted food choices), they ate the same amount of fat, protein and fibre and they had the same refined sugar intake as children instructed to follow a conventional carbohydrate exchange diet.

The myth that all low GI foods are high in fibre and not very palatable also needs dispelling. It is true that legumes and All-Bran™ may not be everyone's favourite foods, but pasta, oats, fruit and many favourite Mediterranean recipes using cracked wheat and chickpeas are low GI and delicious. To dispel such myths, we have included many mouth-watering recipes using legumes and lentils in Part II.

What about resistant starch? What effect does it have on the GI of a food?

Resistant starch is the starch which completely resists digestion in the small intestine. It cannot contribute to the glycemic effect of the food because it is not absorbed. In testing the GI of a food, resistant starch should not be included in the 50 gram carbohydrate serve. By definition, this portion should include only available or glycemic carbohydrate.

Resistant starch is not viscous like some forms of soluble fibre that delay absorption in the small intestine and flatten the blood glucose curve. Hence the mere presence of resistant starch in the food will not affect the GI of a food. Bananas and potato salad both have high amounts of resistant starch but the GI values of these two foods are still relatively high. The difficulty that arises in GI testing is that the carbohydrate content of a food is often estimated by subtracting the sum of the fat, protein, fibre, water and ash from 100. Unfortunately, this will include resistant starch in the carbohydrate value. Measuring resistant starch separately is complex and time consuming. Thankfully, most foods contain only small amounts of resistant starch and the argument is largely academic.

Would a person with diabetes need to reduce their insulin dose if they changed to low GI foods?

Most studies have not shown a need for a significantly reduced insulin dose when consuming a low GI diet. This is probably because the insulin dose is dictated not just by carbohydrates in the diet but by protein and fat as well. A few studies in subjects using insulin pumps have suggested that they could reduce their insulin dosage and maintain the same blood glucose levels. Further studies are needed to say this confidently.

I have recently been diagnosed with coeliac disease (gluten-sensitivity) on top of diabetes. It's extremely hard to find both low GI and wheat-free foods. Any suggestions?

This is not as hard as you think. If you like Asian food—Indian dahls, stir-fries with rice, sushi, noodles—you're in luck, because they are all low GI. Choose vermicelli noodles prepared from rice or mung beans and low GI rices such as Basmati. Use sweet potato instead of potato, use all manner of vegetables without any regard for their GI. Choose fruits and dairy products for their low GI. If you can tolerate dairy products, then take advantage of their universal low GI. If lactose intolerance is a problem, reach for live cultured yoghurts and lactose-hydrolysed milks. Even ice-cream can be enjoyed if you ingest a few drops of lactase enzyme first. See gluten-free foods in the GI tables for more information.

Will the GI be appearing on food labels?

Food manufacturers are increasingly interested in having the GI of their products measured and the GI concept is already being discussed on the back of food labels. As more and more research highlights the benefits of low GI foods, demand for GI information

has increased. Consumers and dietitians are writing and ringing food companies and diabetes organisations asking for GI data. As a result, food manufacturers are beginning to use the GI as a marketing concept.

As consumers, you have a right to information about the nutrient and physiological effects of foods. You have a right to know the GI of a food and to know it has been tested using appropriate standardised methodology. For this reason, the University of Sydney, Diabetes Australia and the Juvenile Diabetes Foundation Australia have joined forces to run the 'GI Symbol Program'. This symbol on foods is your assurance that the food is a nutritious carbohydrate containing food that has been properly GI tested, whether it be high or low GI. Using the information on the food label, you can combine that food in a way that benefits your long-term health. Profits from the licensing of the symbol will be ploughed back into education programs to benefit all consumers.

Wouldn't it be better to use the glycemic load instead of the GI to compare foods?

The glycemic load is the product of the GI and carbohydrate per serve of food. You'll find this value in the tables in Part IV of the book. It provides a measure of the degree of glycemia and insulin demand produced by a normal serving of the food. The glycemic load of a whole day or whole diet can be calculated from diet records and food frequency questionnaires.

Some nutritionists have argued that this is an improvement on the GI because it provides an estimate of both quantity and quality of carbohydrate (the GI gives us just quality) in a diet.

In large scale studies from Harvard University, however, the risk of disease was predicted by both the GI of the overall diet as well as the glycemic load. The use of the glycemic load strengthened the relationships, suggesting that the more frequent the consumption of high carbohydrate, high GI foods, the more adverse the health outcome.

The controversy surrounding the use of the glycemic load concept stems from its implication that the less carbohydrate consumed, even in low GI forms, the lower the risk of developing type 2 diabetes or heart disease. But this is not the correct interpretation of the data. Carbohydrate content alone showed absolutely no relationship to disease risk. The low risk of disease associated with the lowest glycemic load was driven by the consumption of low GI foods, not by low carbohydrate intake. So our message here is: *don't* aim for a very low carbohydrate diet. This type of diet might have a low glycemic load, but it could also have a high saturated fat content and high energy density. Use the glycemic index to compare foods of similar nature (bread with bread, breakfast cereal with breakfast cereal). Use the glycemic load when you note a high GI but low carbohydrate content per serve (e.g. pumpkin).

There is more information about using the glycemic load on page 275 (How to Use the GI tables).

Everybody can benefit from adopting *The New Glucose Revolution* approach to eating. It is the way nature intended us to eat.

PART II

Your Guide to Low GI Eating

Simple tips to help you change to a low GI diet and fifty delicious recipes to help you enjoy low GI foods.

CHAPTER 5

MAKING THE CHANGE TO A LOW GI DIET

Low GI diets are easy to teach and easy to learn. The basic technique is to swap high GI carbohydrates in your diet with low GI foods. This could mean eating muesli at breakfast instead of cornflakes, wholegrain bread instead of white, or fruit in place of biscuits, for example. In our experience helping people modify the GI of their diet, we've identified some other key points that are crucial in putting the GI into practice. Remember:

• *The GI only relates to carbohydrate-rich foods*

The foods we eat contain three main nutrients—protein, carbohydrate and fat. Some foods, such as meat, are high in protein, while bread is high in carbohydrate and butter is high in fat. It is necessary for us to consume a variety of foods (in varying proportions) to provide all three nutrients, but the GI applies only to high carbohydrate foods.

It is impossible for us to measure a GI value for foods which contain negligible carbohydrate. These foods include meats, fish, chicken, eggs, cheese, nuts, oils, cream, butter and most vegetables. There are other nutritional aspects which you could consider in choosing these foods. For example, the amount and type of fats they contain is significant and varied.

- *The GI is not intended to be used in isolation*

The GI of a food does not make it good or bad for us. High GI foods like potato and bread still make a valuable nutritional contribution to our diet. And low GI foods like sausage that are high in saturated fat are no better for us because of their low GI. The nutritional benefits of different foods are many and varied, and it is advisable for you to base your food choices on the overall nutritional content of a food, particularly considering the saturated fat, salt, fibre and GI value.

- *There is no need to eat only low GI foods*

While most of us will benefit from eating carbohydrate with a low GI at each meal, this doesn't mean consuming it at the exclusion of all other carbohydrate. When we eat a combination of low and high GI carbohydrate foods, like baked beans on toast, fruit and sandwiches, lentils and rice, potatoes and corn, the final GI of the meal is intermediate. The high GI of foods like potato is moderated by including a low GI carbohydrate at the same meal. For example, if your main meal contains potato with a GI of 90, then choose a low GI dessert like low fat yoghurt with a GI of 33. Let's assume that half the carbohydrate comes from the potato and half from the yoghurt. The GI for the meal then becomes (50% × 90) + (50% × 33) = 62.

- *Consider both the GI of the food and the amount of carbohydrate it contains, i.e. the glycemic load*

For some foods, the normal serving size contains so little carbohydrate that the GI of that carbohydrate is insignificant. This is generally the case for vegetables like carrots (47), peas (48) and pumpkin (75) which provide about 6 g of carbohydrate per serving. Small amounts of jam (51) or honey (55) also have little glycemic impact. You can calculate the glycemic load by multiplying the GI by the amount of carbohydrate per serve and then dividing by 100. See 'Let's talk Glycemic Load' on page 26 for more information. We have included the glycemic load of foods in the tables in Part IV.

KEY POINTS
- You don't have to avoid all high GI foods to eat a low GI diet.
- You do need to include a low GI food at every meal.
- If you're not already eating low GI foods, about half the carbohydrate choices in your day need to be exchanged from high GI to low GI types.
- If the high GI foods you choose are high in carbohydrate, eat them in smaller quantities to reduce their glycemic load.

Two simple steps to a low GI diet

1. Begin with a healthy, balanced diet based on a variety of foods.

The first step in developing a healthy low GI diet is to begin with a meal plan based on good nutrition principles. It should be low in saturated fat, have a moderate to high carbohydrate content, be high in fibre and contain a sufficient variety of foods to meet vitamin and mineral requirements.

A balanced diet can still include your favourite high GI foods

Following is a guide to the minimum number of serves needed per day to achieve most people's requirements for energy, protein, vitamins and minerals. We stress that these are minimum amounts and more detailed guidelines for the different needs of adults, pregnant and breastfeeding women, children and adolescents are available at www.health.gov.au/pubhlth/strateg/food/guide/.

- Bread, cereals, rice, pasta and noodles: 4 serves, where a serve is equivalent to 2 slices of bread or 1 cup of rice, pasta or porridge.
- Vegetables, including legumes: 5 serves, where a serve is ½ cup of cooked vegetables or 1 cup of raw salad vegetables.
- Fruit: 2 serves, where a serve is 1 medium piece of fruit or a 125 ml juice.
- Milk, yoghurt, cheese: 2 serves, where a serve is 1 cup of milk or, alternatively, 40 grams of cheese.
- Meat, fish, poultry, eggs, nuts, legumes: 1 serve, where a serve is 65–100 grams cooked meat or 2 small eggs or ½ cup cooked legumes or nuts.

2. Substitute low GI alternatives for carbohydrate foods with a high GI

The next step towards a low GI diet is to look at the type of carbohydrate foods you eat. Identify those which you eat the most of as these have the greatest glycemic impact. Consider the high carbohydrate foods you consume at each meal and replace at least one of these with one low GI food (e.g. replace potato with sweet potato, replace a high GI breakfast cereal with oatmeal, use noodles or Basmati rice instead of normal rice). Substituting half the total carbohydrate from high GI to low GI foods will result in a significant reduction in the overall GI of your diet.

Compare the following menus to see how the GI of a diet can be lowered by making a few simple changes in carbohydrate food choices.

High GI Menu

GI value: 74

Breakfast

30 grams Cornflakes with milk

2 slices wholemeal toast with margarine and Vegemite™

Snack

2 Morning Coffee™ biscuits

Light Meal

A wholemeal roll with ham and salad
An apple

Snack

4 slices Crackerbread with cottage cheese and chives

Main Meal

Roast chicken
1 large baked potato
Baked pumpkin
Peas
A lamington

ENERGY VALUE:

7500 kilojoules
Carbohydrate: 50% of energy
Fat: 30% of energy

Low GI Menu

GI value: 44

Breakfast

30 grams All-Bran™ with low fat milk

2 slices of Bürgen Soy-Lin™ bread with margarine and Vegemite™

Snack

2 Highland Oatmeal™ biscuits

Light Meal

A sandwich (Bürgen Loaf™) with ham and salad
Soft serve vanilla yoghurt with strawberries and toasted muesli sprinkle

Snack

A banana

Main Meal

Roast chicken
1 small baked potato
1 piece of baked sweet potato
Peas
2 scoops of low fat ice cream and 1/2 cup of canned peaches

ENERGY VALUE:

7500 kilojoules
Carbohydrate: 50% of energy
Fat: 30% of energy

Lowering the GI of your diet

Bread Include more grainy varieties and sourdough. If you are making your own bread, substitute about 50 per cent of the flour with whole or cracked grains such as kibbled wheat, barley flakes, oat bran, linseeds. Bürgen™ is a low GI commercial brand.

Breakfast cereals Many processed cereals have high GI values. Check the tables in Part IV for low GI varieties and use these more often.

Casseroles Try substituting kidney beans, borlotti beans or lentils for a portion of the meat. Boosts the fibre and drops the fat too!

Flour Bakery products such as scones, cakes, biscuits, doughnuts and pastries are made with highly refined flour which is quickly digested and absorbed. With your own cooking, try to increase the soluble fibre content by partially substituting flour with oat bran, rice bran, or rolled oats and increase the bulkiness of the product with dried fruits, nuts, muesli, All-Bran™ or unprocessed bran.

Fruit Most fruits have a low GI. Tropical fruits, such as mango, pawpaw, pineapple and rockmelon, tend to have higher values than temperate fruits such as apples and oranges. But all fruits are good for you.

Potatoes Their glycemic impact is lessened by eating smaller serves and varying your diet with alternatives such as sweet potato or butter beans. Tiny new potatoes have a lower GI than normal varieties.

Rice Try Basmati or Doongara rice, or pearled barley, quick-cooking wheat, buckwheat, bulghur, couscous or noodles.

Rissoles or meat loaf Add cooked lentils, canned beans, or rolled oats in combination with the minced meat.

Soups These are a great way to incorporate legumes into your diet. Add lentils, barley, split peas, haricot beans and pasta—make a minestrone! Soup can be a very filling meal.

Sugar Enjoy sugar in moderation. It has an intermediate GI. For a low GI alternative, try apple juice or dried fruit to sweeten dishes. Honey, particularly pure floral honeys, also has lower GI values.

These menus are identical in all but the carbohydrate foods they contain. Careful selection of low GI carbohydrate foods and smaller amounts of high GI carbohydrates in the menu on the right bring about a 40 per cent reduction in the overall GI value.

How do we calculate the GI of a meal, menu or recipe?

It is difficult to calculate the precise GI of a combination of foods unless you have access to food composition figures or a nutrient analysis program, and it is seldom necessary. This is, however, one of the most frequently asked questions by our readers, so here's how it's done.

First of all, the GI of a meal is not the sum of the GI values of each food in the meal, nor is it simply an average of their GI values. The GI of a meal, menu or recipe consisting of a variety of carbohydrate foods is a weighted average of the GI values of each food. The weighting is based on the proportion of the total carbohydrate contributed by each food.

For example, let's say we have a meal of peaches (42) and ice-cream (61). Depending on the amounts of each food, we could calculate the total content of the meal carbohydrate from food composition tables. Let's say the meal contains 60 grams of carbohydrate, with 20 grams provided by the peaches and 40 grams by the ice-cream.

To estimate the GI of this dish we multiply the GI of peaches by their proportion of the total carbohydrate:

$$42 \times {}^{20}\!/_{60} = 14$$

and multiply the GI of ice-cream by its proportion of the total carbohydrate:

$$61 \times {}^{40}\!/_{60} = 41.$$

We then add these two figures to give a GI for this dish of 55.

We have estimated a GI rating for the recipes in this book. Because food processing, including heating, mashing, fermenting, acidifying etc, changes the nature of the carbohydrate, a calculation of the precise GI of the recipes is not possible.

A sensible approach to changing the way you eat

Some people change their diet easily, but for the majority of us, change of any kind is difficult. Unlike altering bad habits such as smoking, changing our diet is seldom just a matter of giving up certain foods. A healthy diet contains a wide variety of foods but we need to eat them in appropriate proportions. The decisions behind what we eat are many and complex and often some professional assistance is necessary to make changes. Helping people improve their diet is something dietitians do every day, so seek one out if you need some help. Keep these four guidelines in mind if you are considering changes to your diet:

1. Aim to make changes gradually
Major changes to diet, for example following a pre-printed menu plan, are usually short-lived. Identify one aspect of your diet which you want to work on (for example, eating more vegetables) and make that your focus.

2. Attempt the easiest changes first
Nothing inspires like success, so increase your chances by attacking the easiest changes first. For example, plan to eat a piece of fruit for morning tea each day.

3. Break big goals into a number of smaller, more achievable goals
A big goal may be wanting to lose weight. This is unlikely to happen quickly, but it is attainable through gradual habit change. Smaller goals could be to exercise for 30 minutes every day and to reduce the

saturated fat content of your diet. Even smaller goals (which are the way to begin) could be to do a 15-minute walk twice a week and limit takeaway to only once a week.

4. Accept lapses in your habits
Lapses are not failures but are natural stages in the progression to new habits.

Putting the GI to work in your day

Breakfast: sustaining you through the day

A growing number of people in the population don't eat breakfast. This is an alarming phenomenon given the evidence that people who do eat breakfast are calmer, happier and more sociable. Studies prove that eating breakfast improves mood, mental alertness, concentration and memory. Nutritionists know that having breakfast helps people lose weight and can lower cholesterol levels. We also know it helps stabilise blood glucose levels.

Missing breakfast can cause symptoms of fatigue, dehydration and loss of energy. A high GI breakfast can also leave you hungry by mid-morning. Many breakfast cereals and breads have a high GI which means while they pick you up initially, they won't last long. When the energy runs out and your blood glucose starts to drop, you feel hungry again. Try some low GI choices at breakfast and see how much easier it is to make it through to lunchtime.

Three-quarters of people who skip breakfast say they have 'no time to eat' so we've included lots of quick, healthy, low GI breakfast ideas. Whether you prefer a liquid breakfast on the go, a hearty hot break-fast or simply a muesli bar and an apple on the way to work, we guarantee you'll find something to sustain you through the day!

The GI is about the type of carbohydrate in your diet

> **DID YOU KNOW?**
> Skipping breakfast is not a good way to cut back your food intake. Breakfast-skippers tend to make up for the missed food by eating more snacks during the day and more food overall.

Low GI breakfast basics

1. Start with some fruit or juice
Fruit contributes fibre and, more importantly, vitamin C, which helps your body absorb the nutrient iron.

Lowest GI fresh fruits and juices

Apples	38	Oranges	42
Bananas	52	Peaches	42
Cherries	22	Pears	38
Custard apple	54	Plums	39
Grapefruit	25	Apple Juice	40
Grapes	46	Grapefruit Juice	48
Kiwi fruit	58	Pineapple Juice	46
Mango	51	Tomato Juice	38

2. Try a low GI breakfast cereal
Cereals are important as a source of fibre and vitamin B. When choosing processed breakfast cereals, look for those with a high fibre content.

The top six low GI breakfast cereals

Kellogg's All-Bran™ Original	30
Kellogg's All-Bran™ Soy and Fibre	33
Kellogg's Guardian™	37
Kellogg's All-Bran™ Fruit and Oats	39
Uncle Toby's Porridge	42
Uncle Toby's Healthwise for Heart Health	48
Vogel's Soytana	49

We know the GI for about 90 different cereals and more are being tested all the time. See the tables in Part IV for more comprehensive values.

3. Add milk or yoghurt
Low fat milk or yoghurt will make a valuable contribution to your daily calcium intake and all have a low GI. Lower fat varieties have just as much, or more, calcium as regular types.

4. Add bread or toast if you are still hungry

Lowest GI breads

Bürgen™ Oat Bran and Honey Loaf with Barley (Tip-Top)	31
Bürgen™ Soy Lin, Soy and Linseed Loaf (Tip-Top)	36
Performax™ (Country Life)	38
Multigrain™ 9-Grain (Tip-Top)	43
Ploughman's Whole-Grain (Quality Bakers)	47
Bürgen™ Mixed Grain (Tip-Top)	49

Ten luscious low GI breakfasts

1. Toast Bürgen™ Fruit Loaf, spread lightly with margarine and accompany with a hot chocolate drink made with low fat milk.
2. Lightly toast some wholegrain, English-style muffins. Spread with creamed corn, top with sliced fresh mushroom and a sprinkle of light mozzarella cheese. Grill until cheese melts and creamed corn is bubbly.
3. Soak four pitted prunes and a teaspoon of linseeds in a little hot water until softened. Stir into a bowl of milky porridge and drizzle with a teaspoon of honey.
4. Take a crisp, toasted slice of sourdough bread and rub with a clove of garlic. Smear with avocado and top with slices of ripe red tomato and grilled eye bacon or prosciutto.

5. Top a bowl of vanilla-flavoured, low fat yoghurt with a sliced peach and chopped strawberries then scatter the top with toasted muesli.

6. Combine a tub of low fat fruit yoghurt with two tablespoons of chopped almonds, one diced banana or pear and one cup of Special K™. Divide between two bowls and serve.

7. Spread a generous layer of Nutella™ over Performax™ low GI, wholemeal toast and team it with a mug of low fat milky coffee.

8. Beat together two eggs, a quarter cup of skim milk, two teaspoons of caster sugar and a teaspoon of vanilla essence. Dip four thick slices of fruit loaf into the egg mixture then cook over medium heat in a greased, non-stick frypan for two to three minutes each side, until golden. Serve topped with pan-fried pear or apple slices and a sprinkling of cinnamon.

9. Spread Bürgen™ loaf with fresh ricotta and top with a dollop of blackberry all-fruit conserve.

10. Make a big bowl of steaming porridge then stir in some frozen blueberries or raspberries. Top with a dollop of low fat natural yoghurt and a sprinkling of brown sugar.

Refuelling with a low GI lunch

Although lunch is often a meal grabbed on the run, it is important to refuel after the four or five hours since breakfast. Lunch needn't be a big meal. In fact, if you find yourself feeling like a sleep after lunch, it may help to eat a lighter meal of protein, vegetables and a small serve of carbohydrate. (A cup of coffee helps too!)

Low GI lunch basics

1. Carbohydrate-rich foods with a low GI, such as wholegrain bread, pasta or noodles, grains or legumes.

2. Proteins like fish, lean meat, chicken, cheese or egg.

3. Vegetables to bulk it out and fill you up.

4. Round it off with fruit.

LUNCHING OUT

Buying lunch and want to know how to get a low GI choice? The following list provides examples of low GI foods you can buy for lunch. Many of the traditional dishes on ethnic restaurant menus will have a low GI because they are based on legumes.

Sushi	48	Stuffed vine leaves	30
Moroccan couscous (with chickpeas)	58	Ravioli	39
Rice noodle soup	40	Tabbouli	30
Tortilla with beans and tomato sauce	39	Lentils and rice	24
Thai noodles with vegetables	40	Pasta marinara	40
Spaghetti bolognaise	52	Dhal	40

Ten light and lively low GI lunch ideas

1. Take a piece of Lebanese bread, spread it with hummus, top with thinly sliced lean roast beef and tabbouli and roll up.

2. Make a lentil and sweet potato soup by browning an onion with two cloves of crushed garlic. Add 500 grams sweet potato chunks, half a cup of split red lentils and three and a half cups of vegetable stock. Simmer for 25 minutes, adding one coarsely grated zucchini after 20 minutes.

3. Slice a sweet potato into five mm thick slices. Cut a zucchini in half lengthways and cut a red onion into six segments. Place vegetables in a freezer bag with a clove of crushed garlic, add a tablespoon of olive oil and shake to coat. Spread out on a baking sheet and roast in a hot oven 20–30 minutes until tender. Toss the roast vegetables through boiled pasta with chopped parsley, oregano or basil and a drizzle of olive oil.

4. Divide a 200 gram packet of corn chips (preferably a salt-reduced, low fat one from the health food section) between four ovenproof plates. Top with a 440 gram can of Mexican or chilli-flavoured

Enjoy lean meat, fish and low fat dairy products

kidney beans and sprinkle with grated light mozzarella cheese. Put under a hot grill for two to three minutes then top with dollops of mashed avocado.

5. Take a 100 gram can of tuna in spring water and a 125 gram can of cannelini beans. Drain and combine in a bowl or lunchbox with half a diced Lebanese cucumber, one diced tomato, a handful of baby spinach (or other greens) and chopped parsley. Dress with an equal mix of olive oil and lemon juice and a sprinkle of black pepper.

6. Spread Bürgen™ Soy-Lin with wholegrain mustard. Top with chopped semi-dried tomatoes, char-grilled eggplant, and a slice of mozzarella cheese. Melt the cheese under a grill then add salad greens and another slice of Soy-Lin. Cut in half and serve.

7. Try canned salmon, thinly sliced green apple and red onion with snow pea sprouts on sourdough bread.

8. Sauté two sliced shallots with a teaspoon each of crushed garlic and ginger until aromatic. Add two to three sliced mushrooms, one teaspoon of minced chilli, one tablespoon of soy sauce and one teaspoon sesame oil and cook until the mushrooms soften. Add one cup of vegetable stock, bring to the boil, then stir in a packet of udon noodles, diced cooked chicken or tofu and a handful of shredded spinach.

9. Cook half a cup of split red lentils in boiling water until tender (about 10 minutes). Drain. When cool, mash with two tablespoons mayonnaise, two chopped shallots and a clove of crushed garlic. Season with black pepper. Use on your favourite bread as a sandwich filling with salad greens.

10. Make a vegetarian chickpea burger by combining a can of drained chickpeas with fresh wholemeal breadcrumbs, parsley, garlic and an egg in a food processor. Shape into patties and pan fry. Serve with char-grilled vegetables on a wholemeal bun.

Low GI main meals: choosing the best

What to make for dinner is the perennial question. When organising the ingredients in your mind for a main meal, think of them in the following order.

1. Choose the carbohydrate

   Which will it be? Potato, rice, pasta, noodles, grains, legumes or a combination? Could you add some bread or corn? It isn't just a matter of choosing the food with the lowest GI value. It is best to include a wide variety of foods in your diet to optimise your nutrient intake. Compare the nutritional properties of the following carbohydrate foods and see why variety is important.

Choosing your main meal carbohydrate

Potatoes Australian potatoes all have high GI values (see the tables in Part IV). Tiny, canned new potatoes have the lowest GI (65). Despite their high GI, potatoes are a healthy food providing a fat-free source of carbohydrate along with significant amounts of vitamin C and potassium. Their glycemic impact is lessened by eating moderate quantities and eating other low GI carbohydrates at the same meal.

Rice White rice is bland in flavour, making it an ideal accompaniment to spicy Chinese, Thai and Indian food. Milling of rice removes the bran and germ, resulting in a considerable loss of nutrients. Because of this, brown rice is a much better source of B vitamins, minerals and fibre. Vary your diet to include both brown and white rice. The lower GI rices are Basmati (58) and Doongara (56).

Sweet potato Orange sweet potato (44), a great source of ß-carotene (the plant precursor of vitamin A), is also rich in vitamin C and makes a colourful addition to any dinner. It is a good source of fibre.

Sweet corn Corn on the cob, or loose kernel corn, is generally a popular vegetable with children and is high in fibre. Corn (54) is also a source of B vitamins.

Legumes Chickpeas, lentils and beans are all high in protein and so are a nutritious alternative to meat. Their content of niacin, potassium, phosphorus, iron and zinc is also high while their fibre content is higher than for the other carbohydrate foods listed here. GI values vary—check the tables in Part IV.

Pasta Pasta is higher in protein than rice or potato and is often eaten as a meal without including meat. It is very satisfying and quick to prepare with the addition of vegetables, or a vegetable sauce and a sprinkling of Parmesan. The GI varies from 37 to 55.

Cracked wheat Bulghur (burghul) is parboiled whole or cracked grains of wheat. Because the whole grain is virtually intact, bulghur (48) provides lots of fibre, thiamin, niacin, vitamin E and minerals.

2. Add vegetables—and lots of them

Fresh, frozen, canned—whatever you have, the more the merrier. The main meal tends to be the prime time for eating vegetables, so if they aren't on your dinner plate, chances are you aren't eating enough of them.

3. Include protein for nutrients, flavour and fill-up value

Protein may come in many forms but we urge you to make sure it's low in saturated fat.

Here are some ideas: slivers of lean beef in a stir-fry, a fillet of fresh fish, strips of lean ham, a dollop of ricotta cheese, a tender skinless chicken breast, slices of salmon, a couple of eggs, a handful of nuts, a sprinkle of cheese, or use the protein found in your grains and legumes.

4. Think twice about the fat you add

Check that you are using a healthy oil, such as olive, canola, mustard seed, macadamia, soybean or another mono- or poly-unsaturated type. Don't overdo it—use only the amount you need.

Ten low GI main meals in minutes

1. Quick Thai Noodle Curry

Stir-fry some strips of onion, red capsicum, baby corn and snow peas (or any stir-fry vegetable mix) in a large pan or wok. Add a tablespoon of red curry paste. Prepare your favourite instant noodles according to directions. Add the noodles to the vegetables with enough stock to make a sauce. Stir in a tablespoon of light coconut milk, heat through and it's ready to serve.

Tip: Canned coconut milk or cream (which is high in saturated fat) can be poured into ice-block trays, frozen and then kept in a plastic bag, making it easy to add just a tablespoon to a dish. Alternatively coconut milk powder can be kept in the pantry and mixed as needed.

2. Speedy Spaghetti

Bring a large pot of water to the boil, add some spaghetti and cook according to the directions on the packet. Meanwhile, open a jar of chunky tomato pasta sauce and heat. Make a green salad with lettuce, spring onions and cucumber, or a bag of mixed lettuce. Serve the spaghetti, topped with the pasta sauce, a good sprinkle of Parmesan cheese and the green salad with vinaigrette alongside.

3. Fast Fish and Tiny Taters

Take a boneless fillet of fresh fish. Dust it with seasoned flour. Heat a non-stick pan with a film of oil and pop the fish in to fry. Wash a handful of tiny new potatoes and microwave or steam them until tender. Squeeze lemon juice over the fish, once you have cooked both sides, and sprinkle with pepper. Serve immediately with the potatoes and a salad or mixed vegetables.

4. Quick Pita Pizza

Spread a round of pita bread with pesto or tomato paste. Top with sliced tomato, mushrooms, roasted capsicum, black olives, chopped spring onions and a sprinkle of Parmesan cheese. Heat through under the grill or in a hot oven.

5. Oriental Noodle and Vegetable Stir-Fry

Stir-fry two rashers of diced bacon (all fat removed) or ham. Add a packet of oriental stir-fry frozen vegetable mix, cooking according to the directions on the bag. Mix in some fresh egg noodles, or prepare instant noodles a few minutes before the end of cooking time, and heat through before serving.

Tip: Look for the packets of frozen stir-fry vegetable mixes that have noodles and a sauce sachet included.

6. Time-saving Tortellini

Boil a packet of spinach and cheese (or your favourite filling) tortellini according to packet directions. Heat some bottled tomato pasta sauce and serve this on top of the tortellini with a sprinkle of Parmesan cheese. Add a salad and vinaigrette alongside.

7. Racy Rice and Lentils

Put some Basmati rice on to cook. Heat a heavy-based frypan with a little oil. Add a finely diced onion, crushed garlic and a couple of teaspoons of minced chilli. Sauté until the onion is soft. Meanwhile dice a tomato. Open a packet of Quickpulse™ ready-to-eat (or canned) lentils and add to onion with the tomato. Add ground cumin, salt and pepper to season, heat through and serve alongside the rice.

8. Easy Chicken Pasta

Set half a packet (125 g) of shell pasta on to boil. Meanwhile, thinly slice half a red capsicum, a handful of button mushrooms and a stick of celery. Chop some leftover barbecue chicken into bite-size pieces. Drain the pasta, add the capsicum, mushrooms, celery and chicken and pour over some 'low oil' creamy salad dressing. Top with chopped spring onions and serve.

9. Tomato and Tuna Pasta

Set some pasta on to boil. In a small pan sauté some chopped parsley, garlic and chilli (optional) in a little oil until aromatic. Add a can of chopped tomatoes (undrained) and small can of flaked tuna. Season with pepper and heat through. Serve the tuna and tomato sauce over pasta.

10. Mexican in Minutes

Brown a handful of lean minced meat and a finely diced onion in a pan. Add a small can of Mexican beans and taco seasoning if desired. Heat through. Serve with tomato salsa, shredded lettuce, avocado and grated cheese in taco shells or pita bread.

Desserts: a low GI finish

It's fairly easy to give a meal a low GI twist through dessert. This is because so many of the basic components of dessert, like fruit and dairy products, have a low GI.

In discussions with people about what they eat these days, dessert is seldom mentioned. With busier lifestyles and concerns about weight, dessert is conveniently missed. While this may appear a positive dietary change, there is a negative nutritional consequence.

Desserts can make a valuable contribution to our fruit and dairy intake, commonly underconsumed foods. What's more, desserts are usually carbohydrate-rich which means they help top-up our satiety centre, signifying the completion of eating.

Low GI desserts

Citrus A winter fruit which is an excellent source of vitamin C. Soak segments of a variety of citrus fruit in orange juice with a slurp of brandy, scatter with raisins or sultanas and serve as winter fruit salad.

Cherries A true summer fruit. Serve cherries around a dollop of low fat plain yoghurt drizzled with a floral honey. Add a sprinkle of flaxseeds to increase your day's omega-3 intake.

Stone fruits Apricots, peaches and nectarines in the shops signals the beginning of warmer weather. Fresh sliced peaches or nectarines are delicious with ice-cream or yoghurt. Sprinkle fresh peach halves with cinnamon and try them lightly grilled.

Pears and apples These are at their peak during autumn and winter, but are available all year. Preparation simply involves washing and slicing—they provide the perfect finish to a meal.

Grapes One of the most popular fruits with children because they are so sweet and easy to eat. Put a bowl on the table after a meal or include them in a fruit salad.

Custard, ice-cream and yoghurt Look for low fat varieties for a cool and creamy accompaniment to your fruit.

Something sweet

Sugar or sucrose, a common ingredient in traditional desserts, has a GI of 68. Most sugary foods have low to moderate GI values. Cakes and biscuits made with or without sugar have similar GI values. Recipes incorporating fruit for sweetness rather than sugar, may have more fibre and a lower GI. Remember temperate climate fruits such as apples, pears and stone fruits tend to have the lowest GI values.

Eight quick and easy low GI desserts

1. Combine a punnet of washed, hulled and halved strawberries with a tablespoon of caster sugar in a small saucepan. Stir over medium heat for about five minutes until the strawberries soften and a syrup forms. Serve over light vanilla ice-cream.

2. Remove the core from large green apples and stuff with a combination of sultanas, currants, chopped dried apricots, cinnamon and a teaspoon of brown sugar. Serve with low fat, natural yoghurt or custard.

3. Drain a can of red plums. Spoon into bowls. Pour over some low fat custard then stir in crumbled coconut macaroons.

4. Make a fruit crumble by topping cooked fruit with a crumble mixture of toasted muesli, wheat flakes, a little melted margarine and honey.

5. Slice a firm banana in half lengthways and top with two scoops of light vanilla ice-cream. Spoon fresh passionfruit pulp over the top and sprinkle with toasted almonds.

6. Top canned fruit halves with a combination of shredded coconut, brown sugar and cinnamon. Drizzle with a little of the juice from the can, then bake for 10 minutes till browned.

7. Brush interleaving sheets of filo pastry with low fat milk (rather than butter or margarine). Place stewed or canned apple, sultanas, currants and mixed spice down the centre and wrap as for a strudel. Brush the top with milk and bake in a hot oven for 15 minutes.

8. Lay a selection of sliced fresh fruits (e.g., mango, pineapple, strawberries, kiwi fruit and rockmelon) on a platter and serve with a bowl of 200 grams natural yoghurt combined with a tablespoon of honey.

Snacks: Maintaining between meals

The fine art of grazing! Hands up all those who thought that sensible eating meant keeping to three meals a day? Of course it may be, if the alternative is to skip breakfast, snack all day and then feast before sleeping at night—certainly not the ideal pattern! New evidence, however, suggests that people who graze properly, eating small amounts of nutritious food throughout the day at frequent intervals, may actually be doing themselves a favour. Recent research indicates frequent small meals stimulate the metabolic rate.

A study which compared people eating a diet of three meals a day with those who had three meals and three snacks showed that snacking stimulated the body to use up more energy for metabolism compared to concentrating the same amount of food into three meals. It's as if the more fuel you give your body, the more it will burn.

The problem with grazing is that often we turn to high fat foods like cakes, chocolate, snack bars, crisps or pastries, which add kilojoules with few nutrients. Another criticism is that for those who tend to overeat, increasing the number of times that they face food is tempting disaster. Choosing snack foods which are carbohydrate rich and have a low GI, however, will reduce your chance of overeating. Using our snack suggestions, you can enrich the variety of foods in your diet and feel satisfied before you have overconsumed!

Sustaining snacks

For a snack to keep you satisfied, make a smoothie with low fat yoghurt, milk and a soft fruit like strawberries, rockmelon or banana. You could also try:

- raisin toast
- a juicy orange
- a bunch of grapes
- a slice of Soy-Lin bread with jam
- a small tub of low fat yoghurt

- a can or tub of diced peaches
- a glass of milk and Milo™
- dried apricots
- a handful of sultanas
- a big green apple
- a scoop of light ice-cream in a cone

If your taste is really for something savoury, try:
- baked corn chips
- hummus (process a can of chickpeas with two cloves of garlic, two tablespoons of tahini and two tablespoons of lemon juice) with pumpernickel bread
- raw vegetables (carrot sticks, green beans, zucchini, cucumber) with a low fat dip such as hummus
- a mini can of baked beans
- marinated vegetables such as artichoke hearts, char-grilled capsicum or eggplant (blot off the oil on paper towel) with toasted Turkish bread

CHAPTER 6

COOKING THE LOW GI WAY

The A to Z of foods

In this section we highlight a host of foods which can feature in a low GI diet. These foods have optimum flavour and nutritional value.

Apples One of the most frequently eaten fruits in Australia, apples, like all fruits, make an excellent low GI snack. In a large study of people with type 1 diabetes, those who ate the most apples had the lowest levels of glycated haemoglobin (one of the best measures of diabetes control). Aim to eat at least two serves of fruit every day.

Bacon Bacon is a valuable ingredient in many dishes because of the flavour it offers. You can make a little bacon go a long way by trimming off all fat and chopping it finely. Lean ham is often a more economical and leaner way to go. In casseroles and soups, a ham or bacon bone imparts a fine flavour without much fat.

Cheese At around 30 per cent fat (most of this being saturated), cheese can contribute quite a lot of fat to a recipe. Although there are a number of fat-reduced cheeses available, many of these lose a lot in flavour for a small reduction in fat. It is worth comparing fat per 100 grams between brands to find the tastiest one with the lowest fat content. Alternatively, a sprinkle of a grated, very tasty cheese, or Parmesan, may do the job.

Ricotta and cottage cheeses are low in fat, usually less than seven per cent fat. Try them as an alternative to butter or margarine on a sandwich. They yield a fraction of the fat. It's worth trying some fresh ricotta from a deli—you may find the texture and flavour more acceptable than that of the ricotta available in tubs in the supermarket. Try ricotta in lasagne instead of a creamy white sauce. Flavoured cottage cheeses are ideal low fat toppings for crackers.

Cream and sour cream Keep to very small amounts as these are high in saturated fat. A 300 ml container of cream can be poured into ice-cube trays and frozen, providing small serves of cream easily when you need it. Adding one ice-cube block (about 20 ml) of cream to a dish, adds seven grams of fat. Low fat, evaporated milk is a wonderful alternative for creamy pasta dishes.

Dried beans, peas and lentils These are all low GI and very nutritious. Incorporate them in a recipe, perhaps as a partial substitution for meat, and try a vegetarian dish (such as chickpea curry, dahl, red lentil soup, Mexican burritos or a bean salad) at least once a week. Canned beans, chickpeas and lentils are now widely available. They are convenient to use and a great timesaver.

Eggs Although the yolk is high in cholesterol, the fat in eggs is predominantly monounsaturated and there is no harm in consuming as much as an egg a day within the context of a low fat diet. To enhance your intake of omega-3 fats we suggest using omega-3-enriched eggs.

Fish All seafood is a healthy choice, but salmon, mullet, swordfish, herrings and sardines are richest in beneficial omega-3 fatty acids. Include fish at least once a week.

Grilling Char-grilling and barbecuing are excellent low fat cooking methods (as long as you don't blacken the meat!). Lean cuts of meat, chicken and fish can be quickly cooked this way. Marinating first or basting during cooking will add flavour, moisture and tenderness.

Herbs Fresh herbs are available in most supermarkets these days and there really is no substitute for the flavour they impart.

Ice-cream A source of carbohydrate, calcium, riboflavin, retinol and protein. Higher fat varieties have the lowest GI—but don't use that as an excuse. It's better to choose lower fat varieties.

Jam A dollop of jam on toast contains far fewer kilojoules than lightly spreading butter or margarine on toast. So, enjoy your jam and give fat the flick!

Keep jars of minced garlic, chilli or ginger in the refrigerator to spice up your cooking in an instant.

Lemon juice Try a fresh squeeze with ground black pepper on vegetables rather than a dob of butter. Lemon juice provides acidity that slows gastric emptying and lowers the GI.

Meat Lean meat is the best source of iron (the nutrient used in carrying oxygen in our blood) so we suggest including it at least two to three times a week. It is important that all visible fat is trimmed from meat before cooking.

Nuts Research suggests that those who regularly eat nuts have a lower risk of heart attack. Nuts are high in poly- and monounsaturated fats, vitamin E and fibre. Try sprinkled over your breakfast cereal, salad or dessert and enjoy unsalted nuts as a snack occasionally.

Olive oil Rich in monounsaturates and antioxidants, extra virgin olive oil is the perfect base for vinaigrette dressing, marinades and Mediterranean-style cooking.

Pasta A food to eat more often and a great source of carbohydrate and B vitamins. Fresh or dried, the preparation is easy. Simply boil in water until just tender or *al dente*, drain and top with a dollop of pesto, a tomato sauce or a sprinkle of Parmesan and pepper.

Questions? Ask your dietitian for more recipe ideas.

Red wine A traditional part of the Mediterranean diet, red wine has been found to be cardioprotective, in moderation. This means no more than 100–200 ml in a day. Wine is a great flavouring in cooking too.

Stock Make your own stock. Prepare it in advance, refrigerate it, then skim off the accumulated fat from the top. Prepared stock is available in long-life cartons in the supermarket. Stock cubes are another alternative. Look for brands that have reduced salt.

Tomatoes Tomatoes or tomato paste can be used with abandon. They are low GI and rich in health-giving lycopenes, a form of vitamin A that also serves as an antioxidant.

Unsaturated fats are good for you, but eat them in moderation. Avoid the saturated fats found in fried fast foods and bakery products. Enjoy the monounsaturated fats in avocadoes, olive and canola oils.

Vinegar A vinaigrette dressing (one tablespoon vinegar and two teaspoons of oil) with your salad can lower the blood glucose response to the whole meal by up to 30 per cent. The best types of vinegars for this purpose are red or white wine vinegar, or use lemon juice if you prefer.

Wholegrains This includes barley, bulghur (cracked wheat), corn, oats, rice and wheat. Most wholegrains have a lower glycemic index than refined cereals and they are also nutritionally superior, containing higher levels of fibre, vitamins, minerals and phytoestrogens. Eating one or more serves a day is associated with improvements in insulin sensitivity and lower risk of cancer and heart disease.

Yoghurt Yoghurt is a valuable food in many ways. It is a good source of calcium, 'friendly bacteria', protein and riboflavin. Unlike milk, it is suitable for those who are lactose intolerant. Low fat, natural yoghurt is a suitable substitute for sour cream. If using yoghurt in a hot sauce or casserole, add it at the last minute and do not let it boil, or it will curdle. It is best if you can bring the yoghurt to room temperature before adding to the hot dish. To do this, mix a small amount of yoghurt with a little sauce from the dish then stir this mixture back into the bulk of the sauce.

Zero fat is unhealthy, so learn how to get just the right amount you need. Our bodies need essential fatty acids that can't be sythesised and must be supplied in the diet. Fat adds flavour—use monounsaturated fats such as olive oil, canola oil and flaxseed oil in your cooking.

Your low GI foods

To make low GI choices easy choices, you need to stock the right foods. Here are some ideas for what to keep in your pantry, fridge and freezer.

What to keep in your pantry

Rolled oats Besides their use in porridge, oats can be added to desserts, cakes, loaves and biscuits

Rice Basmati or Doongara

Dried pasta Spaghetti or fettucine and spirals or macaroni

Dried noodles

Couscous Ready in minutes, serve it with casseroles and braised dishes.

Dried legumes Split red lentils, for example, which take only 20 minutes to cook

Canned legumes Kidney beans, mixed beans, baked beans, borlotti beans, butter beans and chickpeas

Canned vegetables Canned sweet corn, tomatoes, asparagus, peas and mushrooms are always handy to boost the vegetable content of a meal

Canned fish Tuna or sardines in spring water, salmon

Tomato paste Use in soups, sauces and casseroles plus bottled tomato pasta sauces

Bottled vegetables Sun-dried tomatoes, char-grilled eggplant or capsicum, marinated artichoke and mushrooms are handy to keep as flavourful additions to pastas and breads

Prepared stock Campbell's 'Real Stock' or stock cubes

Dried fruits Sultanas, dried apricots, fruit medley, raisins, prunes

Canned fruit Peaches, pears, apple

Canned evaporated skim milk Makes an excellent creamy pasta sauce

Oils Canola for general use, some extra virgin olive oil for salad dressings and dishes which benefit from its flavour, sesame oil for Asian-style stir-fries.

Black pepper

Mustard Seeded or wholegrain mustard is useful for a sandwich spread, in salad dressings and sauces

Asian sauces Hoi sin, oyster, soy and fish sauce are a good basic range

Vinegar White wine vinegar and balsamic vinegar are excellent for salads

Curry pastes A tablespoon or so makes a delicious curry base

Spices Ground cummin, turmeric, cinnamon, nutmeg etc should be bought in small quantities as they lose pungency with age and incorrect storage

Honey Those with the lowest GI include Yellow Box and Stringy Bark

Herbs Oregano, basil, thyme and continental parsley are the most useful. Resealable tubes of chopped herbs are handy when only small amounts are required. Ginger, chilli and garlic can be purchased the same way and in jars, if only small amounts are used

Capers, olives and anchovies Can be bought in jars and kept in the fridge and anchovies once opened. They are tasty (but salty) to add to pasta dishes, salads and pizzas

What to keep in your fridge

Milk Skim or fat-reduced milk

Yoghurt Low fat, natural and fruit

Eggs Omega-3-enriched

Cheese Grated light mozzarella is very handy for adding to a toasted sandwich or sprinkling over a bake. A block of fresh Parmesan is indispensable for grating over pasta and will keep for up to a month. Cottage and ricotta cheeses have a short life so are best bought as needed

Fresh pasta or noodles A great standby for a quick meal

What to keep in your freezer

Low fat ice-cream Always ideal for a quick dessert, served with fresh fruit

Spinach Great for adding to pastas

Baby beans Can be added to curries and stir-fries

Peas and corn Handy to add to a quick meal

Berries Make any dessert special

Your low GI food fact finder

Use this to quickly identify low GI foods and discover their other nutritional benefits.

Breads

Bürgen™ varieties (GI of 31–74)   A mixed grain bread from Tip Top Bakeries, Sydney. Available in supermarkets. Bürgen Oat Bran and Honey Loaf with Barley has the lowest GI of all mixed grain breads (GI of 31). Other varieties of Bürgen™ bread also have a low GI.

Fruit loaf (GI of 44–54)   Available in wholemeal and white varieties, but Bürgen Fruitloaf has the lowest GI (GI of 44). The GI of fruit loaf is probably lowered by part substitution of flour (high GI) with fruit (lower GI).

Pita bread (GI of 57)   Unleavened flat bread was found to have a slightly lower GI than regular bread in a Canadian study. Sold in supermarkets in packets of flat rounds.

Ploughman's loaf™ Wholegrain (GI of 47)   A wholemeal bread with additional wholegrains. It is widely available in supermarkets. Other varieties under the Ploughman's label are probably also low GI.

Pumpernickel bread (GI of 41)   Also known as rye kernel bread because the dough it is made from contains 80 to 90 per cent whole rye kernels. It has a strong flavour and is usually sold thinly sliced. Because it is not made with fine flour, its GI is much lower than ordinary bread. Available in supermarkets and delicatessens.

Breakfast cereals

Breakfast cereals   The high degree of cooking and processing of commercial breakfast cereals tends to make the starch in them more rapidly digestible, giving a higher GI. Less processed cereals (muesli, rolled oats) tend to have lower GI values. All-Bran™ and varieties (GI of 30-51), Frosties™ (GI of 55), Guardian™ (GI of 37), Healthwise™ for Heart Health (GI of 48), Komplete (GI of 48), Muesli (GI of 39-66), Oat bran (GI of 55), Rice bran (GI of 19).

Porridge Published GI values range from a low 42 up to 75 for 'one minute oats'. The additional cutting of rolled oats to produce quick cooking oats probably increases the rate of digestion causing a higher GI.

Dairy foods

Custard (GI of 35) Made with milk, so provides calcium, protein and B vitamins plus a little sugar, vanilla flavouring and a starch thickener.

Ice-cream (GI of 36–80) Go for the lower fat varieties. Most dairy products have very low GI values. When we eat dairy foods a protein curd forms in the stomach and slows down its emptying. This has the effect of slowing down absorption and lowering the GI.

Milk (GI of 31) Lactose, the sugar occurring naturally in milk, is a disaccharide which must be digested into its component sugars before absorption. The two sugars that result, glucose and galactose, compete with each other for absorption. This slows down absorption and lowers the GI. The presence of protein and fat in milk also lowers the GI.

Yoghurt (GI of 14-36) A concentrated milk product, soured by the use of specific bacteria. All varieties have a low GI, including those containing sugar. Artificially sweetened brands have both a lower GI and contain fewer kilojoules.

Fruit

Apples (GI of 38) Easy to incorporate into the diet as a low GI food—an average apple will add three grams of fibre to your diet. They are also high in pectin which lowers their GI.

Apple juice (GI of 40)   The main sugar occurring in apples is fructose (6.5 per cent) which itself has a low GI. The high concentration of sugars is known to slow the rate of stomach emptying, hence slowing the absorption and lowering GI.

Apricots (GI of 64, canned; 30, dried)   Apricots are an excellent source of ß-carotene and dried apricots in particular are high in potassium. Like apples, they are high in fructose (5 per cent) which lowers their GI.

Cherries (GI of 22)   The GI for cherries is based on European cherries. Australian cherries which are 6 per cent glucose and 4.4 per cent fructose may have a higher GI value.

Grapefruit (GI of 25)   The low GI of grapefruit may be due to their high acid content which slows absorption from the stomach.

Grapes (GI of 46)   An equal mix of fructose and glucose and a high acid content are characteristics of fruits with a low GI. Grapes are a good example.

Kiwi fruit (GI of 58)   Kiwi fruit contain equal proportions of glucose and fructose and high acidity giving a reasonably low GI. They are also a wonderful source of vitamin C with one kiwi fruit meeting the total recommended daily intake.

Oranges (GI of 42)   Well known as a good source of vitamin C, most of the sugar content of oranges is sucrose. This, and their high acid content, probably accounts for their low GI.

Peach (GI of 42, fresh; 52, canned in light syrup)   Most of the sugar in peaches is sucrose (4.7 per cent). Other aspects like their acid and fibre content may account for their low GI.

Pears (GI of 38, fresh; 43, canned)   Another fruit with a high fructose (7 per cent) content, accounting for the low GI.

Pineapple juice (GI of 46)   Mainly sucrose (8 per cent).

Plums (GI of 39)   The GI for plums comes from a European study. Australian plums contain a fairly equal mixture of glucose, fructose and sucrose. The higher the concentration of sugars, the slower the food is emptied from the stomach and hence the slower the absorption. This may account for the low GI.

Sultanas (GI of 56)   Sultanas are less acidic than grapes and this may account for their slightly higher GI since increased acidity is associated with lower GI values.

Grains

Barley (GI of 25)   'Pearled' barley, which has had the outer brown layers removed, is most commonly used. It is high in soluble fibre which probably contributes to its low GI. Available in supermarkets.

Basmati rice (GI of 58)   Has a low GI attributable to the type of starch it contains (high amylose starch). Available in supermarkets. The only Australian-grown species of rice with a high amylose content is Doongara.

Buckwheat (GI of 54)   Buckwheat is available from health food stores and some supermarkets. It can be cooked as a porridge, or steamed and served with vegetables in place of rice. It can also be ground and used as flour for making pancakes and pasta. Buckwheat in this form is likely to have a higher GI than when whole.

Bulghur (burghul) (GI of 48)   Made by roughly grinding previously cooked and dried wheat. Most commonly recognised as a main ingredient in tabbouli. The intact physical form of the wheat contributes to its low GI.

Doongara rice (GI of 56)   An Australian-grown rice with a high amylose content and low GI. Available in supermarkets and in bulk quantities from wholesalers and some Asian food stores.

Oat bran (GI of 55)   Unprocessed oat bran is available in the cereal section of supermarkets, usually loosely packed in plastic bags. Its carbohydrate content is lower than that of oats and it is higher in fibre, particularly soluble fibre, which is probably responsible for its low GI. A soft, bland product, it is useful as a partial substitution for flour in baked goods to lower the GI.

Oats   See porridge under Breakfast cereals

Parboiled rice (GI of 38–87)   Parboiling involves steeping rice in hot water and steaming it prior to drying and milling. Nutrients from the bran layer are retained in the grain and the cooked product has less tendency to be sticky. Some studies have found parboiled rice to have a lower GI but studies on Australian rice have found only small differences between parboiled and regular rice. The over-riding determinant of the GI of rice is the type of starch present in the grain.

Quick-cooking wheat (GI of 54)   Whole wheat grains which have been physically treated to allow short cooking times, quick-cooking wheat is most often used as a substitute for rice. The whole grain structure also acts as a barrier and so reduces its digestibility and hence lowers the GI.

Rice bran (GI of 19)   Rich in fibre (25 per cent by weight) and oil (20 per cent by weight), rice bran has an extremely low GI. It is available in the cereal section of supermarkets as Sunfarm Rice Bran from Sunrice Australia.

Legumes

Legumes (GI of 10–70)   Also known as pulses. These include dried peas, beans and lentils, most have a GI of 50 or less. Canned varieties have a slightly higher GI than their home-cooked counterpart due to the higher temperature during processing.

Soya beans (GI of 14–20)   These have one of the lowest GI values, possibly due to their higher protein and fat content. The viscous fibre in legumes reduces physical availability of starch to digestive enzymes.

Nuts

Nuts Contain relatively little carbohydrate so they do not have a GI value. Most nuts average about 50 per cent fat but this is predominantly healthy fat of the mono- and polyunsaturated varieties.

Research suggests that a small handful of unsalted nuts (30 grams) on most days of the week is beneficial in lowering cholesterol and reducing risk of heart attack.

Peanuts (GI of 14) are not truly nuts, but legumes. They contain about 25 per cent carbohydrate but have minimal effect on blood glucose level.

Pasta

Pasta (GI of 32–78)   Pasta is made from hard wheat semolina with a high protein content, which gives a strong dough. Protein-starch interactions and minimal disruption to the starch granules during processing contribute to the low GI. There is some evidence that thicker pasta has a lower GI than thin types.

Spaghetti (GI of 38)   While both fresh and dried pastas have a low GI, this is not the case for canned spaghetti. Canned spaghetti is generally made from flour rather than high protein semolina and is very well cooked—two factors which are likely to give it a high GI.

Vegetables

Most vegetables are low in carbohydrate, which makes it difficult to measure their GI. Even those for which a GI has been measured have little effect on blood glucose levels in the quantities usually eaten.

Peas (GI of 48)   Peas are high in fibre and also higher in protein than most other vegetables. Protein-starch interactions may contribute to their lower GI. They also average four per cent sucrose, giving them a sweet flavour.

Sweet corn (GI of 54)   Raw, fresh, frozen or canned varieties would be suitable to use. Corn on the cob has a lower GI than corn chips or cornflakes. The intact whole kernel makes enzymic attack more difficult.

Glycemic load incorporates both the amount and type of carbohydrate   113

Sweet potato (GI of 44) Belonging to a different plant family to regular potato, sweet potatoes are mainly available either white or yellow/orange in colour. The 'sweetness' comes from a high sucrose content. Sweet potato is high in fibre. It has a lower GI than regular potato varieties.

CHAPTER 7

RECIPES

A note about the recipes in this book

All the recipes in this book have been analysed using a computerised nutrient analysis program (Foodworks™, Xyris Software (Australia) Pty Ltd) and the GI, kilojoule, carbohydrate, fat and fibre content per serve is shown. The following information will help put this nutritional profile into context for you. Where a range of servings is given for the recipe, the nutritional information relates to the higher number of serves.

GI We have given each recipe a GI rating, which is our best estimate of the range in which the GI falls. A calculated GI value is not realistic for all recipes because the carbohydrate may be in a different form to that in which the original GI of the food was tested.

Energy This is a measure of how many kilojoules and calories a serving provides. A moderately active woman aged 18 to 54 years consumes about 8000 kilojoules a day; a man about 10 000 kilojoules. Those who burn lots of energy through exercise need a higher kilojoule intake than those who live more sedentary lives.

Carbohydrate It is not necessary to calculate how many grams of carbohydrate you eat on a daily basis; however, if you're an athlete or you have diabetes you may find this information useful. To consume around 50 per cent of energy from carbohydrate, on average, women need about 200 grams a day, while men need about 300 grams. Athletes can consume anywhere from 300 to 700 grams of carbohydrate a day, providing 50–60 per cent of their energy needs. Multiplying the carbohydrate content per serve of the recipe by its GI gives you the glycemic load. See page 26 for an explanation of the glycemic load and the tables in Part IV for glycemic load values.

Fat We have aimed to keep our recipes low in fat, in particular low in saturated fat. For this reason we have used mono- and poly-unsaturated margarines and oils. Omega-3 fatty acids from fish and seafood have many health benefits so we have included a number of recipes containing these foods and used omega-3-enriched eggs.

The amount of fat that is appropriate in your diet depends on your kilojoule intake and the overall composition of your diet. A low fat diet for most people could contain somewhere between 30 and 60 grams of fat per day. If you are not trying to lose weight there is no harm in consuming larger amounts of fat, so long as it is predominantly unsaturated.

Fibre Most of the recipes are high in fibre, both soluble and insoluble. Dietary guidelines recommend a daily fibre intake of at least 30 grams. People with diabetes should aim for 40 grams. A slice of wholemeal bread provides two grams of fibre, an average apple four grams. The average Australian consumes only 20 grams of fibre a day.

BREAKFASTS

Sweet Potato and Corn Hotcakes with Pan-fried Tomato and Basil
Honey Banana Smoothie
Swiss Bircher Muesli with Mixed Fresh Fruit
Raisin-studded Porridge
Buttermilk Pancakes with Glazed Fruit

Sweet Potato and Corn Hotcakes with Pan-fried Tomato and Basil

$\frac{1}{2}$ cup self-raising flour

$\frac{1}{2}$ cup rolled oats

1 egg, lightly beaten

$\frac{1}{2}$ cup low fat milk

1 × 270 g can corn kernels, drained

1 small (150 g) sweet potato, peeled and grated

freshly ground black pepper

3–4 ripe tomatoes, cut into 1 cm thick slices

handful of fresh basil leaves

LOW GI

Per serve:

kJ 386

kCal............90

carb............15 g

fat ....1 g

fibre............2 g

1. Combine the flour and rolled oats in a medium-sized bowl. Using a whisk, stir in the beaten egg and milk, mixing until combined. Stir in the corn kernels and grated sweet potato with the pepper.

2. Brush a non-stick frying pan with oil or spray with cooking spray over medium heat. Add large spoonfuls of the mixture to the pan. Cook 2 minutes or until bubbles begin to form. Turn and cook 1–2 minutes on the other side. Repeat with remaining mixture. Set aside cooked hotcakes in a warm place.

3. Once you are finished cooking the hotcakes, regrease the frying pan and place over medium heat. Add the sliced tomatoes, cooking for a couple of minutes until browned on one side, then turn, sprinkle with basil and cook until softened. Serve the fried tomatoes and basil over the hotcakes.

MAKES 10 HOTCAKES

Honey Banana Smoothie

The 'smoothie'—a quick, but sustaining breakfast. Many variations are possible using different combinations of fruits, milks and yoghurts.

1 large, ripe banana
1 tablespoon All-Bran™ breakfast cereal
1 cup (250 ml) low fat milk, chilled
1/2 cup (125 ml) evaporated low fat milk, well chilled
2 teaspoons honey
few drops vanilla essence

LOW GI
Per serve:
kJ 800
kCal............190
carb............35 g
fat ....0.5 g
fibre............2 g

1. Peel banana and chop roughly.
2. Combine with remaining ingredients in a blender and blend for 30 seconds or until smooth and thick.
3. Serve immediately.

SERVES 2

For this recipe the evaporated milk must be chilled to froth up well.

Swiss Bircher Muesli with Mixed Fresh Fruit

Mushy rolled oats, plump sultanas and crunchy almonds combined with natural yoghurt and milk.

1 cup (80 g) rolled oats
⅔ cup (150 ml) low fat milk
1 tablespoon sultanas
½ cup (100 g) low fat plain yoghurt
¼ cup (40 g) whole almonds, chopped
1 apple, grated
lemon juice (optional)
mixed fresh fruit, such as strawberries, pear, plum,
    passionfruit

LOW GI
Per serve:
kJ 1540
kCal...........365
carb...........50 g
fat ....11 g
fibre...........6 g

1. Combine the oats, milk and sultanas in a bowl. Cover and refrigerate overnight.
2. Add the yoghurt, almonds and apple; mix well.
3. To serve, adjust the flavour with lemon juice. Serve with fresh fruit.

SERVES 2

Raisin-studded Porridge

⅔ cup (60 g) rolled oats
I cup (250 ml) low fat milk, approximately
I small ripe banana, mashed
I heaped tablespoon raisins

LOW GI
Per serve:
kJ 890
kCal............210
carb............38 g
fat ....3 g
fibre............3 g

1. Place the oats in a saucepan or large microwave jug. Add sufficient water to cover plus about ⅔ cup of the milk.
2. Bring to a boil and boil for 2 minutes or microwave on high for I to 2 minutes.
3. Add the banana and cook I to 2 minutes more.
4. Add the remaining milk to make a smooth consistency and stir through raisins.

SERVES 2

Buttermilk Pancakes with Glazed Fruit

Golden light pancakes served with warm, soft stone fruits.

1 cup (100 g) 1-minute oats or unprocessed oat
   bran
2 cups (500 ml) buttermilk
1/2 cup (75 g) dried fruit medley, chopped
1/2 cup (75 g) plain flour, sifted
2 teaspoons sugar
1 teaspoon bicarbonate of soda
1 egg, lightly beaten
2 teaspoons mono- or polyunsaturated margarine,
   melted
low fat milk, (optional)

Glazed peaches

1 tablespoon mono- or polyunsaturated margarine
1 tablespoon brown sugar
6 medium peaches or apricots or nectarines

LOW GI	
Per serve:	
kJ	1770
kCal	420
carb	60 g
fat	12 g
fibre	6 g

1. Combine the oats and buttermilk in a bowl and let stand 10 minutes.
2. Stir in the dried fruit, flour, sugar, bicarbonate of soda, egg and margarine; mix thoroughly. Let stand for up to 1 hour.
3. After standing, add a little low fat milk if the mixture is too thick.
4. Heat a non-stick frying pan and spray with cooking spray or grease lightly with margarine. Pour in about 3 tablespoons of batter, cook over moderate–high heat until bubbly on top and lightly browned underneath. Turn pancake to brown on other side. Repeat with remaining batter.
5. Set aside to keep warm.
6. To make the glazed fruit, melt the margarine and sugar together over medium heat in frying pan. Stir till sugar is dissolved. Add the sliced fruit and cook over medium heat 2–3 mins until softened. Serve warm over the pancakes.

SERVES 4

Dried fruit medley is a mixture of dried fruit and is available from supermarkets and health food stores.

LIGHT MEALS

Pasta with Roasted Pumpkin and Capsicum in a White Wine sauce
Marinated Mushroom and Cracked Wheat Salad
Lentil and Barley Soup
Minestrone
Split Pea Soup
Pasta and Red Bean Salad
Tabbouli
Vegetable Lasagne
Creamy Mushrooms and Pasta
Pasta Primavera
Spicy Noodles

Pasta with Roasted Pumpkin and Capsicum in a White Wine Sauce

650 g (approx ¼ medium) jap pumpkin

1 large (200 g) red capsicum, halved lengthways,
   seeds removed

2 sprigs fresh rosemary

1 clove garlic

1 tablespoon olive oil

250 g pasta shapes (e.g., bows or twists)

White wine sauce:

1 teaspoon olive oil

1 teaspoon margarine

1 large (200 g) red onion, halved and thinly sliced

1 clove garlic, crushed

2 teaspoons seeded mustard

1 sprig fresh rosemary, chopped

½ cup white wine

200 ml low fat evaporated milk

basil leaves

LOW GI

Per serve:

kJ	1745
kCal	410
carb	63 g
fat	8 g
fibre	5 g

1. Preheat a fan-forced grill on medium high.
2. Cut the pumpkin into 3 wedges. Peel and then slice each wedge into 0.5 cm thick slices, to create small triangular shaped pieces of pumpkin. Toss the sliced pumpkin and capsicum in the olive oil with the rosemary and garlic to coat. Lay the pumpkin in a single layer, and the capsicum skin-side up, on a sheet of baking paper on a tray. Place under a fan-forced hot grill for 10 minutes.
3. Put the pasta on to cook in a large saucepan of boiling water.
4. Remove the capsicum from the grill and place in a paper bag, fold down the top and set aside. Return the pumpkin to the grill for another 5–10 minutes or until it is browned and tender.
5. Heat the olive oil and margarine in a large frying pan and sauté the onion and garlic over moderate heat for 2 minutes. Add the mustard, rosemary and white wine and simmer for 2 minutes to reduce slightly.
6. While the wine is reducing, remove the capsicum from the bag and peel off the skin (which should lift easily). Slice into strips.
7. Add the evaporated milk to the frying pan and a handful of fresh basil leaves, stirring over low heat as they wilt. Add the drained hot pasta stirring to coat with the sauce. Then add the capsicum strips and pumpkin and serve.

SERVES 4

Marinated Mushroom and Cracked Wheat Salad

A super nutritious high fibre salad.

125 g button mushrooms, sliced
2 green shallots, finely chopped
1 cup (160 g) cracked wheat (burghul)

Marinade

3 tablespoons lemon juice
3 tablespoons olive oil
1 teaspoon brown sugar
1 clove crushed garlic
2 tablespoons parsley, finely chopped
1 tablespoon mint, finely chopped

LOW GI	
Per serve:	
kJ	810
kCal	195
carb	22 g
fat	10 g
fibre	5 g

1. Combine ingredients for marinade in a bowl. Add mushrooms and shallots, stirring to coat. Cover and refrigerate for about an hour for the mushrooms to soften and the flavours to develop.
2. Meanwhile, place the burghul in a bowl and cover with hot water. Stand for about half an hour for the burghul to absorb the water and soften.
3. Drain the burghul, squeezing out excess water by wrapping in absorbent kitchen paper. Toss the burghul with the marinated mushrooms and spoon into a serving dish.

SERVES 4 TO 6

Lentil and Barley Soup

A satisfying winter soup that makes a meal in itself.

1 tablespoon oil
1 large onion (150 g), finely chopped
2 cloves garlic, crushed, or 2 teaspoons minced garlic
$\frac{1}{2}$ teaspoon turmeric
2 teaspoons curry powder
$\frac{1}{2}$ teaspoon ground cumin
1 teaspoon minced chilli
6 cups (1.5 litres) water
1$\frac{1}{2}$ cups (375 ml) prepared chicken stock
1 cup (200 g) red lentils
$\frac{1}{2}$ cup (100 g) pearl barley
1 × 425 g can tomatoes, undrained and mashed
salt
freshly ground black pepper
chopped fresh parsley or coriander, to serve

LOW GI
Per serve:
kJ 760
kCal............180
carb ....25 g
fat ....5 g
fibre............5 g

1. Heat the oil in a large saucepan. Add the onion, cover and cook gently for about 10 minutes or until beginning to brown, stirring frequently.
2. Add the garlic, turmeric, curry powder, cumin and chilli and cook, stirring, for 1 minute.
3. Stir in the water, stock, lentils, barley, tomatoes, and salt and pepper to taste. Bring to a boil, cover and simmer about 45 minutes or until the lentils and barley are tender.
4. Serve sprinkled with parsley or coriander.

SERVES 4 TO 6

Minestrone

Serve this hearty soup with crusty bread and a green salad.

1/2 cup (100 g) dried haricot beans, or 310 g can,
  rinsed and drained
oil
2 medium onions (240 g), chopped
2 cloves garlic, crushed
2 bacon bones (about 300 g)
10 cups (2.5 litres) water
5 beef stock cubes
3 carrots (360 g), diced
2 sticks celery (160 g), sliced
2 small zucchini (200 g), chopped
4 tomatoes (400 g), diced
1/3 cup (60 g) small macaroni pasta
2 tablespoons fresh parsley, chopped
freshly ground black pepper
grated Parmesan cheese, to serve (optional)

LOW GI
Per serve:
kJ 510
kCal............120
carb............18 g
fat ....2 g
fibre............7 g

1. If using dried haricot beans, soak overnight in water to cover by 5 cm.
2. Heat a little oil in a large heavy-based saucepan. Add the onions and garlic and cook for about 5 minutes or until soft. Add the bacon bones, water, stock cubes and drained beans. Bring to a boil and simmer, covered, about 2 1/2 hours or until beans are tender. (If using canned beans, simply bring to a boil.)
3. Add the carrots, celery, zucchini and tomatoes to the stock. Reduce heat and simmer, covered, for 1 hour.
4. Remove the lid, take out the bacon bones and add the macaroni. Continue to simmer for 10 to 15 minutes or until the macaroni is tender.
5. Stir in the parsley and add pepper to taste. Serve with Parmesan cheese.

SERVES 6

Split Pea Soup

Begin this full flavoured favourite a day ahead, allowing the split peas to soak overnight.

2 cups (500 g) split peas
1 ham bone or 500 g bacon bones
12 cups (3 litres) water
1 teaspoon oil
1 medium onion (120 g), finely chopped
1 medium carrot (120 g), finely chopped
1 stick celery (80 g), finely chopped
1 bay leaf
½ teaspoon dried thyme leaves
juice of ½ lemon
freshly ground black pepper

LOW GI	
Per serve:	
kJ	1100
kCal	260
carb	39 g
fat	3 g
fibre	9 g

1. Wash the split peas, place in a large saucepan with the ham bone or bacon bones and water. Bring to a boil. Allow to cool, refrigerate overnight.
2. Next day, skim any fat from the top and bring to a boil and simmer, covered, for 2 hours.
3. Remove the bones from the soup and trim any meat from them. Return the meat to the soup.
4. Heat the oil in a frying pan, add the onion, carrot and celery and cook for about 10 minutes or until lightly browned. Add the onion mixture to the soup with the bay leaf and thyme. Simmer, covered, for 20 minutes. Remove the bay leaf.
5. Purée the soup in a food processor or blender adding extra water if necessary to make a soup consistency.
6. Add the lemon juice and season to taste with pepper. Reheat if needed before serving.

SERVES 6

Pasta and Red Bean Salad

A summer salad full of flavour. Easy to prepare with canned beans.

1 cup (150 g) cooked pasta (e.g. shells, elbows,
   twists)
1 cup (about 200 g) cooked or canned red kidney
   beans, well drained
3 green shallots, finely chopped
1 tablespoon fresh parsley, finely chopped

Dressing

1 tablespoon olive oil
1 tablespoon wine vinegar
1 teaspoon Dijon mustard
1 clove garlic, crushed
freshly ground black pepper

LOW GI	
Per serve:	
kJ	540
kCal	130
carb	15 g
fat	5 g
fibre	4 g

1. Combine the pasta, beans, shallots and parsley in a serving bowl.
2. For the dressing, combine the oil, vinegar, mustard, garlic and pepper in a screw-top jar; shake well to combine.
3. Pour the dressing over the pasta mixture and toss well.

SERVES 4

Tabbouli

Tabbouli is best if you make it ahead, allowing time for the flavours to develop. It keeps a couple of days in the refrigerator.

$^1/_2$ cup (110 g) cracked wheat (burghul)
1 cup (50 g) fresh flat-leafed parsley or continental
   parsley, finely chopped
1 small onion (100 g) or 3–4 shallots, finely chopped
1 medium tomato (100 g), finely chopped

Dressing

2 tablespoons fresh lemon juice
2 tablespoons olive oil
pinch salt
$^1/_2$ teaspoon freshly ground black pepper

LOW GI
Per serve:
kJ 680
kCal............160
carb...........15 g
fat ....10 g
fibre...........5 g

1. Cover the burghul with hot water and soak for 20-30 minutes to soften. Drain well and roll in a kitchen towel to squeeze out excess water.
2. Combine the burghul, parsley, onion and tomato in a bowl.
3. For the dressing, combine all the ingredients in a screw-top jar; shake well.
4. Add the dressing to the burghul mixture and toss lightly to combine.

SERVES 4

Variations include the addition of a chopped cucumber, a crushed clove of garlic or 2 table-spoons of chopped fresh mint. You can use half lemon juice and half vinegar if preferred.

Vegetable Lasagne

Soft layers of spinach, cheese and lasagne with a luscious vegetable sauce.

1 bunch English spinach, washed and stalks removed
200 g packet instant lasagne sheets
2 tablespoons (20 g) grated Parmesan cheese or low
   fat cheddar cheese

Vegetable Sauce

2 teaspoons oil
2 medium onions (240 g), chopped
2 cloves garlic, crushed, or 2 teaspoons minced garlic
250 g mushrooms, sliced
1 small green capsicum (100 g), chopped
140 g tub tomato paste
1 × 440 g can mixed beans, rinsed and drained
1 × 440 g can tomatoes, undrained and mashed
1 teaspoon mixed herbs

Cheese Sauce

20 g poly- or monounsaturated margarine
1 tablespoon plain flour
1 1/2 cups (375 ml) low fat milk
1/2 cup (60 g) grated low fat cheese
pinch ground nutmeg
freshly ground black pepper

LOW GI
Per serve:
kJ 1420
kCal...........340
carb...........44 g
fat ....10 g
fibre...........9 g

1. Blanch or lightly steam the spinach until just wilted; drain well.
2. For the vegetable sauce, heat the oil in a non-stick frying pan. Add the onions and garlic and cook for about 5 minutes or until soft. Add the mushrooms and capsicum and cook a further 3 minutes, stirring occasionally. Add the tomato paste, beans, tomatoes and herbs. Bring to a boil and simmer, partly covered, for 15 to 20 minutes.
3. Meanwhile, for the cheese sauce, melt the margarine in a saucepan or a microwave bowl. Stir in the flour and cook 1 minute, stirring (for 30 seconds on High, in microwave). Remove from the heat. Gradually add the milk, stirring until smooth. Stir over medium heat until the sauce boils and thickens, or in microwave on High until boiling, stirring occasionally. Remove from the heat, stir in the cheese, nutmeg and pepper.
4. To assemble, pour half the vegetable sauce over the base of a lasagne dish, rectangular slab pan or ovenproof dish (about 16 cm × 28 cm). Cover with a layer of lasagne sheets, then half the spinach. Spread a thin layer of cheese sauce over the spinach. Top with the remaining vegetable sauce and remaining spinach. Place over a layer of lasagne sheets and finish with the remaining cheese sauce. Sprinkle with Parmesan or cheddar cheese.
5. Cover with aluminium foil and bake in a moderate oven (180°C) for 40 minutes. Remove foil and bake for a further 30 minutes or until the top is beginning to brown.

SERVES 6

Dipping the lasagne sheets briefly in hot water before use helps to soften them prior to cooking.

Creamy Mushrooms and Pasta

When mushrooms are in season put this dish together quickly with ingredients from the pantry.

2 cups (300 g) macaroni or other small pasta
2 tablespoons fresh parsley, finely chopped
2 tablespoons finely grated Parmesan cheese

Sauce

2 teaspoons olive oil
I medium onion (120 g), thinly sliced
I clove garlic, crushed, or I teaspoon minced garlic
500 g mushrooms
I teaspoon paprika
2 teaspoons Dijon mustard
2 tablespoons tomato paste
I × 375 ml can evaporated skim milk
1/4 cup (30 g) grated low fat cheddar cheese
1/2 cup (40 g) chopped green shallots
freshly ground black pepper

LOW GI	
Per serve:	
kJ	1860
kCal	440
carb	68 g
fat	7 g
fibre	8 g

1. Add the pasta to a large saucepan of boiling water and boil, uncovered, until just tender. Drain and keep warm.
2. While the pasta is cooking, begin the sauce. Heat the oil in a non-stick frying pan. Add the onions, garlic and mushrooms, and cook for about 5 minutes or until softened.
3. Combine the paprika, mustard, tomato paste and milk in a small jug. Stir into the mushroom mixture with the cheese and cook stirring frequently over low heat for 5 minutes.
4. Add the shallots with pepper to taste.
5. Pour the sauce over the pasta and toss gently to combine. Serve sprinkled with the parsley and Parmesan cheese.

SERVES 4

Mushrooms are a good source of niacin and can be a source of vitamin B12 if they are grown on a mixture containing animal compost.

Pasta Primavera

A simple, light pasta dish that can be on the plate in about 15 minutes.

150 g uncooked spaghetti or other pasta
3 medium tomatoes (160 g)
1 tablespoon of olive oil
1 tablespoon of capers, drained
1 clove garlic, crushed or 1 tablespoon minced garlic
juice of 1 lemon
1 tablespoon sweet chilli sauce
black pepper
fresh basil leaves, shredded
handful of chopped brown onion

LOW GI
Per serve:
kJ 1750
kCal...........415
carb............65 g
fat ....10 g
fibre............7 g

1. Put the spaghetti on to cook in a large saucepan of boiling water, according to packet directions.
2. Meanwhile, dice the tomatoes. Combine in a bowl with the olive oil, capers, garlic, lemon juice, chilli sauce, olives, pepper and basil.
3. Drain the spaghetti and return to its saucepan. Add the tomato combination to it and stir through. Serve hot or warm.

SERVES 2

Spicy Noodles

250 g dried thin egg noodles

2 teaspoons oil

2 cloves garlic, crushed, or 2 teaspoons minced
   garlic

1 teaspoon minced ginger

1 teaspoon minced chilli

6 green shallots, sliced

1 tablespoon smooth peanut butter

2 tablespoons soy sauce

1 cup (250 ml) prepared chicken stock

LOW GI
Per serve:
kJ 1170
kCal............280
carb............45 g
fat ....6 g
fibre...........4 g

1. Add the noodles to a large saucepan of boiling water and boil, uncovered, for about 5 minutes or until just tender.
2. While the noodles are cooking, heat the oil in a non-stick frying pan, add the garlic, ginger, chilli and shallots and stir-fry for 1 minute. Remove from the heat.
3. Stir in the peanut butter and soy sauce and gradually add the stock, stirring until smooth. Stir over heat until simmering, and simmer for 2 minutes.
4. Drain the noodles and add to the spicy sauce, stirring to coat. Serve immediately.

SERVES 4 AS AN ACCOMPANIMENT

Add strips of stir-fried chicken or meat with a packet of Asian-style mixed vegetables.

MAIN MEALS

Moroccan Chicken on Couscous

Spicy Beef Ragout

Steamed Mussels on Ratatouille and Basmati Rice

Spinach, Feta and Bean Frittatas

Thai Tuna and Kumara Tart

Flathead Fillets on Kumara Chips with Oven-roasted Basil Tomatoes

Sweet Chilli Chicken with Kumara Mash and Stir-fried Greens

Pork and Noodle Stir-fry with Cashews

Warm Lamb and Chickpea Salad

Spicy Pilaf with Chickpeas

Moroccan Kebabs

Winter Chilli Hotpot

Vegetarian Cottage Pie

Parsley Cheese Pie

Beef and Lentil Rissoles

Moroccan Chicken on Couscous

2 teaspoons ground cummin

2 teaspoons ground coriander

1 teaspoon ground fennel

1 x 400 g can chickpeas, drained and patted dry

2 cloves garlic, finely chopped

2 red chillies, finely chopped

1 tablespoon olive oil

500 g chicken breast fillets, sinews removed

1/2 bunch flat-leafed parsley, roughly chopped

1 preserved lemon, pith discarded, rinsed and thinly
   sliced

1/2 cup (125 ml) dry white wine

1 cup (200 g) couscous

1/2 cup (90 g) raisins

juice of 1 lemon

salt

freshly ground black pepper

**MODERATE
GI**
Per serve:
kJ 1500
kCal...........360
carb...........43 g
fat ....9 g
fibre...........4 g

1. Combine the cummin, coriander and fennel in a mixing bowl, and toss the chickpeas in the spices.
2. Heat the olive oil in a large wok or frying pan. Add the garlic and chillies and cook, stirring, for 1 minute.
3. Toss the chickpeas into the pan and cook until the aroma of the spices comes through—approximately 2 minutes. Place chickpeas in a large bowl and set aside.
4. Add 1 tablespoon olive oil to the pan and cook the chicken fillets for approximately 4 minutes or until just cooked through. Add to the chickpeas, and stir the chopped parsley and preserved lemon slices through.
5. To make a sauce, deglaze the pan with the wine, simmering for 2 minutes.
6. Pour over the chicken mixture and keep warm.
7. Place the couscous in a large mixing bowl and pour 1 cup of boiling water over the top. As the couscous plumps up, gently fork through the raisins, lemon juice and salt and pepper.

SERVES 6

Spicy Beef Ragout

500 g rump steak, diced

1/3 cup (40 g) plain white flour

salt

freshly ground black pepper

I tablespoon olive oil

2 (350 g) brown onions, finely diced

3 cloves garlic, roughly chopped

I red chilli, roughly chopped

3 large (600 g) kumera, peeled and roughly diced

1 1/2 litres beef stock

2 tablespoons (50 g) tomato paste

I tablespoon grainy mustard

2 stalks celery, sliced

I large (400 g) red capsicum, halved, seeded and
   roughly diced

I cup (170 g) corn kernels

I x 600 g can peeled chopped tomatoes, undrained

I x 400 g can borlotti beans, drained

I cup (70 g) spiral noodles, cooked

1/2 cup kalamata olives

1/2 bunch parsley, roughly chopped

LOW GI	
Per serve:	
kJ	1350
kCal	320
carb	40 g
fat	7 g
fibre	8 g

1. Toss the steak in flour seasoned with salt and black pepper in a large mixing bowl.
2. Heat the oil in a large 6 litre casserole dish and gently cook the onions, garlic and chilli for I minute. Add the steak and brown on all sides.
3. Add the kumera, beef stock, tomato paste, grainy mustard, celery, capsicum, corn kernels and tomatoes. Season with salt and pepper. Simmer gently, with lid on, for 1½ hours, stirring occasionally.
4. Remove the lid and add the borlotti beans, noodles and olives. Simmer for 5 minutes, stir in the parsley and serve immediately.

SERVES 8

Steamed Mussels on Ratatouille and Basmati Rice

1 large (300 g) eggplant, cut into 1 cm cubes
1 large (200 g) red capsicum, halved, seeded and
    diced (1 cm pieces)
4 (300 g) zucchini, sliced into 2 cm rings
1 large (200 g) brown onion, roughly chopped
3 cloves garlic, roughly chopped
1 tablespoon mustard seed oil
1 large (440 g) can chopped tomatoes, undrained
2 cups (500 ml) water
4 bay leaves
2 sprigs fresh thyme
salt
freshly ground black pepper
8 leaves fresh basil
1 cup (110 g) Basmati rice
500 g mussels (approximately 20)
1 cup (250 ml) dry white wine
1 cup (250 ml) water
2 bay leaves
10 black peppercorns

MODERATE GI

Per serve:

kJ	1630
kCal	390
carb	56 g
fat	7 g
fibre	6 g

1. Place the eggplant in a colander, sprinkle with salt and leave for 30 minutes. Wash under cold water, drain and pat dry with kitchen paper.

2. Heat the oil in a large saucepan and add the eggplant, capsicum, zucchini, onion and garlic. Toss in the hot oil for 2 minutes, then add the tomatoes, water and herbs. Season with salt and pepper. Reduce the heat and simmer for 45 minutes, stirring occasionally. Remove the bay leaves and thyme sprigs. Chop the basil leaves and stir through the ratatouille.

3. Bring 2 litres of salted water to the boil and cook the rice for 11 minutes. Immediately drain and keep warm.

4. Prepare the mussels by discarding any broken shells and soaking in cold water. Pull the 'beard' from the side of the shell with a sharp tug towards the pointed end of the mussel.

5. Bring the wine and water, bay leaves and peppercorns to the boil, reduce the heat and add the mussels. Cover the saucepan with the lid, and simmer for approximately 2 minutes, removing each mussel as it fully opens. Discard any unopened shells.

6. To serve, arrange half a cup of rice in the middle of the plate, top with spoonfuls of ratatouille and arrange the cooked mussel shells over the top.

SERVES 4

The ratatouille flavour improves with time, so make it the day before and reheat gently.

Spinach, Feta and Bean Frittatas

1 x 300 g packet chopped frozen spinach, thawed

1 teaspoon nutmeg

150 g reduced-fat feta, crumbled

1 x 400 g can red kidney beans, drained

½ bunch shallots, finely chopped

2 cloves garlic, finely chopped

¼ cup (60 ml) canola oil

5 x 60 g omega-3-enriched eggs, lightly beaten

salt

pepper

¾ cup (85 g) self-raising flour

LOW GI
Per serve:
kJ 950
kCal............227
carb............13 g
fat ....13 g
fibre............5 g

1. Preheat the oven to 180°C.
2. Lightly oil 8 x ¾ cup capacity large muffin tins.
3. In a large mixing bowl, combine the spinach with nutmeg, feta, beans, shallots and garlic.
4. Stir in the canola oil, eggs, salt, pepper and flour.
5. Fill the 8 muffin tins and bake immediately for 35-40 minutes, till golden brown and puffy. Serve hot or cold.

MAKES 8

Thai Tuna and Kumara Tart

1 teaspoon canola oil

2 large (500 g) kumara

5 x 60 g omega-3-enriched eggs

1 x 400 g can lite coconut milk

grated zest of 1 lemon

3 tablespoons fresh coriander, finely chopped

1/2 bunch shallots, roughly sliced

2 cloves garlic, finely sliced

1/2 cup (65 g) self-raising flour

salt

freshly ground black pepper

1/2 cup (100 g) cooked Basmati rice

1 x 425 g can tuna chunks in brine, drained

1 x 440 g can corn niblets, drained

LOW GI	
Per serve:	
kJ	1370
kCal	327
carb	33 g
fat	12 g
fibre	4 g

1. Preheat the oven to 180°C.
2. Oil a 30 cm round ovenproof dish with 1 teaspoon canola oil or, alternatively, oil 12 x 3/4 cup capacity large muffin tins.
3. Peel and steam whole kumara till just tender, approximately 20 minutes. Drain and cut the kumara into chunks.
4. Whisk the eggs, coconut milk, lemon zest, coriander, shallots, garlic, self-raising flour and seasonings together in a large jug till well combined.
5. Arrange chunks of cooked kumara, tuna, rice and corn niblets over the base of the ovenproof dish, or in the muffin tins. Pour over the egg and coconut mixture.
6. Place the tart (or muffin tray) into the preheated oven, and bake for 1 hour (45 minutes for muffins) until puffed and golden brown.
7. Serve cut into wedges or as individual tarts, either hot or cold, with a leafy green salad.

MAKES 1 LARGE TART FOR 8 OR 12 INDIVIDUAL TARTS

Flathead Fillets on Kumara Chips with Oven-roasted Basil Tomatoes

6 (600 g) ripe Roma tomatoes, halved lengthways

I teaspoon olive oil

2 cloves garlic, finely chopped

6 basil leaves, finely sliced

salt

freshly ground pepper

6 small (600 g) flathead fillets

1/3 cup (40 g) plain flour, seasoned with salt and
    freshly ground black pepper

2 x 60g omega-3-enriched eggs, lightly whisked

3 large (approximately 800 g) kumara, peeled and
    thinly sliced

2 tablespoons olive oil

3 cups (60 g) baby spinach leaves

I tablespoon toasted sesame seeds

6 lemon wedges

LOW GI
Per serve:

kJ	1300
kCal	310
carb	26 g
fat	11 g
fibre	4 g

1. Preheat the oven to 180°C.
2. Place the tomatoes, cut side up, on a lightly oiled baking tray. Top the tomatoes with a little olive oil, half the garlic, basil leaves and seasonings. Place in the oven and bake for 30 minutes.
3. Dip the flathead fillets in the seasoned flour and eggs. Cover and set aside in the refrigerator.
4. Heat 1½ tablespoons olive oil in a heavy-based frying pan and spread the kumara slices over, seasoning the layers with salt and pepper and the remaining garlic. Cook until the underside turns golden brown and slightly crisp, then turn once and cook the other side. Keep warm.
5. Heat ½ tablespoon olive oil in a heavy based frying pan and cook the flathead fillets for approximately 4 minutes, turning once only, till golden brown and flaky.
6. Serve with a bed of baby spinach, and then the kumara chips topped with the flathead fillets. Sprinkle with toasted sesame seeds and serve with lemon wedges and oven-roasted basil tomatoes.

SERVES 6

Sweet Chilli Chicken with Kumara Mash and Stir-fried Greens

Kumara Mash

1 medium (approximately 500 g) kumara, peeled and
   cut into chunks
$1/3$ cup low fat milk
1 tablespoon sweet chilli sauce

Sweet Chilli Chicken

2 single chicken breast fillets (approximately 350 g),
   sliced into strips across the grain
1 teaspoon oil
1 cup (250 ml) chicken stock
2 teaspoons salt-reduced soy sauce
1 tablespoon sweet chilli sauce
1 tablespoon cornflour
2 teaspoons grated fresh ginger
few sprigs of fresh coriander leaves

Stir-fried Greens

1 teaspoon oil
large handful of snow peas
bunch of Chinese greens such as choy sum or baby
   bok choy
2 medium zucchini

LOW GI	
Per serve:	
kJ	2230
kCal	530
carb	49 g
fat	15 g
fibre	9 g

1. Boil or microwave the kumara until tender. When cooked, drain and mash with milk and sweet chilli sauce. Keep warm.
2. Heat a wok or large frypan with the oil and stir-fry the chicken until browned. Remove from pan and set aside to keep warm.
3. Heat a further teaspoon of oil in the wok or frypan. When hot add the green vegetables (chopped stalks and sliced zucchini first). Stir-fry until lightly cooked. Combine remaining ingredients in a separate bowl and add to the pan with the cooked chicken and stir till thickened slightly.
4. Serve the chicken and greens over the kumara mash.

SERVES 2

Pork and Noodle Stir-fry with Cashews

1 tablespoon oil

500 g pork strips

1 × 300 g packet hokkien noodles

1 medium (150 g) red capsicum, chopped into thin strips

200 g broccoli, chopped into small florets

1 clove garlic, crushed

2 teaspoons finely grated fresh ginger

150 g snow peas, topped and tailed and sliced diagonally into thirds

200 g button mushrooms, thinly sliced

1 baby bok choy, washed, trimmed and cut lengthways into 8

6 green shallots, chopped diagonally

1 tablespoon salt-reduced soy sauce

1 tablespoon hoisin sauce

1 tablespoon honey

80 g (1/2 cup) roasted cashew nuts

LOW GI
Per serve:
kJ 2430
kCal...........580
carb............56 g
fat ....19 g
fibre...........8 g

1. Heat a large frying pan or wok over high heat. Add half the oil and when the oil is hot, add one-third of the pork strips and stir-fry for 1-2 minutes until just cooked. Repeat with the remaining 2 batches of pork, transferring to a plate covered loosely with foil to keep warm.
2. Prepare the noodles according to the packet directions and drain.
3. Add the remaining oil to the pan over high heat. Add the capsicum, broccoli, garlic and ginger and stir-fry for about 1 minute. Add the remaining vegetables and stir-fry 1-2 minutes until the vegetables are tender crisp, sprinkling in a little water if necessary.
4. Combine the sauces and honey together in a bowl.
5. Return the pork to the pan with the noodles and sauces. Toss until well combined and heated through. Put into bowls to serve and sprinkle with the cashew nuts.

SERVES 4

Warm Lamb and Chickpea Salad

400 g lamb fillet or backstrap

1 tablespoon olive oil

1 onion, finely chopped

3 garlic cloves, crushed

$1/2$ teaspoon ground cumin

$1/2$ teaspoon ground coriander

$1/2$ teaspoon ground ginger

$1/2$ teaspoon paprika

700 g canned chickpeas, drained and rinsed

salt and black pepper to taste

1 tomato, cut into small dice

1 cup fresh coriander, finely chopped

1 cup fresh flat-leafed parsley, finely chopped

1 cup fresh mint, finely chopped

3 tablespoons extra virgin olive oil

juice of 1 lemon

baby spinach leaves, washed, to serve

LOW GI

Per serve:

kJ 1810

kCal............430

carb............23 g

fat ....25 g

fibre............9 g

1. Cook the lamb fillets in a lightly oiled frying pan, over medium heat, about 3 minutes each side. Transfer to a plate and cover with foil to keep warm. Set aside to rest.
2. Heat the tablespoon of olive oil in the frying pan and cook the onion for 5 minutes or until soft. Add the garlic and spices and cook for 5 minutes over low heat, stirring occasionally. Add the chickpeas and heat through, stirring until warm and well coated with the spice mixture. Remove from the heat and add the salt and pepper, tomato, chopped herbs, extra oil and lemon juice.
3. Cut the lamb fillets into thick slices, diagonally. Toss through the chickpea / herb mixture.
4. Arrange the baby spinach leaves on plates and top with the chickpeas and lamb. Serve immediately.

SERVES 4

The fat in this recipe is predominantly from the olive oil dressing and is highly monounsaturated.

Spicy Pilaf with Chickpeas

A meatless, rice dish which serves 3 to 4 people for a light meal or 6 as an accompaniment

1 teaspoon poly- or monounsaturated margarine
2 teaspoons olive oil
1 medium (145 g) brown onion, peeled and finely
   diced
150 g button mushrooms, quartered or halved
1 clove garlic, crushed
⅔ cup Basmati rice
1 teaspoon garam masala
½ a small (300 g) can chickpeas, drained
1 bay leaf
1½ cups chicken stock
1 tablespoon slivered almonds, toasted

LOW GI
Per serve:
kJ 971
kCal...........230
carb............32 g
fat ....8 g
fibre............4 g

1. Heat margarine and oil in a medium-sized frying pan over medium heat. Add the onion, cover and cook 3 minutes, stirring occasionally. Add mushrooms and garlic and cook, uncovered, a further 5 minutes, stirring occasionally.
2. Add the rice and spice, stirring to combine until aromatic. Add the chickpeas and bay leaf and pour over stock. Bring to the boil. Reduce heat to very low. Cover with a tight-fitting lid and simmer (without lifting the lid) for at least 12 minutes or until rice is tender and all liquid has been absorbed.
3. Sprinkle with toasted almonds and serve with a salad.

SERVES 3 TO 4

Slivered almonds can be easily toasted by placing in a dry pan over medium heat. Once the pan gets hot, toss the almonds around to toast them. This will take no more than a minute. Don't leave unattended beause the almonds toast rapidly.

Moroccan Kebabs

4 large pieces of pita bread

375 g premium beef mince

$\frac{1}{2}$ cup (90 g) cracked wheat (burghul)

2 teaspoons Moroccan seasoning

1 medium (120 g) white onion, very finely chopped

1 egg, lightly beaten

3 medium tomatoes, diced

1 tablespoon mint, roughly chopped

2 teaspoons olive oil

2 teaspoons red wine vinegar

lettuce

hummus (optional)

LOW GI
Per serve:
kJ 1984
kCal............470
carb............65 g
fat ....9 g
fibre............11 g

1. Wrap the pita bread in foil and heat in the oven for 15 minutes.
2. Meanwhile, combine beef, burghul, seasoning, onion and egg in a bowl. Shape mixture into 8 patties.
3. Heat a non-stick frying pan with cooking spray and cook patties about 4 to 5 minutes each side.
4. Combine tomato and mint with olive oil and vinegar in a bowl and serve with the patties and lettuce on the pita bread. Spread with hummus.

SERVES 4

Moroccan seasoning is available in jars in the spice section of the supermarket. Alternatively, flavour the patties with 1 clove of crushed garlic and $\frac{1}{2}$ teaspoon each of ground coriander, cumin, paprika, black pepper and dried rosemary.

Hummus can be purchased in the refrigerated section of the supermarket or in delicatessens. Alternatively, see recipe on p 99.

Winter Chilli Hotpot

A hearty vegetarian casserole that can be prepared in around 30 minutes.

1 cup (180 g) dried red kidney
  beans or 440 g can kidney beans, rinsed and
  drained
5 cups (1.25 litres) water
1 bay leaf
1 teaspoon oil
1 onion, finely chopped
2 cloves garlic, crushed or 2 teaspoons minced garlic
2 sticks celery (160 g), sliced
2 squash or 2 small zucchini (200 g), sliced
250 g button mushrooms
800 g can tomatoes, undrained and chopped
1 teaspoon minced chilli
2 tablespoons tomato paste
1½ cups (375 ml) prepared vegetable stock
1¼ cups (250 g) small macaroni pasta
freshly ground black pepper
chopped fresh parsley, to serve

LOW GI	
Per serve:	
kJ	1110
kCal	260
carb	47 g
fat	1.5 g
fibre	12 g

1. If using dried beans, soak overnight in water to cover by 5 cm. Drain. Bring the water to a boil in a large saucepan, add the beans and bay leaf. Boil rapidly for 15 minutes, then reduce heat and simmer for 40 minutes. Drain and set aside.

2. Heat the oil in a non-stick frying pan, add the onion and garlic and cook for about 5 minutes or until soft.

3. Add the celery, squash or zucchini and mushrooms and cook, stirring, for 5 minutes. Stir in the beans (cooked or canned), tomatoes, chilli, tomato paste and stock, and bring to the boil.

4. Add the pasta, reduce heat and simmer for about 20 minutes or until the pasta is tender. Add pepper to taste and serve sprinkled with parsley.

SERVES 4 TO 6

This is a complete meal in itself but you could serve it with a dinner roll or bread to mop up the sauce.

Vegetarian Cottage Pie

An easy version of the traditional favourite using precooked lentils.

4 medium (600 g) potatoes, peeled and cut into chunks

1 teaspoon poly- or monounsaturated oil

1 medium (120 g) onion, finely chopped

2 medium (275 g) zucchini, thinly sliced

120 g mushrooms, sliced

2 cloves garlic, crushed or 2 teaspoons minced garlic

225 g (1/2 packet) Quickpulse™ brown lentils or
  400 g can lentils (drained and rinsed)

2 tablespoons tomato paste

a little water

2 teaspoons (10 g) poly- or monounsaturated
  margarine

1/3 cup (80 ml) low fat milk

salt and pepper to taste

50 g grated reduced-fat cheddar cheese

MODERATE GI

Per serve:

kJ	1042
kCal	250
carb	31 g
fat	7 g
fibre	7 g

1. Boil the potatoes to cook for mashed potato.
2. Then, heat a large, non-stick frying pan and grease the base with the oil. Add the onion, cover and cook over medium heat for 3 to 4 minutes or until transparent. Stir occasionally.
3. Add the zucchini and cook, covered, stirring occasionally, for 3 minutes. Add the mushrooms and garlic and cook a further 2 minutes.
4. Add the lentils and tomato paste, with a little water to help mix through. Cover and cook for 5 minutes.
5. Mash the potatoes with margarine and milk, season with salt and pepper.
6. Spoon lentil mix into a medium-sized (1.5 litre) casserole dish. Top with mashed potato and sprinkle with grated cheese. Finish off under a hot grill until the cheese is melted and bubbling.

SERVES 4

Accompany with freshly steamed broccoli.

Parsley Cheese Pie

A cheese and egg dish incorporating rice. Cheese and eggs make a refreshing alternative to meat in this dish. Serve with a tossed salad.

½ cup (100 g) Basmati rice
1 cup (50 g) chopped fresh parsley
1 cup (125 g) grated low fat cheddar cheese
1 large (150 g) onion, finely chopped
½ cup (130 g) creamed corn
½ cup (130 g) corn kernels
1 large zucchini (180 g), grated
35 g mushrooms, finely chopped
3 eggs
2 cups (500 ml) low fat milk
¼ teaspoon ground nutmeg
1 teaspoon ground cumin
1 egg white, lightly beaten

LOW GI
Per serve:
kJ 870
kCal...........207
carb...........27 g
fat ....4 g
fibre............3 g

1. Add the rice to a saucepan of boiling water and boil, uncovered, for about 12 minutes or until just tender; drain.
2. Combine the rice, parsley, half the cheese, onion, creamed corn, corn kernels, zucchini and mushrooms in a bowl and spoon into a greased 25 cm pie dish.
3. Whisk the eggs, milk, nutmeg and cumin in a bowl. Fold in the lightly beaten egg white and pour evenly over the rice mixture. Sprinkle the remaining cheese on top.
4. Bake in a moderate oven (180°C) for about 1 hour or until set in the centre.

SERVES 6

Beef and Lentil Rissoles

Serve these succulent rissoles hot with vegetables or salad and mustard or chutney.

$\frac{1}{2}$ cup (100 g) red lentils
400 g lean minced beef
1 medium onion (120 g), finely chopped
$\frac{1}{2}$ small capsicum (50 g), finely chopped
1 clove garlic, crushed, or 1 teaspoon minced garlic
2 teaspoons dried mixed herbs
$\frac{1}{3}$ cup (80 ml) tomato sauce
1 egg, lightly beaten
freshly ground black pepper
about $\frac{1}{2}$ cup (70 g) unprocessed oat bran,

LOW GI
Per rissole:
kJ 234
kCal...........56
carb...........4 g
fat ....2 g
fibre...........1 g

1. Cook the lentils in a saucepan of boiling water for about 20 minutes or until soft; drain well.
2. Combine the lentils with the beef, onion, capsicum, garlic, herbs, sauce, egg and pepper in a bowl; mix well.
3. Add enough oat bran to form a burger consistency. Shape the mixture into 24 rissoles and place on a lightly greased baking tray.
4. Bake in a hot oven (200°C) for about 40 minutes, or until cooked through, turning halfway through cooking time. Alternatively, cook the rissoles in a non-stick frying pan over medium-high heat or until browned and cooked through.

MAKES 24 SMALL RISSOLES
Reheat the leftovers and serve sandwiched in Lebanese pita bread with chutney, tomato, cucumber, grated carrot and lettuce.

DESSERTS

Fruit Bread and Butter Pudding

Mixed Berry and Cinnamon Compote

Oat Bran and Honey Loaf Chocolate Pudding

Gingernut and Nectarine Ice-cream

Apple Crumble

Creamy Rice with Sliced Pears

Apricot, Honey and Coconut Slice

Fresh Fruit Cheesecake

Winter Fruit Salad

Yoghurt Berry Jelly

Fruit Bread and Butter Pudding

2½ cups (600 ml) low fat milk

3 x 70 g omega-3-enriched eggs

2 tablespoons caster sugar

1 teaspoon vanilla essence

4 slices (130 g) spicy fruit bread

1 tablespoon margarine

½ cup (100 g) sultanas, soaked in 2 tablespoons
   brandy

1 teaspoon grated cinnamon

LOW GI	
Per serve:	
kJ	745
kCal	175
carb	25 g
fat	4 g
fibre	1 g

1. Preheat the oven to 170°C.
2. Lightly grease a 6 cup (1½ litre) ovenproof dish.
3. Boil the kettle.
4. Whisk the milk, eggs, caster sugar and vanilla essence in a large jug.
5. Remove the crusts from the fruit bread and spread generously with the margarine, cutting each slice in half diagonally. Stack the triangles of bread upright across the prepared dish. Scatter the cut slices with the pre-soaked sultanas, and pour over the custard mixture. Gently push the slices down to soak up the custard. Sprinkle with grated cinnamon.
6. Place a deep baking dish in the oven and position the bread and butter pudding dish in the centre. Pour the boiling water into the baking dish to come at least three-quarters of the way up the sides of the oven-proof dish.
7. Bake for 1 hour until the custard is set, puffy, and a light golden brown.
8. Serve with the Mixed Berry and Cinnamon Compote (see overleaf).

SERVES 6 TO 8.

Mixed Berry and Cinnamon Compote

3/4 cup (185 ml) freshly squeezed orange juice

1 cup (250 g) caster sugar

2 cinnamon sticks

zest of 1 orange, finely sliced

4 cups (500 g) mixed berries (raspberries,
    blackberries, blueberries, strawberries)

LOW GI
Per serve:
kJ 610
kCal 145
carb.............36 g
fat ....neg
fibre ....2 g

1. Place the orange juice, caster sugar, cinnamon sticks and orange zest in a large stainless steel saucepan, and slowly bring to the boil.
2. Add the mixed berries and simmer gently for 2 minutes, just until the berries warm through and swell.
3. Serve warm with Fruit Bread and Butter Pudding (see previous page).

SERVES 6 TO 8

Before you squeeze the oranges for juice, zest the skin, using a potato peeler.

Oat Bran and Honey Loaf Chocolate Pudding

1 tablespoon sultanas or raisins

1 tablespoon rum (optional)

4 slices Burgen™ Oatbran and Honey bread

2 tablespoons Nutella™ hazelnut spread

2 eggs, lightly beaten

½ teaspoon ground cinnamon

½ cup caster sugar

1 cup (250 ml) low fat milk

1 tablespoon custard powder

LOW GI
Per serve:
kJ 1420
kCal...........340
carb...........55 g
fat ....7 g
fibre..........2 g

1. If you want to plump the sultanas or raisins with rum, place them in a small bowl with the alcohol and heat in the microwave for 20 seconds or until the fruit is swollen.

2. Spread the Nutella thickly over 2 slices of the bread. Dot with the sultanas or raisins and sandwich together with the remaining 2 slices of bread. Cut each sandwich into 4 triangular quarters and stand upright in a 1 litre casserole dish, squashing together to fit.

3. Combine the beaten eggs with the remaining ingredients by whisking together in a jug or deep bowl. Pour the egg mixture over the sandwiches in the casserole dish and stand for 10 minutes while the bread absorbs the custard.

4. Stand the casserole dish into another ovenproof dish and add hot water to the larger dish to come halfway up the sides (bain-marie style). Bake for 40 minutes at 200°C until the custard around the bread is set and golden in colour.

SERVES 4

Gingernut and Nectarine Ice-cream

2 medium (200 g) nectarines
1 litre low fat vanilla ice-cream
2 teaspoons honey
125 g low fat natural yoghurt
100 g diced dried fruit medley
4 gingernut biscuits, crushed
almond bread wafers to serve

LOW GI
Per serve:
kJ 620
kCal............148
carb............27 g
fat ....3 g
fibre............2 g

1. Cut the flesh from the stone of the nectarines and chop into small (0.5 cm) dice.
2. Remove ice-cream from freezer and stand for about 10 minutes or until softened slightly. Scoop out into a large bowl.
3. Stir the honey into the yoghurt. Add to the softened ice-cream with the dried fruit, biscuits and nectarines, mixing through quickly. Pour the ice-cream into a metal loaf tin, cover with plastic wrap and return to freezer for at least 4 hours until set.
4. To serve, remove the ice-cream from the freezer and stand the tin in a sink of hot water for 20–30 seconds to soften the outside of the ice-cream. Tip the ice-cream out onto a board and cut thick slices through it with a knife dipped into hot water, between cuts. Lay on plates and garnish with almond bread wafers.

SERVES 8

Apple Crumble

A quick and easy version that makes a delicious low GI dessert.

3 large Granny Smith apples, peeled, cored and sliced
  or a 440 g can of pie apple
½ teaspoon mixed spice

Crumble

1 cup (90 g) rolled oats

½ cup unprocessed oat bran

½ cup brown sugar

1 teaspoon cinnamon

45 g poly- or monounsaturated margarine

LOW GI	
Per serve:	
kJ	1537
kCal	365
carb	60 g
fat	12 g
fibre	7 g

1. Combine the apples and spice and place in a 25 cm pie dish.
2. In a food processor combine the crumble ingredients.
3. Mix to form a crumble and sprinkle over the apples. Bake in a 180°C oven for 30 minutes.

SERVES 4 (GENEROUSLY)

Unprocessed oat bran is available in supermarkets and health food stores.

Creamy Rice with Sliced Pears

2 cups (500 ml) water

I cup (200 g) Basmati rice

¾ cup (185 ml) canned evaporated skim milk

¼ cup (55 g) firmly packed brown sugar

I teaspoon vanilla essence

440 g can pear slices

LOW GI
Per serve:
kJ 1250
kCal............295
carb............65 g
fat negligible
fibre............3 g

1. Bring the water to a boil in a saucepan, add the rice and boil for 15 minutes; drain.

2. Return the rice to the saucepan with the milk. Stir over low heat until all the milk is absorbed. Stir in the sugar and vanilla essence; cool.

3. Using an ice-cream scoop, serve scoops of rice with the pear slices fanned out next to it.

SERVES 4

Apricot, Honey and Coconut Slice

Apricots, honey and yoghurt on a coconut biscuit base.

Base

¼ cup (20 g) desiccated coconut, toasted

125 g Weston's Highland Oatmeal™ biscuits, finely
  crushed

60 g poly- or monounsaturated margarine, melted

Topping

1 cup (125 g) dried apricots

½ cup (125 ml) boiling water

2 x 200 g cartons low fat apricot yoghurt

¼ cup (60 ml) honey

2 eggs

LOW GI	
Per serve:	
kJ	1080
kCal	255
carb	32 g
fat	12 g
fibre	2 g

1. Line an 18 cm x 28 cm rectangular slab pan with foil.
2. For the base, combine the ingredients in a bowl and mix well. Press the mixture evenly over the base of the prepared pan.
3. Bake in a moderate oven (180°C) for about 10 minutes or until browned. Remove from oven and allow to cool.
4. For the topping, cover the apricots with the boiling water, let stand 30 minutes or until soft. Process in a blender or food processor until smooth. Add the yoghurt, honey and eggs and blend until smooth.
5. Spread the topping mixture over the prepared base. Bake in a moderate oven (180°C) for about 30 to 35 minutes or until set.
6. Cool, then refrigerate several hours before serving.

SERVES 8

To toast coconut, cook in a non-stick frypan over low heat, stirring for 2 minutes or until just golden. Remove from the pan to cool.

Fresh Fruit Cheesecake

A delicious lower fat cheesecake that leaves you feeling good after you eat it—not weighed down with fat.

Base

250 g Weston's Highland Oatmeal™ biscuits,
  crushed
90 g poly- or monounsaturated margarine, melted

Filling

2 teaspoons gelatine
2 tablespoons boiling water
200 g carton low fat fruit yoghurt
250 g carton low fat pineapple cottage cheese
$\frac{1}{4}$ cup (60 ml) honey
$\frac{1}{2}$ teaspoon vanilla essence
I cup (200 g) chopped fresh fruit (e.g. apple, orange,
  rockmelon, strawberries, pear, grapes)

LOW GI	
Per serve:	
kJ	1400
kCal	335
carb	35 g
fat	14 g
fibre	1 g

1. For the base, combine the biscuit crumbs and margarine in a bowl. Press evenly into a 23 cm pie dish. Bake in a moderate oven (180°C) for 10 minutes. Cool.
2. For the filling, sprinkle the gelatine over the boiling water in a cup, stand cup in a small pan of simmering water and stir until dissolved; cool slightly.
3. Process the cooled gelatine with the yoghurt, cottage cheese, honey and vanilla essence in a blender or food processor until smooth.
4. Arrange the chopped fruit over the prepared crust and pour over the yoghurt mixture. Refrigerate for about 1 hour or until set.

SERVES 8

Don't use pawpaw, pineapple or kiwi fruit as these tend to prevent gelatine from setting.

Winter Fruit Salad

Oranges, apples and bananas tend to be available all year round and this combination is ideal when other fruits are out of season.

1 orange, peeled and separated into segments
1 medium red apple, cut into bite-size cubes
2 teaspoons sugar
1 teaspoon fresh lemon juice
1 small banana
1 tablespoon shredded coconut

LOW GI
Per serve:
kJ 625
kCal............150
carb.............33 g
fat ....1 g
fibre............5 g

1. Cut orange segments in half. Place apple and orange chunks in a bowl. Sprinkle over the sugar and lemon juice and mix thoroughly. Cover and refrigerate at least 1 hour.
2. Just before serving, stir in the sliced banana. Sprinkle with coconut to serve.

SERVES 2

Yoghurt Berry Jelly

An easy dessert. You could make it with low joule jelly crystals if you wanted to reduce the kilojoule content.

LOW GI

Per serve:
kJ 360
kCal...........85
carb...........16 g
fat negligible
fibre...........1 g

85 g packet berry-flavoured jelly crystals
1 cup (250 ml) boiling water
1 cup (145 g) strawberries or frozen raspberries
1 ½ cups (300 g) low fat berry yoghurt

1. Combine the jelly crystals and the boiling water in a bowl, stir until dissolved; cool, but do not allow to set.
2. Roughly chop the strawberries (frozen raspberries will tend to break up on stirring).
3. Fold the yoghurt and berries through the jelly; mix well. Pour into serving bowls, cover and refrigerate until set.

SERVES 4

SNACKS

Walnut, Banana and Sesame Seed Loaf
Cinnamon Muesli Cookies
Oat and Apple Muffins
Cheese and Herb Oat Scones
Muesli Bars
Muesli Munchies
Chick Nuts

Walnut, Banana and Sesame Seed Loaf

3 tablespoons honey

1 tablespoon canola oil

3 x 60 g omega-3-enriched eggs

3 large bananas, roughly mashed

1 teaspoon ground cinnamon

1 cup (125 g) wholemeal self-raising flour

1 cup (125 g) white self-raising flour

1 cup (100 g) whole walnuts

1 tablespoon sesame seeds

MODERATE GI
Per serve:
kJ 1070
kCal 255
carb..............30 g
fat ....12 g
fibre ....5 g

1. Preheat the oven to 180°C.
2. Lightly oil a 14 cm x 24 cm metal loaf tin, and line with a strip of baking paper.
3. Combine the honey, oil and eggs in a large mixing bowl and whisk together well.
4. Whisk the bananas into the mixture with the cinnamon, and add the flours, 1 cup at a time, whisking quickly.
5. Stir in the walnuts and quickly spoon the mixture into the prepared loaf tin. Sprinkle with sesame seeds.
6. Place on the middle shelf in the preheated oven and bake for 45 minutes.
7. Test with a skewer inserted into the centre of the loaf. If it comes out clean, and the loaf is golden brown, it is ready.
8. Turn out onto a wire rack to cool and slice.

Makes 1 x 775 g loaf.

SERVES 10

Cinnamon Muesli Cookies

2 tablespoons canola oil

3 tablespoons golden syrup

$1/3$ cup (85 ml) orange juice

1 cup (150 g) unsweetened rolled oat muesli

1 cup (125 g) self-raising flour

1 tablespoon cinnamon

icing sugar

MODERATE GI
Per cookie:
kJ 550kJ
kCal...........130
carb...........21g
fat ....4 g
fibre...........2 g

1. Preheat the oven to 180°C.
2. Line a baking tray with baking paper.
3. Measure the oil and golden syrup into a large mixing bowl. Add the orange juice and mix.
4. Add the muesli, flour and cinnamon and mix to a soft dough.
5. Place spoonfuls of the mixture onto the prepared tray, leaving about 2 cm between each cookie.
6. Bake immediately for 15-20 minutes, till just golden brown. Cool on a wire rack and sprinkle with a little icing sugar.

MAKES APPROXIMATELY 12 COOKIES

Oat and Apple Muffins

These are a delicious low fat muffin, with moist chunks of apple through them.

½ cup All-Bran™ cereal
⅔ cup (165 ml) low fat milk
½ cup (75 g) self-raising flour
2 teaspoons baking powder
1 teaspoon mixed spice
½ cup (75 g) unprocessed oat bran
½ cup (80 g) sultanas
1 green apple, peeled and cut into 5 mm cubes
1 egg, lightly beaten
¼ cup (60 ml) honey
½ teaspoon vanilla essence

LOW GI
Per serve:
kJ 430
kCal............ 100
carb .... 22 g
fat .... 1 g
fibre .... 2 g

1. Combine the All-Bran™ and milk in a bowl and let stand for 10 minutes.
2. Sift the flour, baking powder and mixed spice into a large bowl. Stir in the oat bran, sultanas and apple.
3. Combine the egg, honey and vanilla essence in a bowl. Add the egg mixture and All-Bran™ mixture to the dry ingredients and stir with a wooden spoon until just combined. Do not overmix.
4. Spoon the mixture into a greased 12-hole muffin tray. Bake in a moderate oven (180°C) for about 15 minutes or until lightly browned and cooked through. Serve warm or cold.

MAKES 12 MUFFINS

If you find them too dry when cold, warm in the microwave on High for 10 seconds before serving. Warm the honey first to make measuring easy.

Cheese and Herb Oat Scones

These savoury scones make a delicious light lunch with salad or a tasty snack on their own. They are ready to eat as they are!

1 cup (150 g) self-raising flour, sifted

1 1/2 teaspoons baking powder

1 cup (140 g) unprocessed oat bran

30 g poly- or monounsaturated or margarine

1/2 cup (125 ml) low fat milk

2 tablespoons water

1/2 cup (60 g) grated low fat cheddar cheese

2 teaspoons chopped fresh parsley

2 teaspoons chopped fresh basil or 1 teaspoon
  dried basil leaves

1 teaspoon dried rosemary leaves

MODERATE GI

Per serve:

kJ 530

kCal 125

carb.............17 g

fat ....5 g

fibre ....3 g

1. Sift the flour and baking powder into a large bowl, stir in the oat bran. Rub in the margarine.
2. Make a well in the centre and add the milk and half the water. Mix lightly with a knife, adding extra water if necessary, to make a soft dough. Turn the dough onto a lightly floured board and knead gently.
3. Roll out the dough to a rectangle about 1 cm thick. Scatter half the cheese and all the herbs over the entire surface.
4. Beginning from a long side, roll up like a Swiss roll to make a thick sausage. Cut into 3 cm slices to make little rounds.
5. Place the rounds side by side on a greased baking tray and sprinkle with the remaining cheese. Bake in a hot oven (200°C) for about 20 minutes or until golden brown. Serve hot or cold.

MAKES 10 SCONES

Muesli Bars

These bars have a heavy, wholesome texture and make a very sustaining snack.

1/2 cup (75 g) wholemeal plain flour
1/2 cup (75 g) self-raising flour
1 teaspoon baking powder
1/2 teaspoon mixed spice
1/2 teaspoon ground cinnamon
1 1/2 cups (135 g) rolled oats
1 cup (150 g) dried fruit medley or dried fruit of
    choice, chopped
1/4 cup (35 g) sunflower seed kernels
1/2 cup (125 ml) apple juice
1/4 cup (60 ml) oil
1 egg, lightly beaten
2 egg whites, lightly beaten

LOW GI	
Per serve:	
kJ	590
kCal	140
carb	15 g
fat	8 g
fibre	3 g

1. Line a 20 cm x 30 cm slice pan with baking paper.
2. Sift the flours, baking powder and spices into a large bowl. Stir in the oats, fruit and seeds and stir to combine.
3. Add the apple juice, oil and whole egg; mix well. Gently mix in the egg whites until combined.
4. Press the mixture evenly into the prepared pan and press firmly with the back of a spoon. Mark the surface into 12 bars using a sharp knife.
5. Bake in a hot oven (200°C) for about 15 to 20 minutes or until lightly browned. Cool and cut into bars.

MAKES 12 BARS

Muesli Munchies

Crunchy little bite-sized biscuits which make handy low GI snacks.

90 g poly- or monounsaturated margarine
¼ cup (60 ml) honey
I egg
½ teaspoon vanilla essence
2½ cups (300 g) natural muesli
2 tablespoons sunflower seed kernels
¼ cup (40 g) self-raising flour, sifted

LOW GI	
Per serve:	
kJ	590
kCal	140
carb	15 g
fat	8 g
fibre	3 g

1. Melt the margarine and honey in a small saucepan.
2. Whisk the egg and vanilla essence together in a large bowl.
3. Add the margarine mixture, muesli, sunflower seed kernels and flour to the egg mixture; stir until combined.
4. Place small spoonfuls of the mixture onto a lightly greased baking tray, spacing evenly.
5. Bake in a moderately hot oven (190°C) for about 10 minutes or until golden brown. Let stand on tray until firm, then loosen and place on a wire rack to cool.

MAKES 16 BISCUITS

Chick Nuts

Toasted chick peas make a terrifically healthy low GI nibble. Spice them up with flavourings suggested or your own combinations. All you need is some chick peas.

375 g packet dried chick peas

LOW GI
Per ½ cup
kJ 1350
kCal............320
carb............45 g
fat ....6 g
fibre............15 g

1. Soak the chick peas in water overnight. Next day, drain and pat dry with paper towels.
2. Spread the chick peas in a single layer over a baking tray. Bake in a moderate oven (180°C) for about 45 minutes or until completely crisp. (They will shrink to their original size.)
3. Toss with a flavouring (see below) while hot, or cool and serve plain.

Flavour variations

Chick Devils
Sprinkle a mixture of cayenne pepper and salt over the hot chick nuts.

Red Chicks
Sprinkle a mixture of paprika and garlic salt over the hot chick nuts.

PART III
The GI and You

All the latest information and figures on the GI and
diabetes, how it can help you with weight control,
diabetes and heart health.

CHAPTER 8

THE GI AND WEIGHT CONTROL

Obesity is now recognised as a serious and growing health concern for a large proportion of the Australian population. In Australia, two in three men and one in two women are now overweight or obese. Even children are affected—25 per cent of them carry too much body fat. We need to tackle the problem on many fronts, including exercise and diet. The GI can play an important role in weight management by helping to control appetite and insulin levels.

If you are overweight, or consider yourself overweight, chances are that you have looked at countless books, brochures and magazines offering a solution to losing weight. New diets or miracle weight loss solutions seem to appear weekly. They are clearly good for selling magazines, but for the majority of people who are overweight the 'diets' don't work—if they did, there wouldn't be so many!

At best—while you stick to it—a 'diet' will reduce your kilojoule intake. At its worst, a 'diet' will change your body composition for the fatter. This is because many diets employ the technique of drastically reducing your carbohydrate intake to bring about quick weight loss. The weight you lose, however, is mostly water (that was trapped or held with stored carbohydrate) and muscle (as it is broken down to produce the glucose you need to fuel your brain). Once you return to your former way of eating, your body contains a little less muscle mass. With each repetition of a diet you lose more muscle. Over years, the resultant change in body composition to less muscle and proportionately more fat makes weight control increasingly difficult. Your body requires less and less energy to keep the engine idling. This is nature's way of helping animals adapt to the environment in which they live.

> ## The real aim in losing weight is losing body fat. Perhaps it would be better described as 'releasing' body fat. After all, to lose something suggests that we hope to find it again some day!

This chapter is not prescribing yet another 'diet' for you to try, instead we will give you some important facts about food and how your body uses it. Not all foods are equal. When it comes to losing weight, it is not necessarily a matter of reducing how much you eat. Research has shown that the type of food you give your body determines what it is going to burn and what it is going to store as body fat. It has also revealed that certain foods are more satisfying to the appetite than others.

This is where the GI plays a leading role. Low GI foods have two essential advantages for people trying to lose weight:

1. They fill you up and keep you satisfied for longer.
2. They help you burn more body fat and less muscle.

Eating to lose weight with low GI foods is easier because you don't have to go hungry and what you end up with is true fat release.

Why is being overweight a problem?

If you are overweight you are at increased risk of a range of health problems. Among these are heart disease, diabetes, high blood pressure, gout, gallstones, sleep apnoea (when breathing stops for a significant period of time; snoring is a good sign of this) and arthritis. Along with this list of complications, there is an equal number of emotional and psychological problems associated with being overweight.

The proportion of overweight people in our society is increasing, despite the expanding weight-loss industry and an ever increasing range of 'diet' or 'lite' foods. It is clear that the answer to preventing obesity or becoming overweight is not a simple one. Nor is losing weight easy to do. *The New Glucose Revolution* can make it easier, however. We can tell you which foods satisfy hunger for longer and are the least likely to encourage weight gain. When you use the GI as the basis for your food choices there is no need to:

- overly restrict your food intake
- obsessively count kilojoules
- starve yourself

Learning which foods your body works best on is what using the GI is all about.

It is also worthwhile to take control of aspects of your lifestyle that have an impact on your weight. You may not create a new body from your efforts, but you will feel better about the body you've got. Eating well and exercising is the aim of the game.

Why do people become overweight?

Is it genetic?

Is it hormonal?

Is it our environment?

Is it a psychological problem?

Or is it due to an abnormal metabolism?

For most of us, even without much conscious effort, our bodies maintain a constant weight, even if that's higher than we'd prefer. This is despite huge variations in how much we eat. It's as if there's a weight to which our body naturally moves. For a proportion of people who are overweight, this balancing of energy intake and output is operating at a higher threshold. So, regardless of all apparent efforts to control it—every fad diet, every exercise program, even operations and medications—body weight is regained over the years.

Our weight is a result of how much we take in and how much we burn up. So, if we take in too much and don't burn up enough we are likely to put on weight.

The question is: how much, of what, is too much?

The answer is not a simple one: not all foods are equal and no two bodies are the same.

People are overweight for many different reasons. Some people believe they only 'have to look at food', others put on weight from 'just walking past the patisserie', others blame themselves because they just can't refuse highly palatable food. Research has made it clear that a combination of social, genetic, dietary, metabolic, psychological (and emotional) factors combine to influence our weight.

Before we talk more about food, let's look at the role *genetics* plays in weight control. There are many overweight people who tell us resignedly:

- 'well my mother's/father's the same'
- 'I've always been overweight'
- 'it must be in my genes'

Research shows us that these comments have much truth behind them. A child born to overweight parents is much more likely to be overweight than one whose parents were not overweight. It may sound like an excuse, but there is a lot of evidence to back the idea that our body weight and shape is at least partially determined by our genes.

Much of our knowledge in this area comes from studies in twins. Identical twins tend to be similar in body weight even if they are raised apart. Twins adopted out as infants show the body fat profile of their biological parents rather than that of their adoptive parents. When twins were given 1000 extra calories a day for 100 days, some gained 4 kilograms and some gained 12 kilograms, but amazingly, one twin invariably gained similar amounts to that of his/her partner. These findings suggest that our genes are a stronger determinant of weight than our environment (which includes the food we eat). It seems that information stored in our genes governs our tendency to burn off or store excess calories/kilojoules.

Our genetic make-up also underlies our *metabolism* (basically how many kilojoules we burn per minute). Bodies, like cars, differ in this regard. A V-8 consumes more fuel to run than a small 4-cylinder car. A bigger body, generally, requires more kilojoules than a smaller one. When a car is stationary, the engine idles—using just enough fuel to keep the motor running. When we are asleep, our engine keeps running (for example, our brain is still at work) and we use a minimum number of kilojoules. This is our *resting metabolic rate*—the amount of kilojoules we burn without any exercise (when we are at rest). Most of it is necessary fuel for our large brains. When we start exercising, or even just moving around, the number of kilojoules, or the amount of fuel we use, increases. The largest amount (around 70 per cent) of the kilojoules used in a 24-hour period, however, are those used to maintain our resting metabolic rate.

Since our resting metabolic rate is where most of the kilojoules we eat are used, it is a significant determinant of our body weight. The lower your resting metabolic rate, the greater your risk of gaining weight and vice versa. We all know someone who appears to 'eat like a horse' but is positively thin! Almost in awe we comment on their 'fast metabolism', and we may not be far off the mark! Men's bodies, for example, contain more muscle mass and are expensive to run, unlike body fat that is there just for the ride. Maintaining muscle mass by exercising is therefore important to weight control. New research also suggests that our genes dictate the fuel mix that we burn from minute to minute. A mix that contains *more energy derived from fat and less from carbohydrate* (even if the total energy burned per minute is the same) may aid weight control.

All this doesn't mean that if your parents were overweight you should resign yourself to being overweight too. But it may help you understand why you have to watch what you eat while other people seemingly don't have to.

MEASURING THE FUEL WE NEED

Remember, kilojoules are the metric equivalent of calories. They are a measure of the energy in food and the energy we require to keep us alive. Our bodies need a certain number of kilojoules every day to keep our hearts beating and our brains working, just as a car needs so many litres of petrol to run for a day. Food and drink are our source of kilojoules. If we eat and drink too much we may store the additional kilojoules as extra body fat and protein. If we consume fewer kilojoules than we need, our bodies will break down their stores of fat and protein to make up for the shortfall.

So, if you were born with a tendency to be overweight, why does it matter what you eat? The answer is that foods (or more correctly, nutrients) are not equal in their effect on body metabolism. In particular, the foods you eat dictate the fuel mix that you burn for several hours after eating. If you are burning more fat and less carbohydrate, even if the energy content of the food is the same, then chances are you'll be less hungry and less likely to gain body fat over the course of the day. Consequently, your choice of foods is critical for weight control.

Amongst all four major sources of kilojoules in food (protein, fat, carbohydrate and alcohol) fat has the highest energy content per gram, twice that of carbohydrate and protein. A high fat food is therefore said to be 'energy dense', meaning there are a lot of kilojoules in a relatively small amount of food. A typical croissant made with wafer-thin layers of pastry interspersed with lashings of butter contains

---

DID YOU KNOW?

A food's 'energy density' (kilojoules per gram) is more important to weight control than its fat content.

Assessing a food's energy density has become more important than knowing its fat content. Some diets, such as traditional Mediterranean diets, contain quite a lot of fat (mainly from olive oil), but are still a bulky diet based on large serves of fruit and vegetables, including foods like legumes, which have exceptionally low GI values.

Many new low fat foods on the market are not bulky—they have the same energy density as the original high fat food. Examples include low fat yoghurts, ice-creams, and sweet and savoury snack products. So read the label—look for the energy content per 100 gram or per serve as your best guide to a food's 'fattening' power.

You can eat quantity—just consider the quality!

---

over 2000 kilojoules (about 20–25 per cent of total energy needs for the day!). To eat the same amount of energy in the form of apples, you have to eat about 6 large apples. So, getting more energy—kilojoules—than your body needs is relatively easy when eating an energy dense food.

During the 1990s, one of the most notable findings was that high fat foods were less satiating than conventional high carbohydrate foods. For this reason, dieters were advised to stay away from high fat foods and the food industry responded to the call for more low fat foods. Unfortunately, along the way, someone forgot to say that what really counts is the food's final energy density. If a low fat food has the same energy density (kilojoules per gram) as a high fat food, then it's just as easy to overconsume. There are lots of low fat products on the market that are no different from the high fat counterpart when it comes to kilojoules per gram. The best examples are the low fat yoghurts, ice-creams, crackers and biscuits.

Think *energy density* not high fat or low fat

Nutritionists have therefore had to fine-tune the message about diets for weight control:

- eating *bulky* food is more important than simply eating low fat
- the *type* of fat is more critical to long-term health
- the *type* of carbohydrate is more important than the *amount*

WHY EXERCISE KEEPS YOU MOVING
The effect of exercise doesn't end when you stop moving. People who exercise have higher metabolic rates and their bodies burn more kilojoules per minute even when they are asleep!

The need for exercise

A 'fast metabolism' is not necessarily a matter of luck. Exercise, or any physical activity, speeds up our metabolic rate. By increasing our kilojoule expenditure, exercise helps to balance our sometimes excessive kilojoule intake from food.

Exercise also makes our muscles bigger (and therefore more energy demanding) and better at using fat as a source of fuel. By making our muscles more sensitive to insulin, exercise reduces the demand for this hormone and increases the amount of fat we burn. A low GI diet has the same effect. Low GI foods reduce the amount of insulin we need which makes fat easier to burn and harder to store. When we eat a low GI meal, the fuel mix being burnt for the next few hours contains more fat and less carbohydrate. Since body fat is what you want to get rid of when you lose weight, exercise in combination with a low GI diet makes a lot of sense!

Which foods affect weight?

It was widely (and wrongly) believed for many years that sugar and starchy foods like potato, rice and pasta were the cause of obesity. Twenty years ago, every weight-loss diet advocated restriction of these carbohydrate-rich foods. One of the reasons for this carbohydrate restriction stemmed from the 'instant results' of low carbohydrate diets. If your diet is very low in carbohydrate, you will lose weight fast. The problem is that what you primarily lose is carbohydrate and fluid, and not fat. What's more a low carbohydrate diet depletes the limited carbohydrate (glycogen) stores in the muscles making exercise difficult and tiring.

Sugar has been blamed for obesity because it is often found in energy dense foods such as cakes, biscuits, chocolate and ice-cream. These foods, however, contain a mixture of sugar and fat and it's the fat which makes them energy dense. If we substituted starch for all

COUNTING THE KILOJOULES

All foods contain kilojoules. Often the kilojoule content of a food is considered a measure of how fattening it is. Of all the nutrients in food that we consume, carbohydrate yields the fewest kilojoules per gram.

carbohydrate	16 kilojoules per gram
protein	17 kilojoules per gram
alcohol	29 kilojoules per gram
fat	37 kilojoules per gram

the sugar, they would still contain the same energy content. The primary sources of concentrated energy in our diet are *not* sweet. Fatty meats, cheese, French fries, potato crisps, rich sauces, savoury biscuits, butter and margarine contain no sugar.

On the whole, there is scarce evidence to condemn sugar or starchy foods as the cause of obesity. Overweight people show a preference for energy dense foods rather than a preference for foods high in sugar or starch because their bodies have high energy requirements, even at rest, and the easiest way to satisfy their hunger is with high energy foods. In a survey performed at the University of Michigan where obese men and women listed their favourite foods, men preferred mainly fatty meats and women listed cakes, biscuits and doughnuts. The unifying trait was a lot of energy per gram of food.

How can the GI help?

One of the biggest challenges to losing weight can be feeling hungry all the time, but this gnawing feeling is not a necessary part of losing weight. Foods with a low GI are amongst the most filling of all foods and delay hunger pangs for longer.

In the past, it was believed that protein, fat and carbohydrate foods, taken in equal quantities, satisfied our appetite equally. We now know from recent research that the satiating capacity—the degree to which foods make us feel full—of these three nutrients is not equal.

Fatty foods, in particular, have only a weak effect on satisfying appetite relative to the number of kilojoules they provide. This has been demonstrated clearly in experimental situations where people are asked to eat until their appetite is satisfied. They overconsume kilojoules if the foods they are offered are high in fat. When high carbohydrate and low fat foods are offered, they consume fewer kilojoules when given the opportunity to eat until satisfied. So, *conventional* carbohydrate foods are the best for satisfying our appetite without over-satisfying our kilojoule requirement.

Satiety is the feeling of fullness and satisfaction we experience after eating. Conventional carbohydrate foods provide the best satiety.

In studies we conducted, people were given a range of individual foods which contained equal numbers of kilojoules, then their satiety responses were compared. We found that the most filling foods were those that contained fewer kilojoules per gram, i.e. the least energy dense. This included potatoes, porridge, apples, oranges and pasta. Eating more of these foods satisfies appetite without providing excess kilojoules. Foods that provided a lot of kilojoules per gram, like croissants, chocolate and peanuts, were the least satisfying. These foods are more likely to leave us wanting more and to lead to what scientists call 'passive overconsumption', i.e. overeating without realising it.

After energy density, the second best predictor of satiety was a food's GI—the lower the GI, the more the food satisfied people's hunger. Indeed, there are now over 17 studies that confirm low GI foods are able to suppress hunger for longer than high GI foods.

There are probably several mechanisms responsible for this.

- Low GI foods remain longer in the small intestine, triggering receptors that tell the brain there's food still in the gut to be digested.

- High GI foods may stimulate hunger because the rapid rise and then fall in blood glucose levels appears to stimulate counter-regulatory responses to reverse the decline.

- Stress hormones like adrenalin and cortisol are released when glucose levels rebound after a high GI food. Both hormones tend to stimulate appetite.

- Low GI foods may be more satiating simply because they are often less energy dense than their high GI counterparts. The naturally high fibre content of many low GI foods increases their bulk without increasing their energy content.

What's more, even when the kilojoule intake is the same, people eating low GI foods may lose more weight than those eating high GI foods. In a South African study, the investigators divided overweight volunteers into two groups: one group ate a low kilojoule, high GI diet and the other, a low kilojoule, low GI diet. The amount of kilojoules, fat, protein, carbohydrate and fibre in the diet was the same for both groups. Only the GI of the diets was different. The low GI group included foods like lentils, pasta, porridge and corn in their diet and excluded high GI foods like potato and bread. After 12 weeks, the volunteers in the group eating low GI foods had lost, on average, nine kilograms—two kilograms more than people in the group eating the diet of high GI foods.

How did the low GI diet work? The most significant finding was the different effects of the two diets on the level of insulin in the blood. Low GI foods resulted in lower levels of insulin over the course of the day and night.

Insulin is a hormone that is not only involved in regulating blood glucose levels, it also plays a key part in determining the fuel mix that we burn from minute to minute. High levels of insulin mean the body is *forced* to burn carbohydrate, rather than fat. Thus, over the day, even if the total energy burnt is the same, the proportions of fat and carbohydrate are not.

Obese individuals appear to have high glycogen (carbohydrate) stores that undergo major fluctuations during the day. This suggests that glycogen is a critical source of fuel for obese people. If glycogen is burning, this makes it hard to burn the fat in food as well as the fat stored in the body. The next meal restores glycogen to its former high level (especially if the food is high GI) and the cycle repeats itself.

ARE POTATOES FATTENING?

In spite of their high GI, potatoes are highly filling during the first two hours after consumption. One explanation for this is their low energy density—to eat 1000 kilojoules, you need to eat 7 medium-sized potatoes! It is possible, however, that in the period 3–4 hours after consumption, the high insulin response caused by potatoes may cause lower levels of glucose and free fatty acids in the blood. In turn, this may increase the levels of the stress hormones cortisol and noradrenalin, and thereby stimulate appetite—a finding that has been shown in previous studies. So if potatoes are your favourite food, don't cut them out—eat them in moderation, cut your usual portion by half and substitute sweet potato (low GI) instead. Boiled potatoes are a much better choice for weight control than French fries or potato crisps or similar foods with a high energy density.

In our experience of looking at the diets of people who want to lose weight, the change required is often to eat more.

There are other reasons why low GI diets might aid weight loss. When people first begin a diet, their metabolic rate drops in response to the reduction in food intake. One study, however, found that the metabolic rate had dropped less after one week on a low GI diet compared to a conventional high carbohydrate diet. The same study suggested that the low GI diet helped to preserve lean body mass better, which could explain the higher metabolic rate.

New findings also provide evidence that low GI diets are able to reduce abdominal fat specifically. In a French study, overweight men were given in succession a high and low GI weight-maintaining diet (in random order), equivalent in energy and macronutrient composition. After five weeks on each diet, their body fat mass was measured using sophisticated X-ray methods. Those allocated to the low GI diet had lost 500 grams of fat from the abdomen. There was no difference in subcutaneous fat (i.e. the fat under the skin). That evidence was backed up by a large 'observational' study in Europe of people with type 1 diabetes. It found that those who had naturally self-selected a low GI diet had not only better blood glucose control values, but the men in the group had lower waist circumferences, a good index of abdominal fat.

In the table opposite, foods on the left are energy dense—a small amount of food provides a lot of kilojoules. Compare these to the combination of foods of low energy density on the right.

Energy Dense	Low Energy Density
2 Scotch Finger shortbread biscuits	2 slices of Bürgen™ grain bread spread with fresh ricotta cheese and jam
A double-choc Cornetto™ ice-cream	A Splice™ ice-cream and 7 marshmallows
A 200 g tub of full fat fruit yoghurt	A 200 g tub of Diet-Lite yoghurt and one large banana
A snack pack of sultanas	A small bunch ($1/2$ cup) of grapes and a medium-sized apple
6 Jatz™ and cheese	8 Vita-weats™ topped with ham, tomato and cucumber
A small serve of hot chips	I large dry-baked potato with $1/2$ cup of chilli beans, grated cheese, a small orange juice and an apple.

Weight gain in pregnancy

Did you gain a lot of weight during pregnancy and have never lost it all? A new study suggests that weight gain during pregnancy is influenced greatly by the GI of the diet. Women who followed a low GI diet from early on in pregnancy gained only nine kilograms, compared to 20 kilograms gained by those eating an otherwise equivalent high GI diet. What's more, the baby's birth weight and body fat content were also higher if the mother's diet was high GI. This study requires confirmation but it's not all that surprising. It's been known for a long time that a baby's birth weight is related to the mother's blood glucose levels. Women with diabetes (or at risk of developing it) have heavier babies than those without diabetes. Now it seems that *all* the maternal tissues may respond to the high levels of glucose and insulin that occur after eating high GI foods. That includes the fat stores laid down to sustain lactation. While we await more studies, low GI diets during pregnancy can do no harm.

Four tips for losing weight

Tip 1. Focus on what to eat, rather than what not to eat

Typically people approach weight management by looking at which foods they could eat less of. An alternative is to focus on meeting the recommended fruit and vegetable intake first, and then see how much space you have left to fit in the extras.

To eat a healthy diet, ensure you eat at least the minimum of these foods:

1. **Vegetables and legumes—at least 5 servings every day.**
   1 serving means:
   $\frac{1}{2}$ cup cooked vegetables
   1 small potato
   $\frac{1}{2}$ cup cooked dried beans, peas or lentils
   1 cup of salad vegetables

2. **Fruit—at least 2 servings every day.**
   1 serving means:
   1 medium piece (apple, banana, orange)
   2 small pieces (apricots, kiwi fruit, plums)
   1 cup diced pieces or canned fruit
   1–2 tablespoons dried fruit
   $\frac{1}{2}$ cup fruit juice

3. **Breads/cereals/rice/pasta and noodles—4 servings or more every day.**
   1 serving means:
   $1\frac{1}{3}$ cups breakfast cereal flakes (40 grams)
   1 cup cooked pasta, noodles or rice
   1 cup cooked porridge
   2 slices bread
   1 bread roll

Tip 2. Eat at least one low GI food at each meal

Reducing the GI of your diet will reduce insulin levels and increase the potential for fat burning. You can achieve an effective reduction in the GI by substituting at least one high GI carbohydrate choice at each meal with a low GI type. It's the carbohydrate foods that you eat the most of which have the greatest impact—so check your intake using the following table.

What type of carbohydrate did you eat yesterday?

1. Recall the carbohydrate-rich foods that you ate yesterday. Remember to think of snacks as well as the main meals!
2. Tick the check boxes below for the types of foods you ate.

High GI	Low GI
Fruit	**Fruit**
☐ Paw Paw	☐ Apples
☐ Pineapple	☐ Oranges
☐ Rockmelon	☐ Bananas
☐ Watermelon	☐ Grapes
	☐ Kiwi fruit
	☐ Peaches, plums, apricots, cherries
Starchy foods	**Starchy foods**
☐ Potato, including baked, mashed, steamed, boiled and chips	☐ Sweet corn
	☐ Baked beans
☐ Rice	☐ Sweet potato
	☐ Chickpeas, kidney beans, lentils
	☐ Pasta
	☐ Noodles
	☐ Basmati or Doongara rice

Bread Products

☐ White bread
☐ Wholemeal bread
☐ Crumpets
☐ Pikelets
☐ Scones
☐ Bagels
☐ French bread

Bread Products

☐ Wholegrain bread
☐ Fruit loaf, raisin toast
☐ Sourdough bread

Cereals

☐ Weet-Bix™
☐ Cornflakes™
☐ Rice Bubbles™
☐ Coco Pops™
☐ Froot Loops™
☐ Puffed Wheat

Cereals

☐ Special K™
☐ Porridge
☐ Muesli
☐ All-Bran™
☐ Frosties™
☐ Guardian™

Biscuits

☐ Sao™
☐ Water crackers
☐ Cruskits™
☐ Rice cakes
☐ Morning Coffee™
☐ Milk Arrowroot™

Biscuits

☐ Vita-weat™
☐ Rich Tea™
☐ Fruit Slice

Snacks

☐ Dates
☐ Fruit bars
☐ Lollies
☐ Popcorn
☐ Pretzels

Snacks

☐ Dried apricots
☐ Prunes
☐ Nuts
☐ Yoghurt

3. Now add up the number of ticks in each column of foods. The foods in the left column have a high GI. If most of your ticks are in this column, you are eating a high GI diet. Consider altering some of your choices to include more of the foods from the column on the right.

Tip 3. Reduce your fat intake, especially saturated fat

Reducing the amount of fat we eat is an effective way to lower the energy density of our diet. Because fat contains more kilojoules per gram than any other food, it can provide lots of energy for little fill-up value. It is, however, unnecessary and unwise to cut fat out completely. The priority is to reduce sources of saturated fat (butter, cream, cheese, biscuits, cakes, fast foods, chips, sausages, salamis, fatty meats) looking at your consumption of foods high in unsaturated, healthier fats (most oils, margarines, nuts, avocadoes) only if further kilojoule reduction is necessary.

Remember too, that while a low fat diet is important, the kilojoules from other sources are important too. Rice and bread contain little fat, but when your body is burning the carbohydrate in these foods, it doesn't burn as much fat. So even if you do truly follow a low fat diet, you won't lose weight if your kilojoule intake is still high.

Is your diet too high in fat?

Use this fat counter to tally up how much fat your diet contains.

Circle all the foods that you could eat in a day, look at the serving size listed and multiply the grams of fat up or down to match your serving size. For example, with milk, if you estimate you might consume 2 cups of regular milk in a day, this supplies you with 20 grams of fat.

Food	Fat content (grams)	How much did you eat?
Dairy Foods		
Milk, (250 ml) 1 cup		
regular	10	
fat-reduced (<1% fat)	1	
skim	0	

Food	Fat content (grams)	How much did you eat?
Yoghurt, 200 gram tub		
regular	6	
low fat	0	
Ice-cream, 2 scoops, (100 ml/50 grams)		
regular, vanilla	5	
reduced fat, vanilla	3	
Cheese		
regular block cheese, 20 gram slice	7	
reduced-fat block cheese, 30 gram slice	5	
low fat slices (per slice)	2	
cottage, 2 tablespoons	2	
ricotta, 2 tablespoons	2	
Cream/sour cream, 1 tablespoon		
regular	7	
fat reduced	5	

Fats and Oils

Food	Fat content (grams)	How much did you eat?
Butter/margarine, 1 teaspoon	4	
Oil, any type, 1 tablespoon (20 ml)	20	
Cooking spray, per spray	1	
Mayonnaise, 1 tablespoon	6	
Salad dressing, 1 tablespoon	5	

Meat

Food	Fat content (grams)	How much did you eat?
Beef		
steak, 1 medium (160 grams), fat trimmed	5	
minced beef patty, (170 grams),		
cooked, drained	21	
sausage, 1 thick, grilled, (80 grams)	13	
topside roast, 2 slices, lean only, (80 grams)	5	
Lamb		
chump chop, grilled/BBQ, 2, fat trimmed	10	
leg, roast meat, lean only, 2 slices, (60 grams)	6	
loin chop, grilled/BBQ, 2, lean only	6	
Pork		
bacon, 1 rasher, grilled	6	
ham, 1 slice, leg, lean	1	
butterfly steak, fat trimmed	3	
leg, roast meat, 3 slices (80 grams), lean only	6	
large chop, fat trimmed	9	

Food	Fat content (grams)	How much did you eat?
Chicken		
breast, skinless, 150 grams	8	
drumstick, skinless	8	
thigh, skinless	12	
¼ barbecue chicken (including skin)	17	

Fish

grilled fish, 1 average fillet	3	
salmon, 50 grams	5	
fish fingers, 4 grilled	10	
fish fillets, 2, crumbed, oven-baked		
regular	20	
light	16	

Snack Foods

Chocolate (50 gram bar)	25	
Potato crisps, 50 gram bag	15	
Corn chips, 50 gram bag	14	
Peanuts, ½ cup, (70 grams)	36	
French fries, regular serve	20	
Pizza, 2 slices, medium pizza	18	
Pie/sausage roll	17	

Total

How did you rate?

Less than 40 grams	Excellent. 30 to 40 grams of fat per day is an average range recommended for those trying to lose weight.
41–60 grams	Good. A fat intake in this range is recommended for most adult men and women.
61–80 grams	Acceptable. If you are very active, i.e. doing hard physical work (labouring) or athletic training. It is too much if you are trying to lose weight.
More than 80 grams	You're possibly eating too much fat, unless of course you are Superman or Superwoman!

Tip 4. Eat regularly

Regular consumption of low GI foods increases satiety at meals and decreases subsequent energy intake to help prevent excess weight gain. Snacking can help prevent overeating at meal times and helps control appetitie. Of course the choice of foods is important.

Planning low GI meals

Here are some basic tips for low GI meals. Part II has more comprehensive information about changing to a low GI diet, as well as some fabulous low GI recipes. *The New Glucose Revolution Pocket Guide for Losing Weight* also contains some excellent tips and meal plans.

Breakfast

- Start with a bowl of low GI cereal served with skim or low fat milk or yoghurt.
- Try something like All-Bran™, rolled oats (raw or cooked) or Guardian™.
- If you prefer muesli, keep to a small bowl of low fat muesli—check that it doesn't contain added fats.
- Add a slice of toast made from a low GI bread (or two slices for a bigger person) with a dollop of jam, sliced banana, honey, Vegemite™, marmalade, or light cream cheese with sliced apple. Keep butter or margarine to a minimum, or use none at all.
- If you like a hot breakfast, try baked beans, a boiled or poached egg, cooked tomatoes or mushrooms with your toast.

Lunch

- Try a sandwich or roll, with only a small amount of margarine. Choose a bread with lots of wholegrains through it (not just sprinkled on top) if you can, for a low GI. Add plenty of salad fillings.

- For the filling choose from a thin slice of leg ham, pastrami, lean roast beef or chicken or turkey smallgood, or a slice of low fat cheese, salmon or tuna (in brine), or an egg. An extra container of salad or vegetable soup will help to fill you up.
- Finish your lunch with a piece of fruit, or fruit salad with a low fat yoghurt, or a low fat flavoured or plain milk.

Dinner

- The basis of dinner should be high carbohydrate grains and root vegetables.
- Eat as many vegetables as you can, using a small amount of meat, chicken or fish as an accompaniment rather than the main ingredient.
- Use lean meat like topside beef, veal, new-fashioned pork, trim lamb, chicken breast, fish fillets, turkey. Red meat is a valuable source of iron—just choose lean types. A piece of meat, chicken or fish that fits in the palm of your hand (no fingers) fulfils the daily protein requirements of an adult.
- If you prefer not to eat meat, a cup of cooked dried peas, beans, lentils or chickpeas can provide protein and iron without any fat. At the same time they supply low GI carbohydrate and fibre.
- Sanitarium products such as Nutmeat™, Casserole Mince™ and tofu are based on high protein legumes like soya beans and peanuts and are good meat alternatives.
- Boost your fruit intake and get into the habit of finishing your meal with fruit—fresh, stewed or baked.

Snacks

- It is important to include a couple of dairy food serves each day for your calcium needs. If you haven't used yoghurt or cheese in any meals, you may choose to make a low fat milkshake. One or two scoops of low fat ice-cream or custard can also contribute to daily calcium intake.

Eat grainy breads, pasta, beans, fruit and vegetables

- If you like grainy breads, a slice of toast makes a very good choice for a snack. Other snacks can include toasted English-style muffin halves, a crumpet with a small amount of margarine, bagels or fruit loaf.
- Fruit is always a low kilojoule option for snacks. You should aim to consume at least three serves a day. It may be helpful to prepare fruit in advance to make it accessible and easy to eat.
- Low fat crackers (like water or rice crackers) are a low kilojoule snack if you want something dry and crunchy, although they may not be as sustaining as a grainy bread.
- Keep vegetables (like celery and carrot sticks, baby tomatoes, florets of blanched cauliflower or broccoli) ready-prepared to snack on too.

CHAPTER 9

THE GI
AND DIABETES

Diabetes is on its way to becoming one of the most common health problems in the world. Currently, in many developing and newly industrialised nations, there is an epidemic of diabetes and the World Health Organization predicts that the rates of diabetes will double in the next 15-20 years. Already in some developing countries half of the adult population has diabetes. Even in developed countries, the rates of diabetes is increasing at an alarming pace. In Australia diabetes and impaired glucose metabolism affect 1 in 4 people. The disease is even more common in Australia's Aboriginal people and those of Asian descent. Australia has one of the highest recorded prevalences of diabetes for a developed nation. And for every person with known diabetes there is another person with undiagnosed diabetes.

The GI has far-reaching implications for diabetes. Not only is it important in treating people with diabetes, but it may also help prevent people from getting diabetes in the first place and possibly even prevent some of the complications of diabetes.

What is diabetes?

Diabetes is a chronic condition in which there is too much glucose in the blood. Keeping the glucose level normal in the blood requires the right amount of a hormone called insulin. Insulin gets the glucose out of the blood and into the body's muscles where it is used to provide energy for the body. If there is not enough insulin, or if the insulin does not do its job properly, diabetes develops.

Children and young adults usually develop diabetes because they cannot make enough insulin. This is called *type 1 diabetes*. In this type of diabetes the pancreas does not produce enough insulin and insulin injections are needed to replace the insulin deficit. Fifteen per cent of people with diabetes have type 1 diabetes.

Typically, *type 2 diabetes*, or non–insulin-dependent diabetes mellitus, develops after the age of 40. With our society's increasing trend to physical inactivity and obesity, however, this type of diabetes is being found in younger and younger people, and in some indigenous populations, even in children less than ten years of age.

People get type 2 diabetes because their insulin does not work properly (insulin 'resistance'). At first the body will struggle to make extra insulin, but later people with type 2 develop a shortage of insulin. The aim of treatment is to help people with type 2 make the best use of the insulin they have and to try to make it last as long as possible. Overeating, being overweight and not exercising enough are important factors (what we call lifestyle factors) which can lead to this type of diabetes, especially when there is someone else in the family with diabetes. Tablets or insulin injections may be necessary to treat this type of diabetes. Eighty-five per cent of people with diabetes have type 2 diabetes.

ARE YOU AT RISK?

You are at particular risk of type 2 diabetes if any of the following apply to you:

- over the age of 55
- with a family history of diabetes
- overweight
- have high blood pressure
- had diabetes during pregnancy (gestational diabetes)
- of one of the following ethnic backgrounds: Indigenous Australian or Torres Strait Islander, Southeast Asian, Asian Indian, or Pacific Islander.

If you fit into one of these categories, you can reduce your chances of getting diabetes by controlling your weight, exercising more and eating more foods with a low GI. A reduction of the GI of your diet reduces the demand on your pancreas to produce more insulin, perhaps prolonging its function and delaying the development of diabetes. Research from Harvard University has shown that eating low GI foods which were high in fibre was associated with the lowest risk of developing type 2 diabetes (see page 216 in this chapter for more information).

Why do we get diabetes?

To find the answer we need to look back in time. Our ancestors lived and evolved in a very cold climate. Over the last 700 000 years there have been many ice ages—the last ended only 10 000 years ago. During these ice ages there was very little edible plant food around and people had to hunt animals for survival. This gave them a lot of protein in their diet. In other words, during the ice ages our ancestors were carnivores (meat eaters). Their bodies adapted to this way of life to help them survive on this diet—and also to help them survive times when food was scarce.

As it turned out, this protein-based diet would also have favoured those people with genes for insulin resistance. This is because the main way the body copes when there is not much carbohydrate (glucose) in the diet, is to make sure that the important parts, such as the brain, get what little glucose is available. To do this the body redirects glucose away from muscles to the brain. The mechanism of doing this involves making the muscles insulin resistant. Thus the natural selection process benefitted those who were genetically insulin resistant.

Since the end of the last ice age there have been many changes to the type and amount of food that we eat. First, our ancestors began to grow food crops. Agriculture changed their eating pattern from one based on animal protein to one based on carbohydrate in the form of whole cereal grains, vegetables and beans. A dietary change like this would also have changed the glucose levels in their blood. While they ate a high protein diet, the glucose levels in their blood would not have risen significantly after a meal. When they started eating carbohydrate regularly, the blood glucose level would have increased after meals. The amount by which the glucose levels in the blood increased after a meal would have depended on the GI of the carbohydrate. Crops such as spelt wheat grain, which our ancestors grew, had a low GI. These foods would have had minimal effects on glucose levels in the blood and the demand for insulin would have been similarly low.

The second major change came with industrialisation and the advent of high speed steel roller mills. Instead of eating whole grain products, the new milling procedures produced highly refined carbohydrate, which we now know increases the GI of a food, and transforms a low GI food into one with a high GI. When this highly refined food is eaten it causes a greater increase in blood glucose levels. To keep the blood glucose levels normal, the body has to make large amounts of insulin. Many of the commercially packaged foods and drinks with which we now fill our shopping trolleys, have a high GI. All this strains the body's insulin-making capabilities.

Thirdly, the dramatic increase over the past 50 years in the quantity of high fat takeaway and fast foods that we regularly eat has made matters even worse. To our already high GI foods, we have added a lot of fat as well. As explained in Chapter 8, eating a lot of fat will increase body weight, which in turn makes it harder for the insulin to clear the glucose from the blood. In other words, the body becomes even more resistant to the effect of insulin. Continually eating carbohydrate foods with a high GI places enormous pressure on the body's ability to keep producing large amounts of insulin to control the blood glucose levels. Add to this worsening insulin resistance, and you have the perfect recipe for eventually exhausting the body's insulin supply and developing diabetes.

It takes aeons of time for our bodies to adapt to such major changes in diet. Because our European ancestors had thousands of years to adapt to a diet with a lot of carbohydrate, they were in a better position to cope with the changes in the GI of foods. That is why people of European descent have a lower prevalence of type 2 diabetes compared with people whose diets have recently changed to include lots of high GI foods. There is, however, only so much that our bodies can take. As we continue to consume increasing quantities of foods with a high GI, plus excessive amounts of fatty foods, our bodies are coping less well. The result can be seen in the significant increase of people developing diabetes.

Studies from Harvard University, in which thousands of men and women were studied over many years, have shown that people who ate large amounts of refined, high GI foods were two to three times more likely to develop type 2 diabetes or heart disease. The most dramatic increases in diabetes, however, have occurred in populations which have been exposed to these lifestyle changes over a much shorter period of time. In some groups of native American Indians and populations within the Pacific region, up to one adult in two has diabetes because of the rapid dietary and lifestyle changes they have undergone in the twentieth century.

Treating diabetes

Taking care with what you eat is essential if you have diabetes. For some people with type 2 diabetes, this is all they have to do to keep their blood glucose levels in the normal range (of between four and eight millimoles per litre). Others also need to take tablets or injections of insulin. People with type 1 diabetes must have insulin injections. But no matter what the treatment, everyone with diabetes must carefully consider what they eat in order to keep their blood glucose levels under control. Keeping the blood glucose near the normal range helps prevent complications of diabetes such as heart attacks, strokes, blindness, kidney failure and amputations.

For over a hundred years, people with diabetes have been given advice on what to eat. Many diets were based more on unproven (although seemingly logical) theories, rather than actual research. In 1915, for example, the *Boston Medical and Surgical Journal* advocated that the best dietary treatment for someone with diabetes was 'limitation of all components of the diet'. This translated into a very low kilojoule diet interspersed with days of fasting. Unfortunately, malnutrition was often the result!

In the 1920s doctors began recommending high fat diets for their diabetic patients. Ignorant of the dangers of a high fat diet, they knew that fat, at least, didn't break down to become blood glucose. We now know that high fat diets only hastened the development of heart disease, the most frequent cause of death among people with diabetes.

It was not until the 1970s that carbohydrate was considered to be a valuable part of the diabetic diet. Researchers found that not only did the nutritional status of patients improve with a higher carbo-hydrate intake, but their insulin sensitivity improved as well.

The only part of food which directly affects blood glucose levels is carbohydrate. When we eat carbohydrate foods, they are broken down into glucose and cause the blood glucose levels to rise. The body responds by releasing insulin into the blood. The insulin clears the glucose from the blood, moving it into the muscles where it is used for energy, so the blood glucose level returns to normal.

Some people think that because carbohydrate raises the blood glu-cose level, it should not be eaten at all by people who have diabetes. This is not correct. Carbohydrate is a normal part of the diet and helps maintain insulin sensitivity and physical endurance. Mental per-formance is also superior when meals contain carbohydrate, rather than just protein and fat.

The secret to the diabetic diet is not so much the *quantity* but the *type* of carbohydrate.

Traditionally sugar was excluded from diabetic diets because it was thought to be the worst type of carbohydrate. The simple structure of sugar supposedly made it more rapidly digested and absorbed than other types of carbohydrate, like starch. This assumption was not cor-rect. Even in the late 1970s, test meal studies showed that there was a great deal of overlap between the blood glucose responses to sugary and starchy foods. Fifty grams of carbohydrate eaten as potato caused a similar rise in blood glucose as 50 grams of sugar. Ice-cream resulted in a lower blood glucose response than potato! Findings like these sparked research into the GI in an effort to learn more about how the body actually responds to different carbohydrate foods.

Looks at ways you can reduce saturated fat

PAUL'S STORY

I'm 54 and the CEO of a very large public sector organisation with all that that entails, including missed meals, incorrect eating (often a single meal at night), long work hours, stress etc.

After feeling unwell for some time, I consulted my GP and blood tests were offered. They showed a relatively mild onset of type 2 diabetes and a couple of other disorders that, in the scheme of things, were not what you would consider serious but all of which could be attributed to my crazy lifestyle.

My GP referred me to a dietitian and nutritionist who, thankfully with my knowledge now, is well versed in the GI.

Well, to cut the inevitable story short, three months later I have lost almost 12 kilos, am within two or three kilos of final weight, and feel significantly improved health wise, in all respects including self-esteem. My wonderful wife has also lost six or seven kilos and she too doesn't need to lose much more.

Although I have yet to go back for blood tests, neither I nor Penny, my dietitian, have any doubts that there will be a major improvement in the results, so well do I feel.

At my first appointment with Penny, I indicated to her that I was not there just to lose some weight and reduce my type 2 symptoms. That was certainly the primary objective but the main game was to change for the long term my eating and lifestyle habits.

Although it's only early days, thanks primarily to your book, I now believe I have achieved that. Both the philosophy and the practice of GI are relatively simple and easy to understand and very much commonsense. I have read and continue to refer to your books and I'm a fairly regular drop-in to your website.

So that's my story thus far. Keep up the great work.

Regards

Paul

The emphasis through the 1970s, and for much of the 1980s, was on the quantity of carbohydrate in the diet. 'Portion' diets were used to prescribe a set amount of carbohydrate to be eaten at every meal. (A 'carbohydrate portion' is an amount of carbohydrate-rich food which contains 10 to 15 grams of carbohydrate—depending on which country, or state of Australia, you lived in. So, not only was the portion system complicated, portion sizes varied throughout the world!).

An underlying assumption of the carbohydrate portions theory was that equivalent amounts of carbohydrate, irrespective of the type, cause an equal change in the blood glucose level. This reasoning had no scientific backing and has since clearly been shown to be incorrect. Fortunately, good quality scientific research supports today's dietary recommendations for people with diabetes. While the GI research has not negated the significance of the quantity of carbohydrate in the diet, it has shown us the importance of considering the *type* of carbohydrate food as well.

The GI has shown us that the way to increase the quantity of carbohydrate in the diabetic diet, without increasing the glucose levels in the blood, is to choose carbohydrate foods with a low GI.

CASE STUDY

At 50 years of age, Helen had tried many times to lose weight. Her neighbours had started walking on a regular basis but she felt tired all the time and had no energy to do anything more than what she had to. Being 95 kilograms and only 168 centimetres tall ruined her morale. Her mother had diabetes and she knew being overweight put her at greater risk, but every time she lost weight she ended up regaining it. Finally, it was no surprise to her when she was diagnosed with diabetes. In fact it was some relief, here at last was a reason for her tiredness.

On her doctor's suggestion, Helen saw a dietitian for help with her diet. At first glance, what Helen was eating appeared reasonable. Breakfast was

Eat grainy breads, pasta, beans, fruit and vegetables

a slice of wholemeal toast or a wholemeal cracker with margarine and black tea. Lunch was a light meal such as celery, lettuce, a slice of cheese, a slice of cold meat, an egg and a couple of crackers, spread with margarine. For dinner she was having soup and a piece of steak with vegetables. She limited herself to a small cocktail potato. The meal was finished by a piece of fruit.

A closer look at her food record, showed that Helen's diet was in fact poorly balanced. It was dominated by protein and saturated fat and contained insufficient carbohydrate. It didn't contain enough food to provide a good range of nutrients. What's more, Helen herself was struggling with it and often felt hungry since she had cut lollies and biscuits out of her diet.

To improve things, we first looked at the frequency of eating. Helen kept to three meals a day because she had been brought up to believe that was better for her. She agreed to try a small snack of fruit or a slice of bread between meals. Even though she wasn't on medication for diabetes, the effect of spreading her food intake more evenly across the day, between small meals and snacks, could help to stabilise her blood glucose level and help her lose weight.

We then revised the amount of carbohydrate that she ate, and listed a range of low GI carbohydrate foods that were to be her first priority at each meal. The filling value of the carbohydrate left her with less space for the proteins that used to dominate her diet.

Breakfast began with a fresh orange, juiced, and a bowl of oats with sultanas and low fat milk. Helen added a slice of Bürgen™ or raisin toast if she was still hungry.

Lunch was usually a sandwich on Bürgen™ bread with a slice of lean meat and salad and a piece of fruit or a muffin to finish. Sometimes she had a vegetable soup or pasta with a vegetable sauce and salad.

The proportion of foods on her dinner plate was rearranged, shrinking in the meat department and filling out on the vegetable side. She began to think of carbohydrate food as the basis of the meal and varied between pasta, rice and potato. Twice a week she made a vegetarian dish with legumes like a minestrone soup or a vegetable lasagne. An evening snack was usually a yoghurt or fruit.

After a month on her new eating plan Helen felt better—in fact she felt well enough to tackle some exercise. Taking a serious look at her day, she decided to commit the half hour after dinner to a walk, five nights a week.

Over the next six months Helen's weight dropped from 95 kilograms to 80 kilograms. Her blood glucose levels were mainly within the normal range. She no longer struggled with hunger and felt good about the food she was eating.

Lowering the GI of your diet as Helen did is not as hard as it seems, because nearly every carbohydrate food that we typically consume has an equivalent food with a low GI. Our research has shown that blood glucose levels in people with diabetes are greatly improved if foods with a low GI are substituted for high GI foods.

We studied a group of people with type 2 diabetes and taught them how to alter their diet by substituting the high GI foods they were normally eating for carbohydrate foods with a low GI. After three months, there was a significant fall in their average blood glucose levels. They did not find the diet at all difficult and in fact commented on how easy it had been to make the change and how much more variety had been introduced to their diet.

Substituting Low GI Foods for High GI Foods

High GI Food	Low GI Alternative
Bread, wholemeal or white	Wholegrain breads such as Bürgen™ and sourdough breads
Processed breakfast cereal	Unrefined cereal such as oats, or check the GI tables in Part IV for processed cereals with a low GI, e.g. Guardian™
Cakes, biscuits, crackers, doughnuts, scones	Fruit, fresh, canned and dried; milk; yoghurt
Potato, rice	Sweet potato, pasta, legumes, noodles, Basmati and Doongara rice

Similar results have been reported by other researchers in both type 1 and type 2 diabetes. For example, large studies in Australia, Europe and Canada of people with type 1 diabetes have shown that the lower the GI of the diet, the better the diabetes control. In fact the improvement in diabetes control seen after changing to a low GI diet is often better than that achieved with some of the newer and expensive diabetes medications and insulins!

Making this type of change in your everyday diet does not mean that your diet has to be restrictive or unpalatable. There are lots of recipes in Part II of this book that can help you reduce the overall GI of your diet. The following case story is an example of the results you could achieve.

CASE STUDY

Bill, a 62-year-old man, was taking every care with his diabetes. He had changed his diet by reducing his total food intake, had lost weight and was exercising regularly. He was doing finger prick blood glucose level tests at home. Despite his best efforts, he could not achieve a blood glucose level in the desired range of below eight millimoles/litre after breakfast. At first glance he was eating what most dietitians would consider to be a good breakfast for someone with diabetes: two Weet-Bix™ with 250 ml of milk, plus two slices of wholemeal toast with a scrape of margarine. His blood glucose after breakfast, however, was consistently around 11 millimoles/litre. He was advised to make one simple change—to lower the GI of the carbohydrate by changing the Weet-Bix™ to a bowl of rolled oats. This had an immediate impact and his glucose levels after breakfast fell to seven millimoles/litre.

If you are having trouble controlling your blood glucose level after a meal, look up the GI value for the carbohydrates it contains in Part IV. See if you can find substitutes with a lower GI amongst the list. Eating a meal with a lower GI can lower the blood glucose rise after the meal.

Although we haven't mentioned them yet, don't think that fatty foods are not important. They are, especially in people who are overweight. But fatty foods do not increase the glucose levels. Only carbohydrate foods do. Being overweight and eating fatty foods, however, prevents the body's insulin from doing its job and indirectly causes the blood glucose levels to rise. So, eating hot chips or fried rice (mixtures of high GI carbohydrate and fat) causes double trouble. Not only does the high GI of potato and rice increase the blood glucose levels, but the extra fat will also eventually stop the body's insulin from working properly and makes it less effective in clearing the glucose from the blood. Persistently high blood glucose levels may be evident the day after a very high fat evening meal.

The New Glucose Revolution Pocket Guide for People with Type 2 Diabetes can give you more information about low GI diets, including specific meal plans for people with diabetes.

The GI and snacks

The GI is especially important when carbohydrate is eaten by itself and not as part of a mixed meal. Carbohydrate tends to have a stronger effect on our blood glucose level when it is eaten alone. This is the case with between-meal snacks which most people with diabetes are obliged to have. When choosing a between-meal snack, pick one with a low GI. For example, an apple with a GI of 36 is better than a slice of normal toast with a GI of around 70, and will result in less of a jump in the blood glucose level.

Some snack foods with a very low GI (such as peanuts with a GI of 14) have a very high fat content and are not recommended for people with a weight problem. As an occasional snack they are fine (especially as their fat is monounsaturated), but not every day. Peanuts are also very moreish and it is hard to stop at just one handful!

Try the following low fat and low GI snack foods instead:

- raisin toast
- a low fat milkshake or smoothie
- an apple
- low fat fruit yoghurt
- 5 to 6 dried apricot halves
- a small banana
- a mini can of baked beans
- an orange
- a scoop of low fat ice-cream in a cone
- a glass of low fat milk

Many people with diabetes have to resort to tablets to control blood glucose levels. An increased intake of low GI carbohydrate foods can sometimes make tablets unnecessary.

Sometimes, however, despite your best efforts with diet, tablets will still be needed to obtain good blood glucose control. This is eventually the case for most people with type 2 diabetes as they grow older and their insulin secreting capacity declines further.

Hypos—the exception to the low GI rule

In people with diabetes who are treated with insulin or tablets the blood glucose may sometimes fall below four millimoles per litre, which is the lower end of the normal range. When this happens you might feel hungry, shaky, sweaty and be unable to think clearly. This is called a hypo (short for 'hypoglycemia').

A hypo is a potentially dangerous situation and must be treated straightaway by eating some carbohydrate food. In this case, you should pick a carbohydrate with a high GI because you need to increase your blood glucose quickly. Jelly beans (GI of 80) are a good choice. If you are not due for your next meal or snack, you should also have some low GI carbohydrate, like an apple, to keep your blood glucose from falling again until you next eat.

CASE STUDY

Hypos in the night were a particularly worrying problem for Jane. Her evening insulin doses had been adjusted in an effort to stop her blood glucose going too low at night, but she believed experimenting with her supper carbohydrate could also help. After trying all sorts of different foods and many 3 a.m. blood tests, she struck the answer that the GI predicted would work— milk! Jane found that a large glass of milk before going to bed, rather than her usual plain biscuits, was easy to have and maintained her blood glucose at a good level through the night.

Diabetes complications

If blood glucose levels are not properly controlled, diabetes can cause damage to the blood vessels in the heart, legs, brain, eyes and kidneys. For this reason, heart attacks, leg amputations, strokes, blindness and kidney failure are more common in people with diabetes. It can also damage the nerves in the feet, causing pain and irritation in the feet and numbness and loss of sensation.

In addition to high glucose levels, many researchers believe that high levels of insulin also contribute to the damage of the blood vessels of the heart, legs and brain. High insulin levels are thought to be one of the factors which might stimulate the muscle in the wall of the blood vessel to thicken. Thickening of the muscle wall causes the blood vessels to narrow and can slow the flow of blood to the point that a clot can form and stop the blood flow altogether. This is what happens to cause a heart attack or stroke.

We know that foods with a high GI cause the body to produce larger amounts of insulin, resulting in higher levels of insulin in the blood. Therefore, for people with type 2 diabetes, it makes sense that eating foods with a low GI will have the effect of helping to control blood glucose levels, and will do this with lower levels of insulin.

Glycemic load incorporates both the amount and type of carbohydrate

This may have the added benefit of reducing the large vessel damage which accounts for so many of the problems of diabetes.

A word of advice

There are many factors that can affect your blood glucose levels. If you have diabetes and you are struggling to control your blood glucose level it is important to seek medical help. How much exercise you do, your weight, stress levels, total dietary intake and need for medication may have to be assessed.

THE OPTIMUM DIET FOR PEOPLE WITH DIABETES

Plenty of wholegrain cereals, breads, vegetables and fruits

A low fat, low GI diet contains lots of heavy grain breads; cereals like oats, barley, couscous, cracked wheat; legumes like kidney beans and lentils; and all types of fruit and vegetables.

Only small amounts of fat, especially saturated fat

Limit biscuits, cakes, butter, potato chips, takeaway fried foods, full cream dairy products, fatty meats and sausages which are all high in saturated fat. Poly- and monounsaturated oils are healthier types of fats.

A moderate amount of sugar and sugar-containing foods

It's okay to include your favourite sweetener or sweet food—small quantities of sugar, honey, golden syrup, jam—to make meals more palatable and pleasurable.

Only a moderate quantity of alcohol

Only four standard drinks for men and two standard drinks for women per day, with at least two alcohol-free days a week.

Only a moderate amount of salt and salted foods

Try lemon juice, freshly ground black pepper, garlic, chilli, herbs and other flavours rather than relying on salt.

CHAPTER 10

THE GI
AND HYPOGLYCEMIA

These days, hypoglycemia is a popular diagnosis for all sorts of problems which cannot be attributed to a more specific diagnosis. There has been considerable publicity about hypoglycemia which is often blamed for many non-specific health problems, ranging from tiredness to depression. Unfortunately, hypoglycemia is often wrongly blamed, which can delay a proper diagnosis and correct treatment.

Nevertheless, genuine hypoglycemia does occur in a few people, and the GI has a role to play in treating some forms of this condition.

Hypoglycemia is a condition in which the glucose level in the blood falls below normal levels. It derives from the Greek words hypo meaning *under* and glycemia meaning *blood glucose*—hence blood glucose level below normal.

The most common form of hypoglycemia occurs after a meal is eaten. This is called reactive hypoglycemia.

Normally, when a meal containing carbohydrate is eaten, the blood glucose level rises. This causes the pancreas to make insulin which 'pushes' the glucose out of the blood and into the muscles where it provides energy for you to carry out your regular tasks and activities. The movement of glucose out of the blood and into the muscles is finely controlled by just the right amount of insulin to drop the glucose back to normal. In some people, the blood glucose level rises too quickly after eating and causes an excessive amount of insulin to be released. This draws too much glucose out of the blood and causes the blood glucose level to fall below normal. The result is hypoglycemia.

Hypoglycemia causes a variety of unpleasant symptoms. Many of these are stress-like symptoms such as sweating, tremor, anxiety, palpitations and weakness. Other symptoms affect mental function and lead to restlessness, irritability, poor concentration, lethargy and drowsiness.

The diagnosis of true reactive hypoglycemia cannot be made on the basis of vague symptoms. It depends on detecting a low blood glucose level when the symptoms are actually being experienced. This means a blood test.

Because it may be difficult (or almost impossible) for someone to be in the right place at the right time to have a blood sample taken while experiencing the symptoms, a glucose tolerance test is sometimes used to try to make the diagnosis. This involves drinking pure glucose which causes the blood glucose levels to rise. If too much insulin is produced in response, a person with reactive hypoglycemia will experience an excessive fall in their blood glucose level. Sounds simple enough, but there are pitfalls.

Testing must be done under strictly controlled conditions; a low blood glucose is best demonstrated by measuring properly collected capillary (not venous) blood samples. Home blood glucose meters are not sufficient for the diagnosis of hypoglycemia in people without diabetes.

Treating hypoglycemia

The aim of treating reactive hypoglycemia is to prevent sudden large increases in blood glucose levels. If the blood glucose level can be prevented from increasing quickly, then excessive, unnecessary amounts of insulin will not be produced and the blood glucose levels will not plunge to abnormally low levels.

Smooth, steady blood glucose levels can be readily achieved by changing from high to low GI foods in the diet. This is particularly important when eating carbohydrate foods by themselves. Low GI foods like wholegrain bread, low fat yoghurt and low GI fruits are best for snacks.

If you can stop the big swings in blood glucose levels, then you will not get the symptoms of reactive hypoglycemia and chances are you will feel a lot better.

Hypoglycemia due to a serious medical problem is rare. Such conditions require in-depth investigation and treatment of the underlying cause.

An irregular eating pattern is the most common dietary habit that we see in people who have hypoglycemia. The following case study illustrates this very well.

CASE STUDY

Diane, with her hectic working life, often did not find time for proper meals. Finally, her body no longer accepted the strain it was under. Diane began to experience odd bouts of weakness and shakiness where she was unable to think clearly. A visit to the doctor and a glucose tolerance test confirmed that she was suffering from hypoglycemia. The treatment was to change her habits—her eating pattern at least. Diane needed to eat three regular meals

The GI is about the type of carbohydrate in your diet

a day with snacks in between. The thought of eating six times every day seemed an enormous task to Diane—and it took much thought and planning to organise her new diet. What kept her going was how much better she felt almost immediately. The following meal plan is a typical menu for Diane's day.

6 a.m. Breakfast	Banana, milk, yoghurt, honey and vanilla blended into a smoothie for a speedy start to the day
8.30 a.m. At work	An oatbran and apple muffin (home-made on the weekend and frozen individually)
12 noon Lunch	A substantial sandwich, roll or foccacia; occasionally a Mexican dish with beans or a pasta meal if out
3 p.m. At work	Handful of dried fruit (kept in jar in office)
5 p.m. Still at work	Couple of oatmeal biscuits (kept in office) for late days
7.30 p.m. Dinner	Something quick, often pasta, baked beans on toast or meat and vegetables. (Always double check for carbohydrate in the main)
9–10 p.m. Late night snack	Fruit or milkshake for dessert

TO PREVENT REACTIVE HYPOGLYCEMIA REMEMBER:

- Eat regular meals and snacks—plan to eat every three hours.
- Include low GI carbohydrate foods at every meal and for snacks.
- Mix high GI foods with low GI foods in your meals—the combination will give an overall intermediate GI.
- Avoid eating high GI foods on their own for snacks—this can trigger reactive hypoglycemia.

CHAPTER 11

THE GI AND HEART HEALTH: THE INSULIN RESISTANCE SYNDROME

Did you know that heart disease is the single biggest killer of Australians? Every 10 minutes, every day, someone in Australia suffers a cardiovascular event. Most heart disease is caused by atherosclerosis, sometimes referred to as 'hardening of the arteries'.

Most people develop atherosclerosis gradually during their lifetime. If it occurs slowly it may not cause any problems at all, even into great old age. But if its development is accelerated by one or more of many processes (such as high cholesterol or high glucose levels) the condition may cause trouble much earlier in life.

Knowing your blood glucose level is just as important as knowing your cholesterol level to ensure optimum heart health.

Atherosclerosis results in reduced blood flow through the affected arteries. In the heart this can mean that the heart muscle gets insufficient oxygen to provide the power for pumping blood, and it changes in such a way that pain is experienced (central chest pain or angina pectoris). Elsewhere in the body, atherosclerosis has a similar blood flow reducing effect: in the legs it can cause muscle pains on exercise; in the brain it can cause a variety of problems from 'funny turns' to strokes.

An even more serious consequence of atherosclerosis occurs when a blood clot forms over the surface of a patch of atherosclerosis on an artery. This process of thrombosis can result in a complete blockage of the artery, with consequences ranging from sudden death to a small heart attack from which the patient recovers quickly.

The process of thrombosis can occur elsewhere in the arterial system with outcomes determined by the extent of the thrombosis. The probability of developing thrombosis is determined by the 'tendency' of the blood to clot versus the natural ability of the blood to break down clots (fibrinolysis). These two counteracting 'tendencies' are influenced by a number of factors, including the level of glucose in the blood.

People who have gradually developed atherosclerosis of the arteries to the heart (the coronary arteries) may gradually develop reduced heart function. For a while the heart may be able to compensate for the problem, so there are no symptoms, but eventually it begins to fail. Shortness of breath may occur, initially on exercise, and there may sometimes be some swelling of the ankles.

Modern medicine has many effective drug treatments for heart failure so this consequence of atherosclerosis does not have quite the same serious implications as it did in the past.

The insulin resistance syndrome

Surveys show that one in two Australian adults over 25 years of age have at least two features of what is seen to be a silent disease: insulin resistance syndrome. The insulin resistance syndrome (sometimes called the metabolic syndrome or syndrome X) is a collection of metabolic abnormalities that 'silently' increase your risk of heart attack.

If you have hypertension, impaired glucose tolerance, low HDL-cholesterol levels and high triglycerides, then you probably have the insulin resistance syndrome.

Chances are your total cholesterol levels are within the normal range, giving you and your doctor a false impression of your coronary health.

You might also be normal weight (or overweight) but your waist circumference is high (more than 90 cm in women, more than 100 cm in men), indicating excessive fat around the abdomen.

But the red flag is that your blood glucose and insulin levels after a glucose load, or after eating, remain high. Resistance to the action of insulin is thought to underlie and unite all the features of this cluster of metabolic abnormalities.

One of the questions that's often asked is why insulin resistance is so common. We know that both genes and environment play a role. People of Asian or Australian Aboriginal origins appear to be more insulin resistant than those of European extraction, even when they are still young and lean.

But regardless of ethnic background, insulin resistance develops as we age. This has been attributed not to age per se, but to the fact that as we get older, we gain excessive fat around our middle, we become less physically active and we lose some of our muscle mass. It's also likely that diet plays a role—high fat diets have been associated with insulin resistance; high carbohydrate diets with improving insulin sensitivity.

Insulin resistance as we age results in the insulin resistance syndrome and gradually lays the foundations of a heart attack. To understand how and why this happens, we need to understand how heart disease develops.

Why do people get heart disease?

Atherosclerotic heart disease develops early in life when the many factors that cause it have a strong influence. Over many decades doctors and scientists have identified the processes in fine detail and now most of the factors which cause heart disease are well known.

Theoretically, this type of heart disease might be prevented if everyone's risks were assessed in youth and if all the right things were done throughout the rest of their lives. In practice there has been a limited development of the ways to screen people for risk early in life, and the resources needed to achieve prevention are just not available.

A great deal is already being done, however, to identify risk factors (i.e. 'red flags') in healthy people and those with established heart disease. A high cholesterol level is a well-established risk factor, as is a low level of HDL—the 'good' cholesterol. More recently, high glucose levels after eating have been shown to be an important, but under-recognised predictor of both cardiovascular disease and death from any cause. The good news is that those of us who take the necessary action, will reduce our risk.

Risk factors for heart disease

The chance of developing heart disease is increased if you smoke cigarettes or any other tobacco product, have high blood pressure, have diabetes or impaired glucose tolerance, have high blood cholesterol (which may be due to eating too much saturated fat in your diet), are overweight or obese and/or do not take enough physical exercise.

Smoking is now clearly established as a cause of atherosclerosis. Few authorities now dispute the evidence. There are however some interesting dietary aspects: Did you know that smokers tend to eat less fruit and vegetables compared to non-smokers (and thus eat less of the protective antioxidant plant compounds)? Did you know that smokers tend to eat more fat and more salt than non-smokers? These characteristics of the smoker's diet may be caused by a desire to seek stronger food flavours as a consequence of the taste-blunting effect of smoking. While these dietary differences may make the smoker at greater risk of heart disease there is only one piece of advice for anyone who smokes: *stop smoking!*

High blood pressure causes changes in the walls of arteries. The muscle layer (a muscular tube, which when healthy can change its size to control the flow of blood) becomes thickened and atherosclerosis is more likely to develop. Treatments for blood pressure have become more effective over the last thirty years, but it is only now becoming clear which types of treatment for blood pressure are also effective at reducing heart disease risk.

Diabetes and **impaired glucose tolerance** accelerate hardening of the arteries. When glucose levels are raised, even temporarily (such as after eating), oxidising reactions are accelerated and antioxidants such as vitamin E and C are soaked up. In particular, the blood fats are oxidised making them more damaging to artery walls. The walls become inflamed, thicken and gradually lose their elasticity. The constriction of the arteries results in increased blood pressure. If that's not bad enough, high insulin levels increase the tendency for blood clots to form. The resulting increased risk of heart attack is a major reason why we put so much effort into helping people with diabetes achieve normal control of blood glucose.

But you don't need to have diabetes to be at risk—raised blood glucose levels hours after a meal have been associated with increased risk of heart disease in normal 'healthy' people.

High blood cholesterol increases the risk of heart disease. Your blood cholesterol is determined by genetic (inherited) factors, which you cannot change, and lifestyle factors, which you *can* change.

There are some relatively rare conditions in which particularly high blood cholesterol levels occur. People who have inherited these conditions need a thorough examination by a specialist doctor followed by life-long drug treatment.

In most people, high blood cholesterol is partly determined by their genes, which have 'set' the cholesterol slightly high, and lifestyle factors which push it up more.

The most important dietary factor is fat. The diets prescribed for blood cholesterol lowering are low in fat (particularly saturated fat), high in carbohydrate and high in fibre.

Body weight also affects blood cholesterol—in some people being overweight has a significant effect on the levels—attaining a reasonable weight can be helpful. The blood also contains triglycerides, another type of fat which is particularly high after meals. High triglycerides may be linked with increased risk of heart disease in some people.

Overweight and obese people are more likely to have high blood pressure and to have diabetes. They are also at increased risk of getting heart disease. Some of that increased risk is due to the high blood pressure, and the tendency to diabetes, but there is a separate 'independent' effect of the obesity.

When increased fatness develops it can be distributed evenly all over the body or it may occur centrally—in and around the abdomen (tummy). This 'central' form of obesity is particularly associated with heart disease. Thus every effort should be made to get body weights nearer to normal—especially if the extra weight is 'middle-age spread'.

Exercise has several benefits for the heart. Cardiovascular fitness is improved by regular strenuous exercise and the blood supply to the heart may be 'improved'. Exercise is also important in maintaining body weight and has effects on metabolism and some factors related to blood clotting. Getting regular exercise is clearly important.

Treating heart disease and secondary prevention

When heart disease is detected two types of treatment are given. Firstly, the effects of the disease are treated (e.g. medical treatment with drugs and surgical treatment to bypass blocked arteries) and, secondly, the risk factors are treated to slow down the further progression of the disease.

Treatment of risk factors after the disease has already developed is 'secondary prevention'. In people who have not yet developed the disease, treatment of risk factors is 'primary prevention'. Obviously it would be better to give primary preventive treatment in all cases.

Preventing heart disease: primary prevention

More and more people now get regular checks of their blood pressure, and tests to check for diabetes. Increasingly blood fat tests are done to check this risk factor too.

All health professionals give lifestyle advice on stopping smoking, the benefits of exercise and the nature of a good diet. When specific risk factors are discovered, diet and lifestyle advice is given, but may not be followed for long.

It is especially difficult to follow advice if the effect of not following it is likely not to matter for ten or more years, and if the changes needed are not seen as appealing. The changes must be wanted by the individual who will be helped by encouragement from friends and relatives, and the changes must ideally be positive changes—'I want to do this' not 'They've told me to do this'. Any new dimension in heart disease prevention must be seen as a great positive change rather than as a negative one.

GI and heart health

The glycemic index is vitally important for coronary health and the prevention of heart disease.

Firstly, it has benefits for weight control, helping to satisfy appetite and preventing overeating and excessive body weight.

Secondly, it helps reduce post-meal blood glucose levels in both normal and diabetic individuals. This improves the elasticity of the walls of the arteries, making dilation easier and improving blood flow. Thirdly, blood fats and clotting factors can also be improved by low GI diets. Specifically, population studies have shown that HDL levels are correlated with the GI and glycemic load of the diet. Those of us who self-select the lowest GI diets, have the highest and best levels of HDL—the good cholesterol.

Furthermore, research studies in people with diabetes, have shown that low GI diets reduce triglycerides in the blood, a factor strongly linked to heart disease. Lastly, low GI diets have been shown to improve insulin sensitivity in people at high risk of heart disease, thereby helping to reduce the rise in blood glucose and insulin levels after normal meals.

By working on several fronts at one time, low GI diets have a distinct advantage over other types of diets or drugs that target only one risk factor at a time.

One study in particular has provided the best evidence in support of the role of the GI in heart disease. The study was conducted by Harvard University and is commonly referred to as 'The Nurses Study'. The Nurse's Study is an ongoing, long-term study of over 65 000 nurses who provide their personal health and diet information to researchers at Harvard School of Public Health every few years. In this way, diet can be linked with the development of different diseases. It found that those who ate more *high* GI foods, had nearly twice the risk of having a heart attack over a ten-year period of follow-up, compared to those eating low GI diets. This association was independent of dietary fibre and other known risk factors, such as age and body mass index. In other words, even if fibre intake was high, there was still an adverse effect of high GI diets on risk. Importantly, neither sugar nor total carbohydrate intake showed any association with risk of heart attack. Thus there was no evidence that lower carbohydrate or sugar intake was helpful.

One of the most important findings of The Nurses Study, was that the increased risk associated with high GI diets was largely seen in those with a body mass index (BMI) over 23 (to calculate your body mass divide your weight in kilograms by the square of your height in metres). There was no increased risk in those under 23. But the fact remains that the great majority of adults have a BMI greater than 23; indeed a BMI of 23–25 is considered normal weight. The implication therefore is that the insulin resistance that comes with increasing weight is an integral part of the disease process. So, if you are very lean and insulin sensitive, high GI diets won't make you more prone to heart attack. This might explain why traditional-living Asian populations, such as the Chinese who eat high GI rice as a staple food, do not show increased risk of heart disease. Their low BMI and their high level of physical activity conspire to keep them insulin sensitive and extremely carbohydrate tolerant.

The New Glucose Revolution Pocket Guide for Your Heart includes more information on how the GI can help and menu ideas for low GI foods.

The GI and insulin resistance

In this condition the body is insensitive, or 'partially' deaf, to insulin. The organs and tissues that ought to respond to even a small rise in insulin remain unresponsive. The body tries harder by secreting more insulin to achieve the same effect, just as you might raise your voice or shout for a hard of hearing person. Thus high insulin levels are part and parcel of insulin resistance. Tests on patients with heart disease and polycystic ovarian syndrome (PCOS—see box, page 228) show that insulin resistance is very common.

Can a low GI diet help? In a recent study, patients with serious disease of the coronary arteries were given either low or high GI diets before surgery for coronary bypass grafts. They were given blood tests before their diets and just before surgery, and at surgery small pieces of fat tissue were removed for testing. The tests on the fat showed that the low GI diets made the tissues of these 'insulin insensitive' patients more sensitive—in fact they were back in the same range as normal 'control' patients after just a few weeks on the diet.

If people with serious heart disease can be improved would the same happen with younger people? Young women in their thirties were divided into those who did and those who did not have a family history of heart disease. They themselves had not yet developed the condition. They had blood tests followed by low or high GI diets for four weeks, after which they had more blood tests, and then when they had surgery (for conditions unrelated to heart disease) pieces of fat were again removed and tested for insulin sensitivity. The young women with a family history of heart disease were insensitive to insulin (those without the family history of heart disease were normal) but after four weeks on the low GI diet were normal again.

POLYCYSTIC OVARIAN SYNDROME (PCOS)

Polycystic ovarian syndrome occurs in women when multiple cysts form on the ovaries during the menstrual cycle and interfere with normal ovulation. It is often diagnosed when women have irregular periods or find it difficult to fall pregnant.

It is now known that insulin resistance is often severe in women with PCOS and that any means of improving insulin sensitivity (drugs, weight loss) will improve outcomes. Some physicians have found that low GI diets are particularly useful for women with PCOS. At present, there is little research to back this up. However, since low GI diets will help reduce weight and have been shown to improve insulin sensitivity in individuals at risk of coronary heart disease, it makes a lot of sense to try the low GI approach.

In both studies, the diets were designed to try to ensure that all the other variables (like total energy, total carbohydrates) were not different, so that the change in insulin sensitivity was likely to have been due to the low GI diet rather than any other factor.

Work on these exciting findings continues, but what is known so far strongly suggests that low GI diets not only improve body weight and improve blood glucose in people with diabetes, but also improve the sensitivity of the body to insulin. It will take many years of further research to show that this simple dietary change to a low GI diet will definitely slow the progress of atherosclerotic heart disease. In the meantime it is clear that risk factors for heart disease are improved by the low GI diet. Low GI diets are consistent with the other required dietary changes needed for prevention of heart disease.

Low saturated fat and low GI help prevent heart disease.

CHAPTER 12

CHILDREN AND THE GI

Helping our children eat well is one of the most important things we can do for them. In an environment where food is abundant, and physical activity limited, the potential for energy imbalance is great and the consequences enormous. Already at least one in five Australian children is overweight or obese—a serious concern given the medical and psychological consequences.

Overweight children are at risk of sleep apnoea, high blood pressure and elevated blood fats. Many will also have elevated levels of circulating insulin, which is an early warning sign for the potential development of type 2 diabetes, a condition once only seen in adults. All in all, overweight children face adulthood with the prospect of cardiovascular disease and reduced longevity. As if this isn't enough, overweight children are commonly stigmatised as lazy, unhealthy and less intelligent. Loss of self-esteem and subsequent social isolation can make life a misery.

How can the GI help?

The management of obesity in children is about altering energy balance. Energy intake has to decrease and energy expenditure has to increase. Our diet in Australia and New Zealand today tends to be too high in fat and quickly digested carbohydrate foods with little fill-up value. Many of our starchy staples, like potato, white bread, cornflakes and rice, have very high GI values. So too do children's favourites like Burger Rings™, Twisties™ and cordial. Because of their high GI, it is easy to overconsume kilojoules with these foods. In contrast, low GI foods have been proven to be more filling and can reduce overeating.

In a study performed in 12 obese teenage boys in the United States, low GI meals significantly reduced subsequent food intake compared with high GI meals. The boys ate special breakfast and lunch meals that had either a low, medium or high GI and then their food intake during the remainder of the day was measured. Researchers found that the boys ate twice as much food in the afternoon after a high GI breakfast and lunch as they did after a low GI breakfast and lunch. This difference in food intake corresponded with differences in hormonal and metabolic changes thought to be responsible for stimulating excessive appetite.

There were higher levels of the hormones insulin, noradrenaline and cortisol after the high GI meals. The increased insulin response to high GI carbohydrates may promote fat storage and obesity. Higher cortisol levels may result in increased appetite. Differences in these hormones are one possible explanation for significantly greater fat loss in a group of children prescribed a diet based on low GI foods compared with those on a conventional low fat diet. With the low GI diet the children were instructed to eat till they were full, snack when hungry and to eat low GI carbohydrate, protein and fat at every meal and snack. Body mass index and body weight decreased significantly more (over the four month study period) in those advised on a low GI diet.

THE IMPORTANCE OF PHYSICAL ACTIVITY

An increase in physical activity is critical to weight managment for children. This includes the reduction of sedentary behaviours (such as television viewing, computer and video games) and an increase in planned and incidental activity (such as helping with household tasks and dressing themselves).

It helps enormously if parents are involved in physical activity themselves, serving as a means of support and a role model. Active family activities such as walks, swimming, bike rides, cricket matches etc., need to be planned. The number one rule is to make it fun!

If children learn to combine regular physical activity with healthy low GI eating, they will be in top condition throughout their lives.

Some dietary guidelines for childhood

A healthy diet for children:

- allows for good health and growth
- satisfies the appetite
- encourages good eating habits
- allows for varied and interesting meals and snacks
- accommodates the child's usual routines and activities
- maintains a healthy body weight

Children need to eat a wide variety of nutritious foods to grow and develop to their full potential. As a parent you can help by ensuring you:

- offer children plenty of breads, cereals, vegetables and fruits to eat
- include lean meats, fish and dairy foods in their daily diet
- encourage children to drink plenty of water
- choose low salt foods for children
- follow these guidelines yourself, so that children can copy you

Remember: not all carbohydrates are equal

Incorporating low GI foods in your child's diet

The GI of a diet can be easily lowered using a simple system of sub-stitution where at least half of high GI carbohydrate choices are swapped for low GI carbohydrate foods.

Keep the following characteristics of children's eating behaviour in mind, when attempting changes in their diet:

Children are naturally neophobic. They dislike new foods. It is normal for children, especially young children to refuse new foods. Repeated exposure to new foods in a positive environment increases their acceptance. But you have to persevere—at least 5–10 tastes of the food may be needed before it is accepted.

Most children are natural grazers. They usually like to have fre-quent meals and snacks throughout the day. It's not a good idea to make children eat everything on the plate as this can encour-age overconsumption. It is preferable they learn to stay in tune with their appetite and eat according to it.

Children have small stomachs with high nutrient require-ments. Their food intake may vary considerably from meal to meal but studies show it remains surprisingly constant from day to day. So long as the foods offered to children are nutritious, appetite is the best indicator of how much they need to eat.

Be clear on what your role is as a parent in relation to feeding your children. The American nutritionist, Ellyn Satter, expresses it well in these words: 'Parents are responsible for what is provided to eat. Children are responsible for how much, and even whether, they eat.'

The best carbohydrate choices

The following foods have a low GI, are high in micronutrients and provide very little saturated fat. The recommended number of daily serves for children aged 4–11 years is included.

Cereal grains

This group includes wholegrain breads, porridge and barley, oats, popcorn, rice, rye, wheat and anything made from them, such as bread, breakfast cereals, flour, noodles, pasta, polenta, ravioli, semolina.

Serves per day: 3–9

Fruits

This includes apples, apricots, bananas, cherries, grapes, kiwi fruit, oranges, peaches, pears, plums and sultanas. Serve them whole or as juices, frappés and smoothies.

Serves per day: 1–2

Vegetables and legumes

Vegetables and legumes provide valuable amounts of vitamins, minerals and fibre. You can eat most vegetables without thinking about their GI because they are very low in carbohydrate. The higher carbohydrate vegetables are potatoes, corn, taro and sweet potato. Of these, corn and sweet potato are the lower GI choices. All legumes (including baked beans, chickpeas, kidney beans, lentils and split peas) are low GI sources of carbohydrate.

Serves per day: 2–5

Milk and milk products

low fat milk and dairy foods like custard, ice-cream and yoghurt are an excellent source of carbohydrate and calcium. Children under five should be given full fat milk but low fat varieties are quite suitable for older children.

Serves per day: 2–3

It isn't necessary to give children low GI foods alone. On the contrary, meals usually consist of a variety of foods, and we know that eating a low GI food with a high GI food produces an intermediate GI meal.

Eat grainy breads, pasta, beans, fruit and vegetables

To help yourself include low GI foods in the family meals every day:

- become familiar with them
- have them available in the pantry and refrigerator
- experiment with them—try new foods and recipes and enjoy what you eat

The New Glucose Revolution Pocket Guide for Healthy Kids and *The New Glucose Revolution Pocket Guide for Children with Type 1 Diabetes* contain more information about the GI and children, including detailed menu plans and recipe ideas.

Try to include a minimum of one low GI food per meal to reap the benefits.

The role of sugar

Children naturally enjoy sweet foods. Sweetness is not a learned taste; in fact, it could be said that we're all born with a sweet tooth. Our first food, breast milk, is sweet. Infants smile when offered a sweet solution and reject sour and bitter tastes.

Today, scientists researching the glycemic index have shown that sugar is not the dietary demon that it was once made out to be. You and your children can enjoy sugar and foods containing sugar in moderation as part of a balanced low GI diet. In fact, studies show that diets containing moderate quantities of added sugars tend to be richest in micronutrients. Sugar itself has only a moderate GI value and many foods containing sugar, such as yoghurt and flavoured milk, are excellent sources of low GI nutrition.

What is a moderate intake of sugar in a child's diet?

A moderate intake of refined sugar in a child's diet is between 30 and 50 grams a day (6-10 teaspoons a day). This reflects average consumption in Australian children and refers to the sugar found in foods such as soft drinks, cordials, breakfast cereals, confectionery, ice-cream, biscuits, jams, as well as what we add—to breakfast cereal, for example. Adding sugar to a well-balanced low GI diet can make foods more palatable and acceptable to children without compromising their nutritional intake or the benefits of the low GI foods.

Artificially sweetened products

While artificially sweetened products may sometimes be appropriate for children, they are not necessary for the average child. Many of these products are simply flavoured fillers such as diet cordials, soft drinks and lollies and provide few, if any, nutrients. Often they are cited as useful in preventing tooth decay. This is not the case for low joule soft drinks, which are highly acidic and will dissolve dental enamel. Even their role in weight reduction is questionable, as individuals using diet products tend to compensate with extra kilojoules at later meals.

Did you know that diets containing a moderate amount of sugar are associated with:

- the highest level of micronutrients
- a lower GI
- lower intakes of saturated fat
- a lower body weight

A moderate quantity of sugar in a 10-year-old child's diet

This child's menu provides 50 grams of refined sugars. It provides 6300 kilojoules of energy, with 25 per cent of energy from fat and 58 per cent of energy from carbohydrate.

Breakfast

½ cup of Coco Pops™ with reduced fat milk
½ banana
100 ml fruit juice

Snack

1 fruit muesli bar
1 cup of reduced fat milk

Lunch

1 cheese and lettuce sandwich (made from low GI bread)
4 dried apricot halves
1 small apple
1 cup of water

Snack

2 chocolate chip biscuits
1 cup of homemade popcorn
1 fruit smoothie

Dinner

½ cup of spaghetti with meat sauce
green salad, tossed with a little dressing if desired
carrot and celery sticks
½ cup of custard and a canned pear half
water to drink

Supper

1 slice raisin toast with a little margarine

Does sugar affect children's behaviour?

Although some people believe sugar causes attention deficit disorder (ADD) or hyperactivity in children, results from many published studies have failed to provide any scientifically proven support for this. In situations where the investigator, the child and the parent were unaware of the composition of the test food or capsule, refined sugar showed no effect on cognitive performance, nor did it cause or exacerbate ADD.

It is possible that a very small number of children may respond adversely to fluctuations in blood glucose levels caused by sugar. But if this is the case, any carbohydrate, including bread and potatoes, will also be incriminated.

On the whole, there is more evidence that sugar might actually have a calming effect, if it has any effect at all. Glucose or sugar can reduce the distress associated with painful medical procedures in infants. In one study there was a reduction in crying and heart rate in infants subjected to heel pricks when they were given a sugar solution immediately prior to the procedure compared with children who were given just water.

What about fat in a child's diet?

Young children (under five) rely on a certain amount of fat in their diet as a source of kilojoules and should generally not be placed on a low fat diet. A moderate amount of fat is also necessary as a source of essential fatty acids and fat-soluble vitamins. Kids need some fat, but don't go overboard. In fact, a recent study from Flinders University found that children are eating more fat now than they did 10 years ago. Like adults, children, should not regularly consume prepared foods which are high in saturated fat, such as biscuits, cakes, pastries, ready-to-eat meals, confectionery and snack foods.

A low GI 7-day sample menu for kids

Monday

Breakfast

Bowl of Mini-Wheats™ cereal with milk.

Half a banana.

Snack: Muesli Bar. Small carton orange juice.

Lunch

Sandwich of grated carrot and apple with cream cheese on
Performax™ bread. Bottle of water. Small tub of vanilla custard.

Snack: Crumpets with honey.

Dinner

Tuna and rice-bake made with Doongara rice, peas, sweet corn and
strips of red capsicum and a light cheese sauce.

Snack: Frozen yoghurt ice-block.

Tuesday

Breakfast

Bowl of Coco-Pops™ with milk. Sliced apple quarters.

Snack: 130 gram tub of light fromage frais (like Fruche™). Small bunch
of grapes.

Lunch

Multigrain sandwich filled with tuna, creamed corn and lettuce. Small
tub or can of peaches.

Snack: Rockmelon chunks and fat-reduced ice-cream.

Dinner

Cook a casserole using a good-quality chicken stock and chunks of
favourite vegetables, including sweet potato. Serve with Basmati rice
or noodles.

Snack: Fruit kebabs (fresh fruit wedges on a skewer).

Wednesday

Breakfast

Toasted muesli with fruit yoghurt and canned two-fruits.

Snack: Snap-lock bag of popcorn.

Lunch

Sandwich-sized Vita-Weat™ spread with vegemite. Celery, carrot and apple sticks. Orange and mango juice.

Snack: Corn on the cob.

Dinner

Bake Tex Mex potatoes (sweet potato baked with onion, bacon, taco seasoning, baked beans, grated cheese, sour cream and corn chips).

Snack: Nutella on toast.

Thursday

Breakfast

Poached egg on toast.

Snack: Mandarin and a Fruit Finger bar.

Lunch

Apricot and banana jaffles (using raisin bread, ricotta cheese, apricot jam, banana, cinnamon). Bottle of water.

Snack: Strawberry smoothie.

Dinner

Serve grilled or barbecued sausages and mash made with a 50:50 mixture of new potato and sweet potato and served with sweet corn cobs.

Snack: A nashi pear.

Friday

Breakfast

Porridge and sultanas.

Snack: Finger bun.

Lunch

A wholemeal roll with egg, mayonnaise and chives. Yoghurt drink.

Snack: Avocado or hummus dip served with fruit or vegetables.

Dinner

Asian takeaway (chicken, meat or seafood dish, plus stir-fried vegetable dish) with home-cooked low GI rice or noodles.

Snack: Chocolate milk drink.

Saturday

Breakfast

Banana honey smoothie.

Snack: Noodles with margarine or grated cheese.

Lunch

Vegetable soup with a crusty wholegrain roll.

Snack: Cheese wedges and dried fruit (apple, sultana, apricot and pear).

Dinner

Try sweet corn and green pea frittata, made with eggs and fresh vegetables or a can of sweet corn kernels and a packet of frozen peas.

Snack: Watermelon wedges.

Sunday

Breakfast

French toast with fruit.

Snack: Low fat crackers and an apple.

Lunch

Jacket potatoes served with tuna, cheese, baked beans or coleslaw.

Snack: Ice-cream in a cone.

Dinner

Baked beans on toast.

Snack: Peanut butter wholegrain toast.

CHAPTER 13

THE GI AND PEAK SPORTS PERFORMANCE

Australian scientists were the first in the world to apply the concept of the glycemic index to sport and exercise science. It may be no coincidence that Australians are famed for their sporting prowess around the world. They have been world champions in swimming, tennis, cricket, rugby, netball and rowing year after year. Manipulating the GI of the diet can give you the winning edge—whether you are one of the elite or a weekend warrior.

Why is the GI relevant to sporting performance?

The GI ranks the carbohydrates in foods according to their glycemic impact. The rise in blood glucose affects the insulin response to that food and ultimately affects the fuel mix and carbohydrate stores available to the exercising muscles. In sport and exercise, there are times when low GI foods provide an advantage (e.g. *before* the event) and times when high GI foods are better (e.g. *during and after* the event). For best performance, a serious athlete needs to learn about which foods have high and low GI values and when to eat them.

But it's not only the type of carbohydrate that matters—the amount of carbohydrate is equally important. Training diets must be very high in carbohydrate if the GI is to make any difference at all.

Manipulating the GI of your diet can give you the winning edge!

A high carbohydrate diet is essential for peak sporting performance

A high carbohydrate training diet is a must for optimum sports performance because it produces the biggest stores of muscle glycogen. As we have previously described, the carbohydrate we eat is stored in the body in the form of glycogen in the muscles and liver. A small amount of carbohydrate (about 5 grams) circulates as glucose in the blood. When you are exercising at a high intensity, your muscles rely on glycogen and glucose for fuel. Although the body can use fat when exercising at lower intensities, fat cannot provide the fuel fast enough when you are working very hard. The bigger your stores of glycogen and glucose, the longer you can go before fatigue sets in.

Unlike the fat stores in the body which can release almost unlimited amounts of fatty acids, the carbohydrate stores are small. They are fully depleted after two or three hours of strenuous exercise. This drying up of carbohydrate stores is often called 'hitting the wall'. The blood glucose concentration begins to decline at this point. If exercise continues at the same rate, blood glucose may drop to levels which interfere with brain function and cause disorientation and unconsciousness. Some athletes refer to this as a 'hypo' and in cycling it is known as 'bonking'.

All else being equal, the eventual winner is the person with the largest stores of muscle glycogen. Any good book on nutrition for sport will tell you how to maximise your muscle glycogen stores by ingesting a high carbohydrate training diet and by 'carbohydrate loading' in the days prior to the competition. In this chapter we provide instructions for increasing muscle glycogen as well as using the GI to your advantage in sport.

Low GI foods: *before* the event

Low GI foods have been proven to extend endurance when eaten alone one to two hours before prolonged strenuous exercise. When a pre-event meal of lentils (low GI) was compared with one of potatoes (high GI), cyclists were able to continue cycling at high intensity (65 per cent of their maximum capacity) for 20 minutes longer when

Figure 9. Comparison of the effect of low and high GI foods on blood glucose levels during prolonged strenuous exercise.

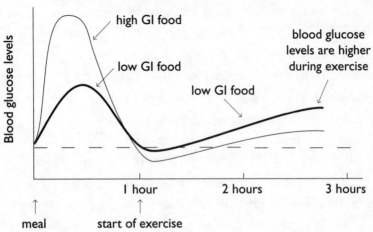

the meal was low GI. Their blood glucose and insulin levels were still above fasting levels at the end of exercise, indicating that carbohydrate was continuing to be absorbed from the small intestine even after 90 minutes of strenuous exercise. Figure 9 shows the blood glucose levels during exercise after consumption of low and high GI foods.

These findings were later confirmed by several other research groups in the United States. Some studies, however, have not been able to show a difference between high and low GI foods. One explanation may be the use of different experimental protocols. Researchers who obtained a positive finding invariably used the 'time to exhaustion' as the criterion for comparison, while those who showed no effect, used the 'time trial' (i.e. the amount of work done or distance travelled over a set time period). While the time trial may be more appropriate for some types of sports events (e.g. a marathon), the time to exhaustion may be closer to reality in other situations (e.g. a tennis match or firefighting).

Despite the fact that they were not able to show a difference in work output between high and low foods, *all of them* showed a difference in blood glucose and insulin levels and all of them showed differences in the ratio of carbohydrate and fat in the fuel mix. In the high GI trials, more carbohydrate and less fat was burnt over the course of the exercise. If this is taken to its logical conclusion, high GI foods must lead to faster carbohydrate depletion and less time before 'hitting the wall'. Anecdotal evidence backs the use of low GI foods before the event. Many elite athletes, including tennis players, have worked out for themselves that pasta gives them the staying power they need for prolonged strenuous events.

Before you read any further, it's important to appreciate the type of event where low GI foods will help. It is one in which the athlete is undertaking a very strenuous form of exercise for longer than 90 minutes. Exercise physiologists define this by saying that the athlete is exercising at more than 65 per cent of their maximum capacity

EVENTS WHERE THE GI CAN GIVE YOU THE EDGE

- running marathon
- swimming marathon
- triathlon
- non-stop tennis competition
- football game (depending on the player's position)
- cross-country skiing
- mountain climbing
- prolonged strenuous aerobics
- and gym work-outs (longer than 90 minutes)

for a prolonged period. Examples of such events include a running or swimming marathon, a triathlon, non-stop tennis competition or football game (depending on the player's position). Some forms of

THE PRE-EVENT MEAL

How much should I eat before the event?
About one gram of carbohydrate for each kilogram of body weight (i.e. 50 grams of carbohydrate if you weigh 50 kilograms, or 75 grams of carbohydrate if you weigh 75 kilograms).

How soon before?
A good starting point is one to two hours before the event.

You should experiment to determine the timing that works best for you.

You will find the amounts of carbohydrate in a nominal serving of food (along with their GI and gylcemic load) in the tables in Part IV of this book.

recreation such as cross-country skiing and mountain climbing may also benefit from using low GI foods. In some occupations that require prolonged strenuous activity for hours and hours (such as police rescue or bush firefighting), low GI foods may also be beneficial.

Low GI foods are best eaten about two hours before the big event—so that the meal will have left the stomach but remains in the small intestine slowly releasing glucose energy for hours afterwards. The slow rate of carbohydrate digestion in low GI foods helps ensure that a small and steady stream of glucose trickles into the bloodstream during the event. Most importantly, the extra glucose will still be available towards the end of the exercise when muscle stores are running close to empty. In this way, low GI foods increase endurance and prolong the time before exhaustion hits.

In sport, it's critical to select low GI foods that do not cause gastrointestinal discomfort (stomach cramps and flatulence). Some low GI foods such as legumes that are high in fibre or indigestible sugars, may produce symptoms in people not used to eating large amounts of them. But there are plenty of low fibre, low GI choices including pasta, noodles and Basmati rice.

Helen O'Connor, a dietitian who has worked with many of Australia's elite footballers, teaches them how to manipulate the GI of their diet. Her book *The Taste of Fitness* is packed with low GI recipes for sports people.

High GI foods: during and after the event

While the pre-event meal should be low GI, scientific evidence indicates that there are times when high GI foods are preferable. This includes during the event, after the event and after normal training sessions. This is because high GI foods are absorbed faster and stimulate more insulin, the hormone responsible for getting glucose back into the muscles for either immediate or future use.

During the event

High GI foods should be used during events lasting longer than 90 minutes. This form of carbohydrate is rapidly released into the blood-stream and ensures that glucose is available for oxidation in the muscle cells. Liquid foods are usually tolerated better than solid foods while racing because they are emptied more quickly from the stomach. Sports drinks are ideal during the race because they replace water and electrolytes as well. The old standby of bananas strapped to the bike doesn't have much scientific basis. The GI of bananas is only 55 and some of their carbohydrate is completely resistant to digestion (which could give you gas and a pain in the belly). If you feel hungry for something solid during a cycling race, try jelly beans (GI of 80) or another form of high glucose confectionery.

Consume 30 to 60 grams of carbohydrate per hour during the event.

The GI of Sports Drinks and Sports Bars

Drinks	GI
Gatorade®	78
Isostar®	70
Sports Plus®	74
Sustegen Sport®	43
Build-Up™	41
Bars	
Power Bar®	56
Ironman PR®	39
Sustain™ (Kelloggs)	57

After the event (recovery)

In some competitive sports, athletes compete on consecutive days and glycogen stores need to be at their maximum each time. Here it is important to restock the glycogen store in the muscles as fast as possible after the event. High GI foods are best in this situation. Sports scientists at the Australian Institute of Sport in Canberra have shown

Look at ways you can reduce saturated fat

that high GI foods resulted in faster replenishment of glycogen into the fatigued muscles. Muscles are more sensitive to glucose in the bloodstream in the first hour after exercise, so a concerted effort should be made to get as many high GI foods in as soon as possible.

Suggested foods include most of the sports drinks on the market (which replace water and electrolyte losses too), or high GI rice (e.g. Calrose or Jasmine), breads and breakfast cereals with a high GI such as cornflakes and rice bubbles. Potatoes cooked without fat are a good choice too, but their high satiety means it is hard to eat lots of them. Soft drinks have an intermediate GI, so they won't be ideal but they won't do any harm either. Alcohol is the worst choice.

A word about alcohol

Alcohol interferes with glycogen resynthesis and lowers blood glucose levels, sometimes to dangerous levels. Keep alcohol intake moderate—no more than one to three standard drinks per day and try to have two alcohol-free days a week. A standard drink is equivalent to one glass of wine (120 ml), one middy of beer (285 ml) or one nip of spirits (30 ml).

Beer is not a good source of carbohydrate, there's less than 10 g in a middy.

RECOVERY FORMULA

Aim to ingest about 1 gram of carbohydrate per kilogram of body weight each 2 hours after exercise. If you weigh between 50 and 75 kilograms, you need 50 to 75 grams of carbohydrate for each 2 hours after exercise.

A word about serving size

Serious athletes need to choose a larger than normal serve. You may not feel like a big meal of rice or pasta and this is the time when sports drinks and soft drinks on the market can help. Choose what you can tolerate and what is easy and practical for you to bring or buy. The main point is to make sure you eat and drink carbohydrate soon after the exercise session.

TO MAXIMISE GLYCOGEN REPLENISHMENT AFTER THE COMPETITION

1. Ingest carbohydrate as soon as you can after the event and maintain a high carbohydrate intake for the next 24 hours.
2. Consume at least 10 grams of carbohydrate per kilogram of body weight over the 24 hours following prolonged exercise.
3. Choose high GI foods in the replenishment phase.
4. Avoid alcohol (alcohol delays glycogen resynthesis).

The training diet and carbohydrate loading

It's not just your pre- and post-event meals that influence your performance. Consuming a high carbohydrate diet every day will help you reach peak performance. The GI of the carbohydrate is not the issue here, only the amount of carbohydrate. Science has proven over and over again (unlike the case for many dietary supplements) that eating lots of high carbohydrate foods maximises muscle glycogen stores and thereby increases endurance. Carbohydrate stores need to be replenished after each training session, not just after a race. If you train on a number of days per week, make sure you consume a high carbohydrate diet throughout the whole week.

When athletes fail to consume adequate carbohydrate each day, muscle and liver glycogen stores eventually became depleted. Dr Ted

Eat grainy breads, pasta, beans, fruit and vegetables

Costill at the University of Texas showed that the gradual and chronic depletion of stored glycogen may decrease endurance and exercise performance. Intense work-outs often two to three times a day, draw heavily on the athlete's muscle glycogen stores. Athletes on a low carbohydrate diet will not perform their best because muscle stores of fuel are low.

If the diet provides inadequate amounts of carbohydrate, the reduction in muscle glycogen will be critical. An athlete training heavily should consume about 500 to 800 grams of carbohydrate a day (about two to three times normal) to help prevent carbohydrate depletion. In practice, few Australian athletes achieve this enormous figure. As a comparison, a typical Australian man or woman eats only 240 grams of carbohydrate each day.

How to choose a high carbohydrate diet?

In this section we give some extra pointers because very active people need to eat much larger amounts of carbohydrate than usual.

You may feel that you already know a lot about diet. But athletes, like everyone else, can have their facts wrong. Many foods that you believe are good sources of carbohydrate are even better sources of fat. For example, chocolate is 55 per cent carbohydrate, but also 30 per cent fat. And fat won't help you win the race.

Dietary advice aimed at the general public needs to be modified for the serious sports person. Athletes have far greater energy needs, perhaps double that of the average office worker. Many high carbohydrate and low fat foods which are recommended for the average person are too bulky and satiating for athletes. It is their bulk that makes it difficult to consume the required amount of food. For example, a 75 gram carbohydrate portion of potatoes is equivalent to 600 grams in weight of potatoes—about four normal servings. Most people can't eat that much at a time. On the other hand, white bread is easy to eat in large amounts. A 75 gram carbohydrate portion of white bread is only five slices. Other foods that you might have believed were not so good for you, like soft drinks, confectionery, honey, sugar, flavoured milk and ice-cream are actually very concentrated sources of carbohydrate that can be used to supplement your diet.

COULD A HIGH GI DIET BE HARMFUL TO ATHLETES?

No. Athletes by virtue of their high activity levels, have optimal insulin sensitivity. When they eat high carbohydrate, high GI foods, blood glucose and insulin levels rise far less in them than in the average person. Hence their bodies are not exposed to the dangerous levels that produce disease in sedentary, insulin resistant individuals.

CASE STUDY

Ian was manager of the Victorian Under-18 Men's Hockey Team. In addition to his role as manager, he was also in charge of the team's fitness and nutrition programs. He had done quite a lot of reading about the glycemic index and decided to base the whole diet around this.

Despite some early grumbling and moaning, the players stuck to the diet almost 100 per cent during the whole two weeks of the Australian championships in Darwin in July. Ian planned the diet very carefully so that they got all the right foods at the right time—low GI before the game and high GI immediately after, along with jelly beans at half time!

He noticed that the benefits became very apparent early in the championship. The players themselves were noticing that they were not running out of energy during the game and were recovering a lot quicker than they had in the past.

About halfway through the tournament other people started to wonder just where this Victorian team was getting all its energy from!

Ian said: 'At first they thought it was amusing and perhaps a little strange that we were eating Coco Pops™ and Rice Bubbles™ at the team bus in the carpark immediately after each game, but soon their amusement turned to

You don't have to eat only low GI foods

curiosity. People kept commenting on how fit the team was. But I knew that it wasn't just their fitness. I had not had as much time as I would have liked to work on their fitness, and in fact I remember being concerned just before we went away that their fitness levels may not have been high enough. I knew that what I was seeing in Darwin was not just their fitness—it was the combination of fitness and a sustained energy supply. A 'whole body fitness' was what we had achieved. It clearly demonstrated to me that you cannot do one without the other.

We ended up winning the championship by a relatively easy margin, and our fitness and energy levels were certainly a major contributing factor.

One of the things I liked about using the glycemic index as the basis of the diet was that the players were able to very quickly understand the basic principles, and by the end of the first week they knew exactly what to do.

I gave the players a questionnaire to complete at the conclusion of the tounament, and I thought you would be interested to hear some of their comments.

- 'I felt that when I played each game I was at my peak. I believe the diet played a major part in this.'
- 'I found I had more energy coming into and during the game.'
- 'Energy and glycogen levels were at perfect level.'
- 'I never felt flat or without energy.'
- 'Felt really good after every game, never felt run down during the game.'
- 'Everything made me feel good before, during and after the game.'
- 'Diet was major reason we did do well in the championships.'
- 'Feel better after games, recovery is better, better energy in the game.'
- 'I was never short of energy. My glycogen levels were constantly maintained and replenished at the necessary points. I always felt fit and healthy.'
- 'Kept my energy level high in the game and also after the game.'
- 'After the game, recovery is far more rapid.'

Is your diet fit for peak performance?

Take the diet fitness quiz and see how well you score. It's a good idea to use this quiz regularly to pick up on areas where you may need to improve your diet.

1. Circle your answer.

* I eat at least 3 meals a day with no longer than 5 hours in between
  Yes/No

Eating patterns

Carbohydrate checker

* I eat at least 4 slices of bread each day
  (1 roll = 2 slices of bread)   Yes/No
* I eat at least 1 cup of breakfast cereal each day
  or an extra slice of bread   Yes/No
* I usually eat 2 or more pieces of fruit each day   Yes/No
* I eat at least 3 different vegetables or have a salad
  most days   Yes/No
* I include carbohydrates like pasta, rice and potato in my
  diet each day   Yes/No

Protein checker

* I eat at least 1 and usually 2 serves of meat or
  meat alternatives (poultry, seafood, eggs, dried
  peas/beans or nuts) each day   Yes/No

Fat checker

* I spread butter or margarine thinly on bread
  or use none at all   Yes/No
* I eat fried food no more than once per week   Yes/No
* I use polyunsaturated or monounsaturated oil
  (Canola or olive) for cooking. (Circle yes if you
  never fry in oil or fat)   Yes/No
* I avoid oil-based dressings on salads   Yes/No

- I use reduced fat or low fat dairy products   Yes/No
- I cut the fat off meat and take the skin off chicken   Yes/No
- I eat fatty snacks such as chocolate, chips, biscuits or
  rich desserts/cakes etc no more than twice a week   Yes/No
- I eat fast or takeaway food no more than once
  per week   Yes/No

Iron checker

- I eat lean red meat at least 3 times per week or 2 servings
  of white meat daily or, for vegetarians, include at least 1–2
  cups of dried peas and beans (e.g. lentils, soy beans,
  chickpeas) daily   Yes/No
- I include a vitamin C source with meals based on bread,
  cereals, fruit and vegetables to assist the iron absorption in
  these 'plant' sources of iron   Yes/No

Calcium checker

- I eat at least 3 serves of dairy food or soy milk alternative
  each day (1 serve = 200 ml milk or fortified soy milk;
  1 slice (30 g) hard cheese; 200 g yoghurt)   Yes/No

Fluids

- I drink fluids regularly before, during and after exercise   Yes/No

Alcohol

- When I drink alcohol, I would mostly drink no more
  than is recommended for the safe drink-driving limit   Yes/No
  (Circle yes if you don't drink alcohol)

2. Score 1 point for every 'yes' answer

Scoring scale

18–20 Excellent   15–17 Room for improvement

12–14 Just made it   00–12 Poor

Note: Very active people will need to eat more breads, cereals and fruit than on this quiz, but to stay healthy no one should be eating less.
(Published in *The G.I. Factor and Sports Nutrition.* Adapted from *The Taste of Fitness* by Helen O'Connor and Donna Hay)

PART IV
The GI Tables

HOW TO USE THE TABLES

We have included two sets of tables, a condensed list of the 400 most popular foods and a comprehensive list which is a complete listing of all the foods that have ever been tested for their GI. Approximately 1500 individual foods and mixed meals are included in the expanded, comprehensive list.

The condensed list of tables is arranged in alphabetical order for easy access. This is the list to consult when you want to locate the GI value of a popular food quickly.

In the expanded tables, in response to reader requests, we have listed foods, not in exact A to Z order, but in food categories: bakery products; beverages; breads; breakfast cereals and bars; cereal grains; cookies; crackers; dairy products; fruit and fruit products; legumes and nuts; meal replacement products; mixed meals and convenience foods; nutritional support products; pasta and noodles; protein foods; snack foods and confectionery; sports bars; soups; sugars; vegetables; and indigenous and ethnic foods.

Within food categories, we have grouped the foods in alphabetical order to help you choose the low GI versions within each food group ('this for that') and also to mix and match. If your favourite food has a high GI, check out its glycemic load. If that's relatively low compared with other foods in that group, then you don't have to worry unduly about its high GI. If it's both high GI and high GL, try to cut down the serving size or team it with a very low GI food (e.g. rice and lentils).

In both tables, you'll find not only the GI but also the glycemic load (GL = carbohydrate content × GI/100). The glycemic load has been calculated using a 'nominal' serving size and the carbohydrate content of that serve, both of which are also listed in the tables. In this way, you can choose foods with either a low GI and/or a low GL. Where there are no carbohydrate or GL figures supplied, refer to the mean figures shown.

In the condensed tables we have given the average result for a particular food. The average may be the mean of ten studies of that food worldwide or of only two to four studies. In a few instances, Australian data is different from that of the rest of the world and we show our data rather than the average.

In the expanded tables, we have broken with tradition and included all the data available, not just average figures and not just Australian data. Here you will find GI values from all over the world, including the United States, Canada, New Zealand, Italy, Sweden, Japan and China, among others. Australians are lucky to have more of their foods tested than any other country. Ethnic and indigenous food and dishes have also been included, so they are truly international tables and the most comprehensive lists available anywhere.

In these new editions of the tables we've also included foods that have very little carbohydrate and have therefore been automatically omitted from previous editions. However, since so many people ask us for the GI of these foods, we decided to include them and show their GI as 0, indicated by a zero [0]. Many vegetables such as avocados and broccoli and protein foods such as chicken, cheese and tuna are among the low or no carbohydrate category.

A word about glycemic load

Some readers will undoubtedly want to know what total GL they should aim for. This depends on many factors—your total energy intake and the carbohydrate intake you are aiming for (moderate or high as discussed on page 21). If you are aiming for 250 grams of carbohydrate per day from low GI sources alone (foods <55), then the total glycemic load for the whole day should be less than $250 \times 55/100 = 138$ (rounded up).

Remember, however, that you don't need to eat all your carbohydrate from low GI sources. If half of your carbohydrate is from low GI sources you are doing well. In this case, you should aim for a glycemic load of about $250 \times 65/100 = 163$ (rounded up).

Remember, too, that the 'nominal' serving size is just that—it may not be yours. If in doubt, weigh out your own and adjust the carbohydrate per serving and GL proportionately.

Don't make the mistake of using GL alone. If you do, you might find yourself eating a diet with very little carbohydrate but a lot of fat, especially saturated fat, and excessive amounts of protein. That's a mistake for the reasons we have already outlined on page 19. For your overall health, the fat, fibre and micronutrient content of your diet is also important. A dietitian can guide you further with healthy food choices.

If you can't find a GI value for a food you eat on many occasions, please write to the manufacturer and encourage them to have the GI of the food tested by an accredited laboratory such as Sydney University Glycemic Index Research Service (SUGiRS) (www.glycemicindex.com).

You might also encourage companies to join the GI symbol program (www.gisymbol.com.au), which flags healthy foods that have been properly GI tested. Royalties from that program are ploughed back into communicating the GI message.

The GI values in these tables are correct at the time of publication. However, the formulation of commercial foods can change and the GI may be altered. You can rely on those foods showing the GI symbol. You will find revised and new data on our webpage (www.glycemicindex.com).

Acknowledgment

These tables would not be as comprehensive as they are without the efforts of Dr Susanna Holt of the Human Nutrition Unit, University of Sydney. Dr Holt is the Research Manager of Sydney University Glycemic Index Research Service (SUGiRS) and responsible for the high quality and large quantity of the Australian data included in the tables.

CONDENSED TABLES

Food	GI Glucose = 100	Nominal serve size (g)	Available carb per serve	GL per serve
All-Bran™, breakfast cereal	30	30	15	4
All-Bran Fruit 'n' Oats™, breakfast cereal	39	30	17	7
All-Bran Soy 'n' Fibre™, breakfast cereal	33	30	14	4
Angel food cake, 1 slice	67	50	29	19
Apple, 1 medium	38 (av)	120	15	6
Apple, dried	29	60	34	10
Apple juice, pure, unsweetened, reconstituted	40	250mL	29	12
Apple muffin	44	60	29	13
Apple, oat and sultana muffin (from mix)	54	50	26	14
Apricots, fresh, 3 medium	57	120	9	5
Apricots, canned in light syrup	64	120	19	12
Apricots, dried	30	60	27	8
Apricot, coconut and honey muffin (from mix)	60	50	26	16
Arborio, risotto rice, boiled	69	150	53	36
Bagel, white	72	70	35	25
Baked beans, canned in tomato sauce	48 (av)	150	15	7
Banana, raw, 1 medium	52 (av)	120	24	12
Banana cake, 1 slice	47	80	38	18
Banana, oat and honey muffin (from mix)	65	50	26	17
Barley, pearled, boiled	25 (av)	150	42	11
Basmati rice, white, boiled, 1 cup	58	150	38	22
Beef	[0]	120	0	0
Beetroot, canned	64	80	7	5
Bengal gram dhal, chickpea	11	150	36	4
Black bean soup	64	250	27	17
Black beans, boiled	30	150	23	7
Blackbread, Riga	76	30	13	10
Blackeyed beans, soaked, boiled	42	150	30	13
Blueberry muffin	59	57	29	17
Bran Flakes™, breakfast cereal	74	30	18	13
Bran muffin	60	57	24	15
Breakfast Bar, Fibre Plus™ bar	78	30	23	18
Breton wheat crackers	67	25	14	10
Broad beans	79	80	11	9
Broken rice, white, cooked in rice cooker	86	150	43	37
Buckwheat	54 (av)	150	30	16
Buckwheat, pancakes, gluten-free, made from packet mix	102	77	22	22

[0] indicates that the food has so little carbohydrate that the GI cannot be tested. The GL is therefore 0.

Food	GI Glucose = 100	Nominal serve size (g)	Available carb per serve	GL per serve
Bulghur, boiled 20 min	48 (av)	150	26	12
Bun, hamburger	61	30	15	9
Bürgen® Oat Bran & Honey Loaf with Barley	31	30	10	3
Bürgen® Soy-Lin, kibbled soy (8%) and linseed (8%) loaf	36	30	9	3
Bürgen® Fruit Loaf	44	30	13	6
Bürgen® Mixed Grain	49 (av)	30	11	6
Burger Rings™, barbeque-flavoured	90	50	31	28
Butter beans, dried, cooked 1.25 h	31	150	20	6
Calrose rice, white, medium grain, boiled	83	150	43	36
Capellini pasta, boiled	45	180	45	20
Carrots, peeled, boiled	49	80	5	2
Cheese	[0]	120	0	0
Cherries, raw	22	120	12	3
Chickpeas, canned in brine	42	150	22	9
Chickpeas, dried, boiled	28 (av)	150	30	8
Chicken nuggets, frozen, reheated in microwave oven 5 min	46	100	16	7
Chocolate, milk	42	50	31	13
Chocolate, white, Milky Bar®	44	50	29	13
Chocolate butterscotch muffins, made from packet mix	53	50	28	15
Chocolate cake made from packet mix with chocolate frosting	38	111	52	20
Chocolate mousse, 2% fat	31	50	11	3
Chocolate pudding, made from powder and whole milk	47	100	16	7
Coca Cola®, soft drink	53	250	26	14
Coco Pops™	77	30	26	20
Condensed milk, sweetened	61	250	136	83
Cordial, orange, reconstituted	66	250	20	13
Corn chips, plain, salted	42	50	25	11
Cornflakes™, breakfast cereal	77	30	25	20
Cornflakes Crunchy Nut™, breakfast cereal	72	30	24	17
Cornmeal, boiled in salted water 2 min	68	150	13	9
Corn pasta, gluten-free	78	180	42	32
Corn Pops™, breakfast cereal	80	30	26	21
Corn Thins, puffed corn cakes, gluten-free	87	25	20	18
Couscous, boiled 5 min	65 (av)	150	35	23

[0] indicates that the food has so little carbohydrate that the GI cannot be tested. The GL is therefore 0.

Food	GI Glucose = 100	Nominal serve size (g)	Available carb per serve	GL per serve
Cranberry juice cocktail	52	250	31	16
Crispix™, breakfast cereal	87	30	25	22
Croissant	67	57	26	17
Crumpet	69	50	19	13
Crunchy Nut Cornflakes™ bar	72	30	26	19
Crunchy Nut™ Cornflakes	72	30	24	17
Cupcake, strawberry-iced	73	38	26	19
Custard, home made from milk, wheat starch, and sugar	43	100	17	7
Custard, prepared from powder with whole milk, no bake	35	100	17	6
Custard, TRIM™, reduced-fat	37	100	15	6
Custard apple, raw, flesh only	54	120	19	10
Dark rye, Blackbread, Riga	76	30	13	10
Dark rye, Schinkenbrot, Riga	86	30	14	12
Dates, dried	103	60	40	42
Desiree potato, peeled, boiled 35 min	101	150	17	17
Dietworks Hazelnut & Apricot bar	42	50	22	9
Digestives plain, 2 biscuits	59 (av)	25	16	10
Doongara, rice, white	56 (av)	150	39	22
Egg Custard, prepared from powder with whole milk, no bake	35	100	17	6
Eggs	[0]	120	0	0
English Muffin™ bread	77	30	14	11
Ensure™, vanilla drink	48	250mL	34	16
Ensure™ bar, chocolate fudge brownie	43	38	20	8
Ensure Plus™, vanilla drink	40	237mL	47	19
Ensure Pudding™, old-fashioned vanilla	36	113	26	9
Fanta®, orange soft drink	68	250	34	23
Fettuccine, egg, cooked	32	180	46	15
Figs, dried, tenderised	61	60	26	16
Fish	[0]	120	0	0
Fish Fingers	38	100	19	7
Flan cake	65	70	48	31
French baguette, white, plain	95	30	15	15
French fries, frozen, reheated in microwave	75	150	29	22
French vanilla cake made from packet mix with vanilla frosting	42	111	58	24
French vanilla ice-cream, premium, 16% fat	38	50	9	3
Froot Loops™, breakfast cereal	69	30	26	18

[0] indicates that the food has so little carbohydrate that the GI cannot be tested. The GL is therefore 0.

Food	GI Glucose = 100	Nominal serve size (g)	Available carb per serve	GL per serve
Frosties™, sugar-coated Cornflakes	55	30	26	15
Fructose, pure	19 (av)	10	10	2
Fruit cocktail, canned	55	120	16	9
Fruit Fingers, Heinz Kidz™, banana	61	30	20	12
Fruit loaf, Bürgen™	44	30	13	6
Fruit Loaf, dense continental style wheat bread with dried fruit	47	30	15	7
Fruit and Spice Loaf, thick sliced	54	30	15	8
Gatorade® sports drink	78	250	15	12
Glucodin™ glucose tablets	102	50	50	50
Gluten-free white bread, sliced	80	30	15	12
Gluten-free multigrain bread	79	30	13	10
Gluten-free muesli, with 1.5% fat milk	39	30	19	7
Gluten-free corn pasta	78	180	42	32
Gluten-free rice and maize pasta	76	180	49	37
Gluten-free split pea and soy pasta shells	29	180	31	9
Gluten-free spaghetti, rice and split pea, canned in tomato sauce	68	220	27	19
Glutinous rice, white, cooked in rice cooker	92 (av)	150	48	44
Gnocchi	68	180	48	33
Golden Wheats™, breakfast cereal	71	30	23	16
Grapefruit, raw	25	120	11	3
Grapefruit juice, unsweetened	48	250	20	9
Grapes, green	46 (av)	120	18	8
Green pea soup, canned	66	250	41	27
Guardian™	37	30	12	5
Hamburger bun	61	30	15	9
Haricot/navy beans	38 (av)	150	31	12
Healthwise™ breakfast cereal for bowel health	66	30	18	12
Healthwise™ breakfast cereal for heart health	48	30	19	9
Helga's™ Classic Seed Loaf	68	30	14	9
Helga's™ traditional wholemeal bread	70	30	13	9
Honey	55 (av)	25	18	10
Honey & Oat bread, Vogel's	55	30	14	7
Honey Rice Bubbles™, breakfast cereal	77	30	27	20
Honey Smacks™, breakfast cereal	71	30	23	11
Ice-cream, regular fat	61 (av)	50	13	8
Ice-cream, low fat, vanilla, 'light'	50	50	6	3

[0] indicates that the food has so little carbohydrate that the GI cannot be tested. The GL is therefore 0.

Food	GI Glucose = 100	Nominal serve size (g)	Available carb per serve	GL per serve
Ice-cream, premium, French vanilla, 16% fat	38	50	9	3
Ice-cream, premium, 'ultra chocolate', 15% fat	37	50	9	4
Instant potato, prepared	85 (av)	150	20	17
Instant rice, white, cooked 6 min	87	150	42	36
Ironman PR bar®, chocolate	39	65	26	10
Isostar® sports drink	70	250	18	13
Jam, apricot fruit spread, reduced sugar	55	30	13	7
Jam, strawberry	51	30	20	10
Jasmine rice, white, cooked in rice cooker	109	150	42	46
Jatz™, plain salted cracker biscuits	55	25	17	10
Jelly Beans	78 (av)	30	28	22
Jevity™, fibre-enriched drink	48	237mL	36	17
Just Right™, breakfast cereal	60	30	22	13
Just Right Just Grains™, breakfast cereal	62	30	23	14
Kaiser rolls	73	30	16	12
Kavli™ Norwegian Crispbread	71	25	16	12
Kidney beans, canned	52	150	17	9
Kidz™, Heinz, Fruit Fingers, banana	61	30	20	12
Kidney beans, boiled	28 (av)	150	25	7
Kiwi fruit	58	120	12	7
Komplete™, breakfast cereal	48	30	21	10
K-Time Just Right™ breakfast cereal bar	72	30	24	17
K-Time Strawberry Crunch™ breakfast cereal bar	77	30	25	19
Kudos Whole Grain Bars, chocolate chip	62	50	32	20
Lactose, pure	46 (av)	10	10	5
Lamb	[0]	120	0	0
Lamingtons, sponge dipped in chocolate and coconut	87	50	29	25
L.E.A.N Fibergy™ bar, Harvest Oat	45	50	29	13
L.E.A.N Life long Nutribar™, Peanut Crunch	30	40	19	6
L.E.A.N Life long Nutribar™, Chocolate Crunch	32	40	19	6
L.E.A.N Nutrimeal™, drink powder, Dutch Chocolate	26	250	13	3
Lebanese bread, white, 1 round	75	30	16	12
Lentils, canned	44	250	21	9
Lentils, green, boiled	30 (av)	150	17	5
Lentils	29 (av)	150	18	5
Lentils, red, boiled	26	150	18	5

[0] indicates that the food has so little carbohydrate that the GI cannot be tested. The GL is therefore 0.

Food	GI Glucose = 100	Nominal serve size (g)	Available carb per serve	GL per serve
Life Savers®, peppermint candy	70	30	30	21
Light rye	68	30	14	10
Lima beans, baby, frozen, reheated in microwave oven	32	150	30	10
Linguine pasta, thick, cooked	46	180	48	22
Linguine pasta, thin, cooked	52	180	45	23
Linseed rye	55	30	13	7
Lucozade®, original sparkling glucose drink	95	250	42	40
Lungkow beanthread noodles	26	180	45	12
Lychees, canned in syrup, drained	79	120	20	16
M & M's®, peanut	33	30	17	6
Macaroni, cooked	47 (av)	180	48	23
Macaroni and Cheese, boxed	64	180	51	32
Maltose, 50 g	105	10	10	11
Mango (*Mangifera indica*)	51	120	15	8
Marmalade, orange (Australia)	48	30	20	9
Mars Bar®	62	60	40	25
Melba toast, Old London	70	30	23	16
Milk, full-fat cow's milk, fresh	31	250mL	12	4
Milk, skim	32	250	13	4
Milk, low fat, chocolate, with sugar, Lite White™	34	250	26	9
Milk, condensed, sweetened	61	50	27	17
Milk Arrowroot™ biscuits	69	25	18	12
Milky Bar®, Chocolate, white	44	50	29	13
Millet, boiled	71	150	36	25
Milo™, chocolate powder, dissolved in water	55	250	16	9
Mini Wheats™, whole wheat breakfast cereal	58	30	21	12
Mini Wheats™, blackcurrant whole wheat breakfast cereal	72	30	21	15
Mixed grain loaf, Bürgen®	49 (av)	30	11	6
Morning Coffee™, 3 biscuits	79	25	19	15
Mousse, butterscotch, 1.9% fat	36	50	10	4
Mousse, chocolate, 2% fat	31	50	11	3
Mousse, hazelnut, 2.4% fat	36	50	10	4
Mousse, mango, 1.8% fat	33	50	11	4
Mousse, mixed berry, 2.2% fat	36	50	10	4
Mousse, strawberry, 2.3% fat	32	50	10	3
Muesli bar containing dried fruit	61	30	21	13
Muesli, gluten-free with 1.5% fat milk	39	30	19	7

[0] indicates that the food has so little carbohydrate that the GI cannot be tested. The GL is therefore 0.

Food	GI Glucose = 100	Nominal serve size (g)	Available carb per serve	GL per serve
Muesli, toasted	43	30	17	7
Muesli, Swiss Formula	56	30	16	9
Multi-Grain 9-Grain	43	30	14	6
Mung bean noodles (Lungkow beanthread), dried, boiled	39	180	45	18
Nesquik™, chocolate dissolved in 1.5% fat milk	41	250	11	5
Nesquik™, strawberry dissolved in 1.5% fat milk	35	250	12	4
New potato, unpeeled and boiled 20 min	78	150	21	16
New potato, canned, heated in microwave 3 min	65	150	18	12
No Bake Egg Custard, prepared from powder with whole milk	35	100	17	6
Noodles, instant 'two-minute' Maggi®	46	180	40	19
Noodles, mung bean (Lungkow beanthread), dried, boiled	39	180	45	18
Noodles, rice, freshly made, boiled	40	180	39	15
Norco Ice-cream, Prestige Light Vanilla	47	50	10	5
Norco Ice-cream, Prestige Light Toffee	37	50	14	5
Norco Ice-cream, Prestige Macadamia	39	50	12	5
Nutella®, chocolate hazelnut spread	33	20	12	4
Nutrigrain™, breakfast cereal	66	30	15	10
Oat 'n' Honey Bake™, breakfast cereal	77	30	17	13
Oat Bran & Honey Loaf with Barley, Bürgen®	31	30	10	3
Oat bran, raw	55 (av)	10	5	3
Oatmeal™, Highland biscuits	55	25	18	10
Orange, 1 medium	42 (av)	120	11	5
Orange cordial, reconstituted	66	250	20	13
Orange juice, unsweetened, reconstituted	53	250mL	18	9
Pancakes, prepared from shake mix	67	80	58	39
Pancakes, buckwheat, gluten-free, made from packet mix	102	77	22	22
Parsnips	97	80	12	12
Party pies, beef	45	100	27	12
Pastry	59	57	26	15
Paw paw (Carica papaya)	56	120	8	5
Peach, fresh, 1 large	42 (av)	120	11	5
Peach, canned in heavy syrup	58	120	15	9

[0] indicates that the food has so little carbohydrate that the GI cannot be tested. The GL is therefore 0.

Food	GI Glucose = 100	Nominal serve size (g)	Available carb per serve	GL per serve
Peach, canned in light syrup	52	120	18	9
Peach, canned in reduced-sugar syrup, SPC Lite	62	120	17	11
Peanuts, roasted, salted	14 (av)	50	6	1
Pear, raw	38 (av)	120	11	4
Pear halves, canned in natural juice	43	120	13	5
Pear halves, canned in reduced-sugar syrup, SPC Lite	25	120	14	4
Peas, dried, boiled	22	150	9	2
Peas, green, frozen, boiled	48 (av)	80	7	3
Pelde brown rice, boiled	76	150	38	29
Performax™ Country Life Bakery	38	30	13	5
Pikelets, Golden brand	85	40	21	18
Pineapple, raw	66	120	10	6
Pineapple juice, unsweetened	46	250	34	15
Pinto beans, canned in brine	45	150	22	10
Pinto beans, dried, boiled	39	150	26	10
Pita bread, white	57	30	17	10
Pizza, cheese	60	100	27	16
Pizza, Super Supreme, pan (11.4% fat)	36	100	24	9
Pizza, Super Supreme, thin and crispy (13.2 % fat)	30	100	22	7
Ploughman's™ Wholegrain, original recipe	47	30	14	7
Ploughman's™ Wholemeal, smooth milled (Quality Bakers, Australia)	64	30	13	9
Plums, raw	39	120	12	5
Pontiac potato, peeled, boiled 35 min	88	150	18	16
Pontiac potato, peeled and microwave on high for 6–7.5 min	79	150	18	14
Pontiac potato, peeled, cubed, boiled 15 min, mashed	91	150	20	18
Pop Tarts™, Double Chocolate	70	50	36	25
Popcorn, plain, cooked in microwave oven	72	20	11	8
Pork	[0]	120	0	0
Porridge	42	250	21	9
Potato, baked	85 (av)	150	30	26
Potato crisps, plain, salted	57	50	18	10
Pound cake	54	53	28	15
Power Bar®, chocolate	56 (av)	65	42	24
Premium Soda Crackers	74	25	17	12

[0] indicates that the food has so little carbohydrate that the GI cannot be tested. The GL is therefore 0.

Food	GI Glucose = 100	Nominal serve size (g)	Available carb per serve	GL per serve
Pretzels, oven-baked, traditional wheat flavour	83	30	20	16
Prunes, pitted, 6	29	60	33	10
Pudding, instant, chocolate, made from powder and whole milk	47	100	16	7
Pudding, instant, vanilla, made from powder and whole milk	40	100	16	6
Pudding, Sustagen™, instant vanilla, made from powdered mix	27	250	47	13
Puffed crispbread	81	25	19	15
Puffed rice cakes, white	82	25	21	17
Puffed Wheat, breakfast cereal	80	30	21	17
Pumpernickel rye kernel bread	41	30	12	5
Pumpkin	75	80	4	3
Quik™, chocolate (Nestlé, Australia), dissolved in 1.5% fat milk	41	250	11	5
Quik™, strawberry (Nestlé, Australia), dissolved in 1.5% fat milk	35	250	12	4
Raisins	64	60	44	28
Ravioli, durum wheat flour, meat filled, boiled	39	180	38	15
Real Fruit Bars, strawberry processed fruit bars	90	30	26	23
Rice and maize pasta, Ris'O'Mais, gluten-free	76	180	49	37
Rice Bran, extruded	19	30	14	3
Rice Bubbles™, breakfast cereal	87	30	26	22
Rice Bubble Treat™ bar	63	30	24	15
Rice cakes, white	82	25	21	17
Rice Krispies™, breakfast cereal	82	30	26	22
Rice noodles, freshly made, boiled	40	180	39	15
Rice pasta, brown, boiled 16 min	92	180	38	35
Rice vermicelli, Kongmoon	58	180	39	22
Rich Tea, 2 biscuits	55	25	19	10
Risotto rice, arborio, boiled	69	150	53	36
Rockmelon/cantaloupe, raw	65	120	6	4
Roggenbrot, Vogel's	59	30	14	8
Roll (bread), Kaiser	73	30	16	12
Rolled oats	42	250	21	9
Roll-Ups®, processed fruit snack	99	30	25	24
Romano beans	46	150	18	8
Rye bread	58 (av)	30	14	8

[0] indicates that the food has so little carbohydrate that the GI cannot be tested. The GL is therefore 0.

Food	GI Glucose = 100	Nominal serve size (g)	Available carb per serve	GL per serve
Ryvita™ crackers	69	25	16	11
Salami	[0]	120	0	0
Sao™, plain square crackers	70	25	17	12
Sausages, fried	28	100	3	1
Scones, plain, made from packet mix	92	25	9	7
Sebago potato, peeled, boiled 35 min	87	150	17	14
Semolina (*Triticum aestivum*), steamed	55	67 (dry)	50	28
Shellfish (prawns, crab, lobster etc)	[0]	120	0	0
Shortbread biscuits	64	25	16	10
Shredded Wheat, breakfast cereal	75 (av)	30	20	15
Shredded Wheatmeal™ biscuits	62	25	18	11
Skittles®	70	50	45	32
Snickers Bar®	41	60	36	15
So Natural™ soy milk, full-fat (3%), 120 mg calcium, Calciforte	36	250	18	6
So Natural™ soy milk, reduced-fat (1.5%), 120 mg calcium, Light	44	250	17	8
So Natural™ soy milk, full-fat (3%), 0 mg calcium, Original	44	250	17	8
So Natural™ soy smoothie drink, banana, 1% fat	30	250	22	7
So Natural™ soy smoothie drink, chocolate hazelnut, 1% fat	34	250	25	8
So Natural™ soy yoghurt, peach and mango, 2% fat, sugar	50	200	26	13
Soda Crackers, Premium	74	25	17	12
Soft drink, Coca Cola®	53	250	26	14
Soft drink, Fanta®, orange	68	250	34	23
Sourdough rye	48	30	12	6
Sourdough wheat	54	30	14	8
Soy milk, So Natural™ full-fat (3%), 120 mg calcium, Calciforte	36	250	18	6
Soy milk, So Natural™ reduced-fat (1.5%), 120 mg calcium, Light	44	250	17	8
Soy milk, So Natural™ full-fat (3%), 0 mg calcium, Original	44	250	17	8
Soy smoothie drink, So Natural™ banana, 1% fat	30	250	22	7
Soy smoothie drink, So Natural™ chocolate hazelnut, 1% fat	34	250	25	8

[0] indicates that the food has so little carbohydrate that the GI cannot be tested. The GL is therefore 0.

Food	GI Glucose = 100	Nominal serve size (g)	Available carb per serve	GL per serve
Soy yoghurt, So Natural™ peach and mango, 2% fat, sugar	50	200	26	13
Soy beans, dried, boiled	20	150	6	1
Soy beans, canned	14	150	6	1
Soy-Lin, Bürgen® kibbled soy (8%) and linseed (8%) loaf	36	30	9	3
Spaghetti, gluten-free, rice and split pea, canned in tomato sauce	68	220	27	19
Spaghetti, white, boiled 5 minutes	38 (av)	180	48	18
Spaghetti, wholemeal, boiled 5 minutes	37	180	42	16
Special K™, breakfast cereal	54	30	21	11
Spirali pasta, durum wheat, white, boiled to al denté texture	43	180	44	19
Split pea and soy pasta shells, gluten-free	29	180	31	9
Split Pea soup	60	250	27	16
Split peas, yellow, boiled 20 min	32	150	19	6
Sponge cake, plain	46	63	36	17
Sports Plus®, sport drink	74	250	17	13
Star Pastina, white, boiled 5 minutes	38	180	48	18
Stoned Wheat Thins	67	25	17	12
Strawberry jam	51	30	20	10
Stuffing, bread	74	30	21	16
Sucrose	68 (av)	10	10	7
Sultana Bran™, breakfast cereal	73	30	19	14
Sultanas	56	60	45	25
Sunbrown Quick™ rice, boiled	80	150	38	31
Sunflower and barley bread, Riga	57	30	11	6
Super Supreme pizza, pan (11.4% fat)	36	100	24	9
Super Supreme pizza, thin and crispy (13.2 % fat)	30	100	22	7
Sushi, salmon	48	100	36	17
Sustagen™ Hospital with extra fibre, drink made from powdered mix	33	250mL	44	15
Sustagen™ milk, Dutch Chocolate	31	250mL	41	13
Sustagen™ pudding, instant vanilla, made from powdered mix	27	250	47	13
Sustagen Sport®, sport drink	43	250	49	21
Sustain™, breakfast cereal	68	30	22	15
Sustain™ cereal bar	57	30	25	14
Swede (rutabaga)	72	150	10	7

[0] indicates that the food has so little carbohydrate that the GI cannot be tested. The GL is therefore 0.

Food	GI Glucose = 100	Nominal serve size (g)	Available carb per serve	GL per serve
Sweet corn, whole kernel, canned, diet-pack, drained	46	150	28	13
Sweet potato, *Ipomoea batatas*	44	150	25	11
Sweetened condensed milk	61	250	136	83
Taco shells, cornmeal-based, baked	68	20	12	8
Tapioca, boiled with milk	81	250	18	14
Tapioca (*Manihot utilissima*), steamed 1 h	70	250	18	12
Team™, breakfast cereal	82	30	22	17
Tofu-based frozen dessert, chocolate with high-fructose (24%) corn syrup (USA)	115	50	9	10
Tomato soup	38	250	17	6
Tortellini, cheese	50	180	21	10
Total™, breakfast cereal	76	30	22	17
TRIM™ custard, reduced-fat	37	100	15	6
Tuna	[0]	120	0	0
Twisties™, cheese-flavoured, extruded snack, rice and corn	74	50	29	22
Twix® Cookie Bar, caramel	44	60	39	17
Ultra chocolate ice-cream, premium 15% fat	37	50	9	4
Vaalia™, reduced-fat apricot and mango yoghurt	26	200	30	8
Vaalia™, reduced-fat French vanilla yoghurt	26	200	10	3
Vaalia™, diet, mango yoghurt, sweetened with acesulfame K and Splenda	23	200	14	3
Vaalia™, diet, mixed berry yoghurt, sweetened with acesulfame K and Splenda	25	200	13	3
Vaalia™, diet, strawberry yoghurt, sweetened with acesulfame K and Splenda	23	200	13	3
Vaalia™, diet, vanilla yoghurt, sweetened with acesulfame K and Splenda	23	200	13	3
Vaalia™, reduced-fat tropical passionfruit yoghurt drink	38	200	29	11
Vanilla cake made from packet mix with vanilla frosting	42	111	58	24

[0] indicates that the food has so little carbohydrate that the GI cannot be tested. The GL is therefore 0.

Food	GI Glucose = 100	Nominal serve size (g)	Available carb per serve	GL per serve
Vanilla pudding, instant, made from powder and whole milk	40	100	16	6
Vanilla wafers, 6 biscuits	77	25	18	14
Veal	[0]	120	0	0
Vermicelli, white, boiled	35	180	44	16
Vita-Brits™, breakfast cereal	68	30	20	13
Vitari, wild berry, non-dairy, frozen fruit dessert	59	100	21	12
Vogel's Honey & Oats	55	30	14	7
Vogel's Roggenbrot	59	30	14	8
Waffles	76	35	13	10
Water crackers	78	25	18	14
Watermelon, raw	72	120	6	4
Weis Mango Frutia™, low fat frozen fruit dessert	42	100	23	10
Weet-Bix™, breakfast cereal	69	30	17	12
Wheat-bites™, breakfast cereal	72	30	25	18
White bread, wheat flour	70	30	14	10
Wholemeal bread, wheat flour	77	30	12	9
Wild About Fruit Apple Juice, pure, clear, unsweetened	44	250	30	13
Wild About Fruit Apple Juice, pure, cloudy, unsweetened	37	250	28	10
Wonderwhite™ bread	80	30	14	11
Yam, peeled, boiled	37 (av)	150	36	13
Yoghurt drink, Vaalia™, reduced-fat tropical passionfruit	38	200	29	11
Yoghurt, low fat, fruit with artificial sweetener	14	200	13	2
Yoghurt, low fat, fruit with sugar	33	200	31	10
Yoghurt, low fat (0.9%), wild strawberry	31	200	30	9

[0] indicates that the food has so little carbohydrate that the GI cannot be tested. The GL is therefore 0.

EXPANDED TABLES

Food	GI Glucose = 100	Nominal serve size (g)	Available carb per serve	GL per serve
BAKERY PRODUCTS				
Cakes				
Angel food cake (Loblaw's, Toronto, Canada)	67	50	29	19
Banana cake, made with sugar	47	80	38	18
Banana cake, made without sugar	55	80	29	16
Chocolate cake, made from packet mix with chocolate frosting (Betty Crocker)	38	111	52	20
Cupcake, strawberry-iced	73	38	26	19
Lamingtons (sponge dipped in chocolate and coconut)	87	50	29	25
Pound cake (Sara Lee)	54	53	28	15
Sponge cake, plain	46	63	36	17
Vanilla cake, made from packet mix with vanilla frosting (Betty Crocker)	42	111	58	24
Croissant	67	57	26	17
Crumpet	69	50	19	13
Doughnut, cake type	76	47	23	17
Flan cake	65	70	48	31
Muffins				
Apple, made with sugar	44	60	29	13
Apple, made without sugar	48	60	19	9
Apple, oat, sultana, made from packet mix	54	50	26	14
Apricot, coconut and honey, made from packet mix	60	50	26	16
Banana, oat and honey, made from packet mix	65	50	26	17
Bran	60	57	24	15
Blueberry	59	57	29	17
Carrot	62	57	32	20
Chocolate butterscotch, made from packet mix	53	50	28	15
Corn muffin, low-amylose	102	57	29	30
Corn muffin, high-amylose	49	57	29	14
Oatmeal, muffin, made from mix (Quaker Oats)	69	50	35	24
Pancakes, prepared from shake mix	67	80	58	39
Pancakes, buckwheat, gluten-free, made from packet mix (Orgran)	102	77	22	22
Pastry	59	57	26	15
Pikelets, Golden brand (Tip Top)	85	40	21	18
Scones, plain, made from packet mix	92	25	9	7
Waffles, Aunt Jemima	76	35	13	10
BEVERAGES				
Coca Cola®, soft drink (Australia)	53	250	26	14

[0] indicates that the food has so little carbohydrate that the GI cannot be tested. The GL is therefore 0.
▲ indicates brand not specified

Food	GI Glucose = 100	Nominal serve size (g)	Available carb per serve	GL per serve
Coca Cola®, soft drink/soda (USA)	63	250	26	16
Cordial, orange, reconstituted (Berri)	66	250	20	13
Fanta®, orange soft drink (Australia)	68	250	34	23
Lucozade®, original (sparkling glucose drink)	95	250	42	40
Smoothie, raspberry (Con Agra)	33	250	41	14
Smoothie drink, soy, banana (So Natural)	30	250	22	7
Smoothie drink, soy, chocolate hazelnut (So Natural)	34	250	25	8
Solo™, lemon squash, soft drink (Australia)	58	250	29	17
Up & Go, cocoa malt flavor (Sanitarium)	43	250	26	11
Up & Go, original malt flavor (Sanitarium)	46	250	24	11
Xpress, chocolate (So Natural, Australia)	39	250	34	13
Yakult® (Yakult, Australia)	46	65	12	6

Juices

Apple juice

Food	GI Glucose = 100	Nominal serve size (g)	Available carb per serve	GL per serve
Apple juice, pure, unsweetened, reconstituted (Australia)	39			
Apple juice, unsweetened	40			
Apple juice, unsweetened (Canada)	41			
mean of three studies	40	250	29	12
Apple juice, pure, clear, unsweetened (Wild About Fruit, Australia)	44	250	30	13
Apple juice, pure, cloudy, unsweetened (Wild About Fruit, Australia)	37	250	28	10
Carrot juice, freshly made (Sydney, Australia)	43	250	23	10
Cranberry juice cocktail (Ocean Spray®, Australia)	52	250	31	16
Cranberry juice cocktail (Ocean Spray®, USA)	68	250	36	24
Cranberry juice drink (Ocean Spray®, UK)	56	250	29	16
Grapefruit juice, unsweetened (Sunpac, Canada)	48	250	22	11

Orange juice

Food	GI Glucose = 100	Nominal serve size (g)	Available carb per serve	GL per serve
Orange juice (Canada)	46	250	26	12
Orange juice, unsweetened, (Quelch®, Australia)	53	250	18	9
Pineapple juice, unsweetened (Dole, Canada)	46	250	34	16
Tomato juice, canned, no added sugar (Berri, Australia)	38	250	9	4

Sports drinks

Food	GI Glucose = 100	Nominal serve size (g)	Available carb per serve	GL per serve
Gatorade® (Australia)	78	250	15	12
Isostar® (Switzerland)	70	250	18	13
Sports Plus® (Australia)	74	250	17	13
Sustagen Sport® (Australia)	43	250	49	21

[0] indicates that the food has so little carbohydrate that the GI cannot be tested. The GL is therefore 0.
▲ indicates brand not specified

Food	GI Glucose = 100	Nominal serve size (g)	Available carb per serve	GL per serve
Drinks made from drinking mix powders				
Build-Up™ with fiber, (Nestlé)	41	250	33	14
Complete Hot Chocolate mix with hot water (Nestlé)	51	250	23	11
Hi-Pro energy drink mix, vanilla, (Harrod)	36	250	19	7
Malted milk in full-fat cow's milk (Nestlé, Australia)	45	250	26	12
Milo™ (chocolate nutrient-fortified drink powder)				
Milo™ (Nestlé, Australia), in water	55	250	16	9
Milo™ (Nestlé, Auckland, New Zealand), in water	52	250	16	9
Milo™ (Nestlé, Australia), in full-fat cow's milk	35	250	25	9
Milo™ (Nestlé, New Zealand), in full-fat cow's milk	36	250	26	9
Nutrimeal™, meal replacement drink, Dutch Chocolate (Usana)	26	250	17	4
Quik™, chocolate (Nestlé, Australia), in water	53	250	7	4
Quik™, chocolate (Nestlé, Australia), in 1.5% fat milk	41	250	11	5
Quik™, strawberry (Nestlé, Australia), in water	64	250	8	5
Quik™, strawberry (Nestlé, Australia), in 1.5% fat milk	35	250	12	4
BREADS				
Bagel, white, frozen (Canada)	72	70	35	25
Baguette, white, plain (France)	95	30	15	15
French baguette with chocolate spread (France)	72	70	37	27
French baguette with butter and strawberry jam (France)	62	70	41	26
Pain au lait (Pasquier, France)	63	60	32	20
Bread stuffing, Paxo (Canada)	74	30	21	16
Barley Breads				
Coarse barley kernel bread				
75% kernels	27	30	20	5
80% scalded intact kernels (20% white wheat flour)	34	30	20	7
80% intact kernels (20% white wheat flour)	40	30	20	8
Barley kernel bread, 50% kernels				
50% kernels (Canada)	43	30	20	9
50% kibbled barley (Australia)	48	30	20	10
Sunflower and barley bread (Riga, Sydney, Australia)	57	30	11	6
Barley flour breads				
100% barley flour (Canada)	67	30	13	9
Wholemeal barley flour (80%) bread (Sweden)	67	30	20	13
Wholemeal barley bread, flat, thin, soft	50	30	15	7

[0] indicates that the food has so little carbohydrate that the GI cannot be tested. The GL is therefore 0.
▲ indicates brand not specified

Food	GI Glucose = 100	Nominal serve size (g)	Available carb per serve	GL per serve
Wholemeal barley bread, flat, thin, soft, high fibre (Sweden)	43	30	11	5
Wholemeal barley flour bread	70	30	20	14
Wholemeal barley flour bread with sourdough (lactic acid)	53	30	20	10
Wholemeal barley flour bread with lactic acid	66	30	19	12
Wholemeal barley flour bread with calcium lactate	59	30	20	12
Wholemeal barley flour bread with sodium propionate	65	30	20	13
Wholemeal barley flour bread with higher dose sodium propionate	57	30	19	11
Buckwheat Bread				
Buckwheat bread, with 50% white wheat flour (Sweden)	47	30	21	10
Fruit Breads				
Bürgen™ Fruit loaf (Tip Top, Australia)	44	30	13	6
Fruit and Spice Loaf, thick sliced (Buttercup, Australia)	54	30	15	8
Continental fruit loaf, wheat bread with dried fruit (Australia)	47	30	15	7
Happiness™ (cinnamon, raisin, pecan bread) (Natural Ovens, USA)	63	30	14	9
Muesli bread, made from packet mix in bread oven (Con Agra Inc., USA)	54	30	12	7
Hamburger bun (Loblaw's, Toronto, Canada)	61	30	15	9
Kaiser rolls (Loblaw's, Canada)	73	30	16	12
Melba toast, Old London (Best Foods Canada Inc.)	70	30	23	16
Gluten-free Bread				
Gluten-free multigrain bread (Country Life Bakeries, Australia)	79	30	13	10
Gluten-free white bread, unsliced (gluten-free wheat starch) (UK)	71	30	15	11
Gluten-free white bread, sliced (gluten-free wheat starch) (UK)	80	30	15	12
mean of two studies	76	30	15	11
Gluten-free fibre-enriched, unsliced (gluten-free wheat starch, soya bran) (UK)	69	30	13	9
Gluten-free fibre-enriched, sliced (gluten-free wheat starch, soya bran) (UK)	76	30	13	10
mean of two studies	73	30	13	9

[0] indicates that the food has so little carbohydrate that the GI cannot be tested. The GL is therefore 0.
▲ indicates brand not specified

Food	GI Glucose = 100	Nominal serve size (g)	Available carb per serve	GL per serve
Oat Bread				
Coarse oat kernel bread, 80% intact oat kernels (Sweden)	65	30	19	12
Oat bran bread				
50% oat bran (Australia)	44	30	18	8
45% oat bran and 50% wheat flour (Sweden)	50	30	18	9
mean of two studies	47	30	18	9
Rice Bread				
Rice bread, low-amylose Calrose rice (Pav's, Australia)	72	30	12	8
Rice bread, high-amylose Doongara rice (Pav's, Australia)	61	30	12	7
Rye Bread				
Rye kernel (pumpernickel) bread				
Coarse rye kernel bread, 80% intact kernels (Sweden)	41	30	12	5
Rye kernel bread (Pumpernickel) (Canada)	41	30	12	5
Wholegrain pumpernickel (Holtzheuser Brothers Ltd., Toronto, Canada)	46	30	11	5
Rye kernel bread, pumpernickel (80% kernels) (Canada)	55	30	12	7
Cocktail, sliced (Kasselar Food Products, Toronto, Canada)	55	30	12	7
Cocktail, sliced (Kasselar Food Products, Canada)	62	30	12	8
mean of six studies	50	30	12	6
Wholemeal rye bread				
Wholemeal rye bread (Canada)	41			
Wholemeal rye bread (Canada)	62			
Wholemeal rye bread (Canada)	63			
Wholemeal rye bread (Canada)	66			
mean of four studies	58	30	14	8
Specialty rye breads				
Blackbread, Riga (Berzin's, Sydney, Australia)	76	30	13	10
Bürgen™ Dark/Swiss rye (Tip Top Bakeries, Australia)	55			
Bürgen™ Dark/Swiss rye (Tip Top Bakeries, Australia)	74			
mean of two studies	65	30	10	7
Klosterbrot wholemeal rye bread (Dimpflmeier, Canada)	67	30	13	9
Light rye (Silverstein's, Canada)	68	30	14	10
Linseed rye (Rudolph's, Canada)	55	30	13	7
Roggenbrot, Vogel's (Stevns & Co, Sydney, Australia)	59	30	14	8

[0] indicates that the food has so little carbohydrate that the GI cannot be tested. The GL is therefore 0.
▲ indicates brand not specified

Food	GI Glucose = 100	Nominal serve size (g)	Available carb per serve	GL per serve
Schinkenbrot, Riga (Berzin's, Sydney, Australia)	86	30	14	12
Sourdough rye (Canada)	57			
Sourdough rye (Australia)	48			
mean of two studies	53	30	12	6
Volkornbrot, wholemeal rye bread (Dimpflmeier, Canada)	56	30	13	7
Wheat Breads				
Coarse wheat kernel bread, 80% intact kernels (Sweden)	52	30	20	10
Cracked wheat kernel (bulghur) bread				
50% cracked wheat kernel (Canada)	58	30	20	12
75% cracked wheat kernels (Canada)	48	30	20	10
mean of two studies	53	30	20	11
Spelt wheat breads				
White spelt wheat bread (Slovenia)	74	30	23	17
Wholemeal spelt wheat bread (Slovenia)	63	30	19	12
Scalded spelt wheat kernel bread (Slovenia)	67	30	22	15
Spelt multigrain bread® (Pav's, Australia)	54	30	12	7
White wheat flour bread				
White flour (Canada)	69	30	14	10
White flour (USA)	70	30	14	10
White flour, Sunblest™ (Tip Top, Australia)	70	30	14	10
White flour (Dempster's Corporate Foods Ltd., Canada)	71	30	14	10
White flour (South Africa)	71	30	13	9
White flour (Canada)	71	30	14	10
mean of six studies	70	30	14	10
White wheat flour bread, hard, toasted (Italian)	73	30	15	11
Wonder™, enriched white bread (USA)	71			
Wonder™, enriched white bread (USA)	72			
Wonder™, enriched white bread (USA)	77			
mean of three studies	73	30	14	10
White Turkish bread (Turkey)	87	30	17	15
White bread with enzyme inhibitors				
White bread + acarbose (200mg) (Mexico)	18	30	17	3
White bread + acarbose (200mg) (Mexico)	50	30	17	8
mean in two groups of subjects	34	30	17	6

[0] indicates that the food has so little carbohydrate that the GI cannot be tested. The GL is therefore 0.
▲ indicates brand not specified

Food	GI Glucose = 100	Nominal serve size (g)	Available carb per serve	GL per serve
White bread roll + 3 mg trestatin (pancreatic alpha-amylase inhibitor)	48	30	12	6
White bread roll + 6 mg trestatin	29	30	12	4
White bread with soluble fibre				
White bread + 15 g psyllium fibre	41	30	17	7
White bread + 15 g psyllium fibre	65	30	17	11
mean in two groups of subjects	53	30	17	9
White bread eaten with vinegar as vinaigrette (Sweden)	45	30	15	7
White bread eaten with powdered dried seaweed	48	30	15	7
White bread containing Eurylon® high-amylose maize starch (France)	42	30	19	8
White fibre-enriched bread				
White, high-fibre (Dempster's, Canada)	67			
White, high-fibre (Weston's Bakery, Toronto, Canada)	69			
mean of two studies	68	30	13	9
White resistant starch-enriched bread				
Fibre White™ (Nature's Fresh, New Zealand)	77	30	15	11
Wonderwhite™ (Buttercup, Australia)	80	30	14	11
Wholemeal (whole wheat) wheat flour bread				
Wholemeal flour (Canada)	52	30	12	6
Wholemeal flour (Canada)	64	30	12	8
Wholemeal flour (Canada)	65	30	12	8
Wholemeal flour (Canada)	67	30	12	8
Wholemeal flour (Canada)	67	30	12	8
Wholemeal flour (Canada)	69	30	12	8
Wholemeal flour (Canada)	71	30	12	8
Wholemeal flour (Canada)	72	30	12	8
Wholemeal flour (USA)	73	30	14	10
Wholemeal flour (South Africa)	75	30	13	9
Wholemeal flour (Tip Top Bakeries, Australia)	77	30	12	9
Wholemeal flour (Tip Top Bakeries, Australia)	78	30	12	9
Wholemeal flour (Kenya)	87	30	13	11
mean of thirteen studies	71	30	13	9
Wholemeal Turkish bread	49	30	16	8
Specialty wheat breads				
Bürgen® Mixed Grain bread (Australia)				
Bürgen® Mixed Grain (Tip Top, Australia)	34			

[0] indicates that the food has so little carbohydrate that the GI cannot be tested. The GL is therefore 0.
▲ indicates brand not specified

Food	GI Glucose = 100	Nominal serve size (g)	Available carb per serve	GL per serve
Bürgen® Mixed Grain	45			
Bürgen® Mixed Grain	69			
mean of three studies	49	30	11	6
Bürgen® Oat Bran & Honey Loaf with Barley (Tip Top, Australia)	31	30	10	3
Bürgen® Soy-Lin, kibbled soy (8%) and linseed (8%) loaf (Tip Top)	36	30	9	3
English Muffin™ bread (Natural Ovens, USA)	77	30	14	11
Healthy Choice™ Hearty 7 Grain (Con Agra Inc., USA)	55	30	14	8
Healthy Choice™ Hearty 100% Whole Grain (Con Agra Inc., USA)	62	30	14	9
Helga's™ Classic Seed Loaf (Quality Bakers, Australia)	68	30	14	9
Helga's™ traditional wholemeal bread (Quality Bakers, Australia)	70	30	13	9
Hunger Filler™, whole grain bread (Natural Ovens, USA)	59	30	13	7
Molenberg™ (Goodman Fielder, Auckland, New Zealand)	75			
Molenberg™ (Goodman Fielder, New Zealand)	84			
mean of two studies	80	30	14	11
Multigrain Loaf, spelt wheat flour (Australia)	54	30	15	8
Multigrain (50% kibbled wheat grain) (Australia)	43	30	14	6
Nutty Natural™, whole grain bread (Natural Ovens, USA)	59	30	12	7
Performax™ (Country Life Bakeries, Australia)	38	30	13	5
Ploughman's™ Wholegrain, original recipe (Quality Bakers, Australia)	47	30	14	7
Ploughman's™ Wholemeal, smooth milled (Quality Bakers, Australia)	64	30	13	9
Semolina Bread (Kenya)	64			
Sourdough wheat (Australia)	54	30	14	8
Soy & Linseed bread (packet mix in bread oven) (Con Agra Inc., USA)	50	30	10	5
Stay Trim™, whole grain bread (Natural Ovens, USA)	70	30	15	10
Sunflower & Barley bread, Riga brand (Berzin's, Australia)	57	30	13	7
Tip Top Holsom's 9 Grain	43	30	14	6
Vogel's Honey & Oats (Stevns & Co., Australia)	55	30	14	7
Vogel's Roggenbrot (Stevns & Co., Australia)	59	30	14	8
Whole-wheat snack bread (Ryvita Co Ltd., UK)	74	30	22	16

[0] indicates that the food has so little carbohydrate that the GI cannot be tested. The GL is therefore 0.
▲ indicates brand not specified

Food	GI Glucose = 100	Nominal serve size (g)	Available carb per serve	GL per serve
100% Whole Grain™ bread (Natural Ovens, USA)	51	30	13	7
White wheat flour flatbread (Sweden)	79	30	16	13
Unleavened Breads				
Lebanese bread, white (Seda Bakery, Australia)	75	30	16	12
Middle Eastern flatbread	97	30	16	15
Pita bread, white (Canada)	57	30	17	10
Wheat flour flatbread (India)	66	30	16	10
Amaranth : wheat (25:75) composite flour flatbread (India)	66	30	15	10
Amaranth : wheat (50:50) composite flour flatbread (India)	76	30	15	11

BREAKFAST CEREALS AND RELATED PRODUCTS

Food	GI	Nominal serve	Available carb	GL
All-Bran™ (Kellogg's, Australia)	30	30	15	4
All-Bran™ (Kellogg's, USA)	38	30	23	9
All-Bran™ (Kellogg's Inc., Canada)	50	30	23	9
All-Bran™ (Kellogg's Inc., Canada)	51	30	23	9
mean of four studies	42	30	21	9
All-Bran Fruit 'n' Oats™ (Kellogg's, Australia)	39	30	17	7
All-Bran Soy 'n' Fibre™ (Kellogg's, Australia)	33	30	14	4
Amaranth, popped, with milk (India)	97	30	19	18
Barley porridge				
Wholemeal barley flour porridge (100% regular barley) (Sweden)	68	50 (dry)	34	23
Wholemeal high-fibre barley flour porridge (Sweden)	55	50 (dry)	15	8
Barley porridge made from thin dehulled flakes (Sweden)	62	50 (dry)	28	17
Barley porridge made from thick dehulled flakes (Sweden)	65	50 (dry)	28	18
Bran Buds™ (Kellogg's, Canada)	58	30	12	7
Bran Buds with psyllium (Kellogg's, Canada)	47	30	12	6
Bran Chex™ (Nabisco, Canada)	58	30	19	11
Bran Flakes™ (Kellogg's, Australia)	74	30	18	13
Cheerios™ (General Mills, Canada)	74	30	20	15
Chocapic™ (Nestlé, France)	84	30	25	21
Coco Pops™ (cocoa-flavoured puffed rice)				
Coco Pops™ (Kellogg's, Australia)	77	30	26	20
Corn Bran™ (Quaker Oats, Canada)	75	30	20	15
Corn Chex™ (Nabisco, Canada)	83	30	25	21

[0] indicates that the food has so little carbohydrate that the GI cannot be tested. The GL is therefore 0.
▲ indicates brand not specified

Food	GI Glucose = 100	Nominal serve size (g)	Available carb per serve	GL per serve
Cornflakes™				
Cornflakes™ (Kellogg's, New Zealand)	72	30	25	18
Cornflakes™ (Kellogg's, Australia)	77	30	25	20
Cornflakes™ (Kellogg's, Canada)	80	30	26	21
Cornflakes™ (Kellogg's, Canada)	86	30	26	22
Cornflakes™ (Kellogg's, USA)	92	30	26	24
mean of five studies	81	30	26	21
Cornflakes, high-fibre (Presidents Choice, Canada)	74	30	23	17
Cornflakes, Crunchy Nut™ (Kellogg's, Australia)	72	30	24	17
Corn Pops™ (Kellogg's, Australia)	80	30	26	21
Cream of Wheat™ (Nabisco, Canada)	66	250	26	17
Cream of Wheat™, Instant (Nabisco, Canada)	74	250	30	22
Crispix™ (Kellogg's, Canada)	87	30	25	22
Energy Mix™ (Quaker, France)	80	30	24	19
Froot Loops™ (Kellogg's, Australia)	69	30	26	18
Frosties™, sugar-coated cornflakes (Kellogg's, Australia)	55	30	26	15
Fruitful Lite™ (Hubbards, New Zealand)	61	30	20	12
Fruity-Bix™, berry (Sanitarium, New Zealand)	113	30	22	25
Golden Grahams™ (General Mills, Canada)	71	30	25	18
Golden Wheats™ (Kellogg's, Australia)	71	30	23	16
Grapenuts™				
Grapenuts™ (Post, Kraft, Canada)	67	30	19	13
Grapenuts™ (Kraft, USA)	75	30	22	16
mean of two studies	71	30	21	15
Grapenuts™ Flakes (Post, Canada)	80	30	22	17
Guardian™ (Kellogg's, Australia)	37	30	12	5
Healthwise™ for bowel health (Uncle Toby's, Australia)	66	30	18	12
Healthwise™ for heart health (Uncle Toby's, Australia)	48	30	19	9
Honey Rice Bubbles™ (Kellogg's, Australia)	77	30	27	20
Honey Smacks™ (Kellogg's, Australia)	71	30	23	11
Hot cereal, apple & cinnamon (Con Agra Inc., USA)	37	30	22	8
Hot cereal, unflavoured (Con Agra Inc., USA)	25	30	19	5
Just Right™ (Kellogg's, Australia)	60	30	22	13
Just Right Just Grains™ (Kellogg's, Australia)	62	30	23	14
Komplete™ (Kellogg's, Australia)	48	30	21	10
Life™ (Quaker Oats Co., Canada)	66	30	25	15
Mini Wheats™, whole wheat (Kellogg's, Australia)	58	30	21	12
Mini Wheats™, blackcurrant (Kellogg's, Australia)	72	30	21	15

[0] indicates that the food has so little carbohydrate that the GI cannot be tested. The GL is therefore 0.
▲ indicates brand not specified

Food	GI Glucose = 100	Nominal serve size (g)	Available carb per serve	GL per serve
Muesli				
Muesli (Canada)	66	30	24	17
Alpen Muesli (Wheetabix, France)	55	30	19	10
Muesli, gluten-free (Freedom Foods, Australia)	39	30	19	7
Muesli, Lite (Sanitarium, New Zealand)	54	30	18	10
Muesli, Natural (Sanitarium, New Zealand)	57	30	19	11
Muesli, Natural (Sanitarium, Australia)	40	30	19	8
mean of two studies	49	30	20	10
Muesli, No Name (Sunfresh, Canada)	60	30	18	11
Muesli, Swiss Formula (Uncle Toby's, Australia)	56	30	16	9
Muesli, toasted (Purina, Australia)	43	30	17	7
Nutrigrain™ (Kellogg's, Australia)	66	30	15	10
Oat 'n' Honey Bake™ (Kellogg's, Australia)	77	30	17	13
Oat bran				
Oat bran, raw (Quaker Oats, Canada)	50	10	5	2
Oat bran, raw	59	10	5	3
mean of two studies	55	10	5	3
Porridge made from rolled oats				
Porridge (Uncle Toby's, Australia)	42	250	21	9
Porridge (Canada)	49	250	23	11
Traditional porridge oats (Lowan, Australia)	51	250	21	11
Porridge (Hubbards, New Zealand)	58	250	21	12
Porridge (Australia)	58	250	21	12
Porridge (Canada)	62	250	23	14
Porridge (Canada)	69	250	23	16
Porridge (USA)	75	250	23	17
mean of eight studies	58	250	22	13
Wholemeal oat flour porridge (Sweden)	74	50 (dry)	32	24
Oat porridge made from thick flakes (Sweden)	55	250	27	15
Oat porridge made from roasted thin flakes (Sweden)	69	250	27	19
Oat porridge made from roasted thick flakes (Sweden)	50	250	27	14
Oat porridge made from roasted and steamed thin oat flakes (Sweden)	80	250	27	22
Oat porridge made from steamed thick (1.0 mm) dehulled oat flakes (Sweden)	53	250	27	14
Instant Porridge				
Quick Oats (Quaker Oats, Canada)	65			
One Minute Oats (Quaker Oats, Canada)	66			
mean of two studies	66	250	26	17

[0] indicates that the food has so little carbohydrate that the GI cannot be tested. The GL is therefore 0.
▲ indicates brand not specified

Food	GI Glucose = 100	Nominal serve size (g)	Available carb per serve	GL per serve
Pop Tarts™, Double Chocolate (Kellogg's, Australia)	70	50	36	25
Pro Stars™ (General Mills, Canada)	71	30	24	17
Puffed Wheat				
Puffed Wheat (Quaker Oats, Canada)	67	30	20	13
Puffed Wheat (Sanitarium, Australia)	80	30	21	17
mean of two studies	74	30	21	16
Raisin Bran™ (Kellogg's, USA)	61	30	19	12
Red River Cereal (Maple Leaf Mills, Canada)	49	30	22	13
Rice Bran, extruded (Rice Growers, Australia)	19	30	14	3
Rice Bubbles™ (puffed rice)				
Rice Bubbles™ (Kellogg's, Australia)	81			
Rice Bubbles™ (Kellogg's, Australia)	85			
Rice Bubbles™ (Kellogg's, Australia)	95			
mean of three studies	87	30	26	22
Rice Chex™ (Nabisco, Canada)	89	30	26	23
Rice Krispies™ (Kellogg's, Canada)	82	30	26	22
Shredded Wheat				
Shredded Wheat (Canada)	67	30	20	13
Shredded Wheat™ (Nabisco, Canada)	83	30	20	17
mean of two studies	75	30	20	15
Special K™—*formulation of this cereal varies in different countries*				
Special K™ (Kellogg's, Australia)	54	30	21	11
Special K™ (Kellogg's, USA)	69	30	21	14
Special K™ (Kellogg's, France)	84	30	24	20
Soy Tasty™ (Sanitarium, Australia)	60	30	20	12
Soytana™ (Vogel's, Australia)	49	45	25	12
Sultana Bran™ (Kellogg's, Australia)	73	30	19	14
Sustain™ (Kellogg's, Australia)	68	30	22	15
Team™ (Nabisco, Canada)	82	30	22	17
Thank Goodness™ (Hubbards, New Zealand)	65	30	23	15
Total™ (General Mills, Canada)	76	30	22	17
Ultra-bran™ (Vogel's, Australia)	41	30	13	5
Wheat-bites™ (Uncle Toby's, Australia)	72	30	25	18
Wheat biscuits (plain flaked wheat)				
Vita-Brits™ (Uncle Toby's, Australia)	61	30	20	12
Vita-Brits™ (Uncle Toby's, Australia)	68	30	20	13
Weet-Bix™ (Sanitarium, Australia)	69	30	17	12
Weet-Bix™ (Sanitarium, Australia)	69	30	17	12

[0] indicates that the food has so little carbohydrate that the GI cannot be tested. The GL is therefore 0.
▲ indicates brand not specified

Food	GI Glucose = 100	Nominal serve size (g)	Available carb per serve	GL per serve
Weetabix™ (Weetabix, Canada)	74	30	22	16
Weetabix™ (Weetabix, Canada)	75	30	22	16
Whole wheat Goldies™ (Kellogg's, Australia)	70	30	20	14
mean of seven studies	70	30	19	13
Wheat biscuits (flaked wheat) with additional ingredients				
Good Start™, muesli wheat biscuits (Sanitarium, Australia)	68	30	20	14
Hi-Bran Weet-Bix™, wheat biscuits (Sanitarium, Australia)	61	30	17	10
Hi-Bran Weet-Bix™ with soy and linseed (Sanitarium, Australia)	57	30	16	9
Honey Goldies™ (Kellogg's Australia)	72	30	21	15
Lite-Bix™, plain, no added sugar (Sanitarium, Australia)	70	30	20	14
Oat bran Weet-Bix™ (Sanitarium, Australia)	57	30	20	11
Sultana Goldies™ (Kellogg's Australia)	65	30	21	13
BREAKFAST CEREAL BARS				
Crunchy Nut Cornflakes™ bar (Kellogg's, Australia)	72	30	26	19
Fibre Plus™ bar (Uncle Toby's, Australia)	78	30	23	18
Fruity-Bix™ bar, fruit and nut (Sanitarium, Australia)	56	30	19	10
Fruity-Bix™ bar, wild berry (Sanitarium, Australia)	51	30	19	9
K-Time Just Right™ bar (Kellogg's, Australia)	72	30	24	17
K-Time Strawberry Crunch™ bar (Kellogg's, Australia)	77	30	25	19
Rice Bubble Treat™ bar (Kellogg's, Australia)	63	30	24	15
Sustain™ bar (Kellogg's, Australia)	57	30	25	14
CEREAL GRAINS				
Amaranth				
Amaranth (*Amaranthus esculentum*) popped, with milk	97	30	22	21
Barley				
Pearl Barley				
Barley, pearled (Canada)	22			
Barley (Canada)	22			
Barley, pot, boiled in salted water 20 min	25			
Barley (Canada)	27			
Barley, pearled (Canada)	29			
mean of five studies	25	150	42	11
Barley (*Hordeum vulgare*) (India)	37			

[0] indicates that the food has so little carbohydrate that the GI cannot be tested. The GL is therefore 0.
▲ indicates brand not specified

Food	GI Glucose = 100	Nominal serve size (g)	Available carb per serve	GL per serve
Barley (*Hordeum vulgare*) (India)	48			
mean of two groups of subjects	43	150	42	26
Barley, cracked (Malthouth, Tunisia)	50	150	42	21
Barley, rolled (Australia)	66	50 (dry)	38	25
Buckwheat				
Buckwheat (Canada)	49			
Buckwheat (Canada)	51			
Buckwheat (Canada)	63			
mean of three studies	54	150	30	16
Buckwheat groats, boiled 12 min (Sweden)	45	150	30	13
Corn/Maize				
Maize (*Zea mays*), flour made into chapatti (India)	59	–	–	–
Maize meal porridge/gruel (Kenya)	109	–	–	–
Cornmeal				
Cornmeal, boiled in salted water 2 min (Canada)	68	150	13	9
Cornmeal + margarine (Canada)	69	150	12	9
mean of two studies	69	150	13	9
Sweet corn				
Sweet corn, 'Honey & Pearl' variety (New Zealand)	37	150	30	11
Sweet corn, on the cob, boiled 20 min (Australia)	48	150	30	14
Sweet corn (Canada)	59	150	33	20
Sweet corn (USA)	60	150	33	20
Sweet corn (USA)	60	150	33	20
Sweet corn (South Africa)	62	150	33	20
mean of six studies	53	150	32	17
Sweet corn, canned, diet-pack (USA)	46	150	28	13
Sweet corn, frozen, reheated in microwave (Canada)	47	150	33	16
Taco shells, cornmeal-based, baked (Old El Paso, Canada)	68	20	12	8
Couscous				
Couscous, boiled 5 min (USA)	61			
Couscous, boiled 5 min (Tunisia)	69			
mean of two studies	65	150	35	23
Millet				
Millet, boiled (Canada)	71	150	36	25
Millet flour porridge (Kenya)	107	–	–	–

[0] indicates that the food has so little carbohydrate that the GI cannot be tested. The GL is therefore 0.
▲ indicates brand not specified

Food	GI Glucose = 100	Nominal serve size (g)	Available carb per serve	GL per serve
Rice, white				
Arborio, risotto rice, boiled (Sun Rice, Australia)	69	150	53	36
White (*Oryza sativa*), boiled (India)	69	150	43	30
Rice, boiled white				
Type NS ▲ (France)	45	150	30	14
Type NS ▲ (India)	48	150	38	18
Type NS ▲ (Canada)	51	150	42	21
Type NS ▲ (France)	52	150	36	19
Type NS ▲ (Canada)	56	150	42	23
Type NS ▲ (Pakistan)	69	150	38	26
Type NS ▲ (Canada)	72	150	42	30
Type NS ▲, boiled in salted water (India)	72	150	38	27
Type NS ▲, boiled 13 min (Italy)	102	150	30	31
Type NS ▲ (Kenya)	112	150	42	47
Type NS ▲, boiled (France)	43	150	30	13
Type NS ▲, boiled (France)	47	150	30	14
Type NS ▲, boiled in salted water, refrigerated 16–20h, reheated (India)	53	150	38	20
Type NS ▲, boiled 13 min, then baked 10 min (Italy)	104	150	30	31
Long grain, boiled				
Long grain, boiled 5 min (Canada)	41	150	40	16
Long grain, boiled 15 min (Mahatma, Australia)	50	150	43	21
Gem long grain (Dainty Food, Canada)	55	150	40	22
Long grain (Uncle Bens, New Zealand)	56	150	43	24
Long grain, boiled 25 min (Surinam)	56	150	43	24
Gem long grain (Dainty, Canada)	57	150	40	23
Long grain, boiled 15 min	58	150	40	23
Gem long grain (Dainty, Canada)	60	150	40	24
Gem long grain (Dainty, Canada)	60	150	40	24
Long grain, boiled 7 min (Star, Canada)	64	150	40	26
mean of 10 studies	56	150	41	23
Rice, long grain, quick-cooking varieties				
Long grain, parboiled 10 min cooking time (Uncle Ben's, Belgium)	68	150	37	25
Long grain, parboiled, 20 min cooking time (Uncle Ben's, Belgium)	75	150	37	28
Long grain, microwaved 2 min (Express Rice, Masterfoods, UK)	52	150	37	19

[0] indicates that the food has so little carbohydrate that the GI cannot be tested. The GL is therefore 0.
▲ indicates brand not specified

Food	GI Glucose = 100	Nominal serve size (g)	Available carb per serve	GL per serve
Rice, specialty rices				
Cajun Style, Uncle Ben's® (Effem Foods, Canada)	51	150	37	19
Garden Style, Uncle Ben's® (Effem Foods, Canada)	55	150	37	21
Long Grain and Wild, Uncle Ben's® (Effem Foods, Canada)	54	150	37	20
Mexican Fast and Fancy, Uncle Ben's® (Effem Foods, Canada)	58	150	37	22
Saskatchewan wild rice (Canada)	57	150	32	18
Broken rice (Lion Foods, Thailand)	86	150	43	37
Glutinous rice (Thailand)	98	150	32	31
Jasmine rice (Thailand)	109	150	42	46
Rice, white low-amylose				
Calrose, white, medium grain, boiled (Rice Growers, Australia)	83	150	43	36
Sungold, Pelde, parboiled (Rice Growers, Australia)	87	150	43	37
Waxy (0–2% amylose) (Rice Growers, Australia)	88	150	43	38
Pelde, white (Rice Growers, Australia)	93	150	43	40
White, low-amylose, boiled (Turkey)	139	150	43	60
Rice, white high-amylose				
Bangladeshi rice variety BR16 (28% amylose)	37	150	39	14
Bangladeshi rice variety BR16, long-grain (27% amylose)	39	150	39	15
mean of two studies	38	150	39	15
Doongara, white (Rice Growers, Australia)	50			
Doongara, white (Rice Growers, Australia)	64			
Doongara, white (Rice Growers, Australia)	54			
mean of three studies	56	150	39	22
Koshikari (Japonica), short-grain, (Japan)	48	150	38	18
Basmati				
Basmati, boiled (Mahatma, Australia)	58	150	38	22
Precooked basmati rice, Uncle Ben's Express® (UK)	57	150	41	24
Quick-cooking basmati, Uncle Ben's® Superior (Belgium)	60	150	38	23
Rice, brown				
Brown (Canada)	66	150	33	21
Brown, steamed (USA)	50	150	33	16
Brown (*Oriza Sativa*), boiled (South India)	50	150	33	16
mean of three studies	55	150	33	18
Calrose brown (Rice Growers, Australia)	87	150	38	33

[0] indicates that the food has so little carbohydrate that the GI cannot be tested. The GL is therefore 0.
▲ indicates brand not specified

Food	GI Glucose = 100	Nominal serve size (g)	Available carb per serve	GL per serve
Doongara brown, high-amylose (Rice Growers, Australia)	66	150	37	24
Pelde brown (Rice Growers, Australia)	76	150	38	29
Parboiled, cooked 20 min, Uncle Ben's Natur-reis ® (Belgium)	64	150	36	23
Sunbrown Quick™ (Rice Growers, Australia)	80	150	38	31
Instant/puffed rice				
Instant rice, white, boiled 1 min (Canada)	46	150	42	19
Instant rice, white, cooked 6 min (Trice brand, Australia)	87	150	42	36
Puffed, white, cooked 5 min, Uncle Ben's Snabbris® (Belgium)	74	150	42	31
mean of three studies	69	150	42	29
Instant Doongara, white, cooked 5 min (Rice Growers, Australia)	94	150	42	35
Parboiled rice				
Parboiled rice (Canada)	48	150	36	18
Parboiled rice (USA)	72	150	36	26
Converted, white, Uncle Ben's® (Canada)	45	150	36	16
Converted, white, boiled 20–30 min, Uncle Ben's® (USA)	38	150	36	14
Converted, white, long grain, boiled 20–30 min, Uncle Ben's® (USA)	50	150	36	18
Boiled, 12 min (Denmark)	39	150	36	14
Boiled, 12 min (Denmark)	42	150	36	15
Boiled, 12 min (Denmark)	43	150	36	16
Boiled, 12 min (Denmark)	46	150	36	17
Long grain, boiled 5 min (Canada)	38	150	36	14
Long grain, boiled, 10 min (USA)	61	150	36	22
Long grain, boiled 15 min (Canada)	47	150	36	17
Long grain, boiled 25 min (Canada)	46	150	36	17
mean of thirteen studies	47	150	36	17
Parboiled, low-amylose				
Bangladeshi rice variety BR2, parboiled (12% amylose)	51	150	38	19
Parboiled, Sungold (Rice Growers, Australia)	87	150	39	34
Parboiled, high-amylose				
Parboiled, high-amylose (28%), Doongara (Rice Growers, Australia)	50	150	39	19
Bangladeshi rice variety BR16 (28% amylose)	35	150	37	13

[0] indicates that the food has so little carbohydrate that the GI cannot be tested. The GL is therefore 0.
▲ indicates brand not specified

Food	GI Glucose = 100	Nominal serve size (g)	Available carb per serve	GL per serve
Bangladeshi rice variety BR16, traditional method (27% amylose)	32	150	38	12
Bangladeshi rice variety BR16, pressure parboiled (27% amylose)	27	150	41	11
Bangladeshi rice variety BR4 (27% amylose)	33	150	38	13
mean of 5 studies	35	150	39	14
Rye, whole kernels				
Rye, whole kernels (Canada)	29	50 (dry)	38	11
Rye, whole kernels, pressure cooked (Canada)	34	50 (dry)	38	13
Rye, whole kernels (Canada)	39	50 (dry)	38	15
mean of three studies	34	50 (dry)	38	13
Wheat				
Wheat, whole kernels				
Wheat, whole kernels *(Triticum aestivum)* (India)	30	50 (dry)	38	11
Wheat, whole kernels (Canada)	42	50 (dry)	33	14
Wheat, whole kernels, pressure cooked (Canada)	44	50 (dry)	33	14
Wheat, whole kernels (Canada)	48	50 (dry)	33	16
mean of four studies	41	50 (dry)	34	14
Wheat, type NS ▲ (India)	90	50 (dry)	38	34
Wheat, precooked kernels				
Durum wheat, precooked, cooked 20 min (France)	52	50 (dry)	37	19
Durum wheat, precooked, cooked 10 min (France)	50	50 (dry)	33	17
Durum wheat, precooked in pouch, reheated (France)	40	125	39	16
Quick-cooking (White Wings, Australia)	54	150	47	25
Semolina				
Semolina, roasted at 105°C then gelatinised with water (India)	55			
Semolina, steamed and gelatinised (India)	54			
mean of two studies	55	150	11	6
Cracked wheat (bulghur)				
Bulghur, boiled (Canada)	46			
Bulghur, boiled in 800 mL water 20 min (Canada)	46			
Bulghur, boiled 20 min (Canada)	46			
Bulghur, boiled 20 min (Canada)	53			
mean of four studies	48	150	26	12

[0] indicates that the food has so little carbohydrate that the GI cannot be tested. The GL is therefore 0.
▲ indicates brand not specified

Food	GI Glucose = 100	Nominal serve size (g)	Available carb per serve	GL per serve
COOKIES				
Arrowroot				
Arrowroot (McCormicks's, Canada)	63	25	20	13
Arrowroot plus (McCormicks's, Canada)	62	25	18	11
Milk Arrowroot™ (Arnotts, Australia)	69	25	18	12
mean of three studies	65	25	19	12
Barquette Abricot (LU, France)	71	40	32	23
Bebe Dobre Rano Chocolate (LU, Czech Republic)	57	50	33	19
Bebe Dobre Rano Honey and Hazelnuts (LU, Czech Republic)	51	50	34	17
Bebe Jemne Susenky (LU, Czech Republic)	67	25	20	14
Digestives				
Digestives (Canada)	55			
Digestives (Canada)	59			
Digestives, Peak Freans (Nabisco, Canada)	62			
mean of three studies	59	25	16	10
Digestives, gluten-free (Nutricia, UK)	58	25	17	10
Evergreen met Krenten (LU, Netherlands)	66	38	21	14
Golden Fruit (Griffin's, New Zealand)	77	25	17	13
Graham Wafers (Christie Brown, Canada)	74	25	18	14
Gran'Dia Banana, Oats and Honey (LU, Brazil)	28	30	23	6
Grany en-cas Abricot (LU, France)	55	30	16	9
Grany en-cas Fruits des bois (LU, France)	50	30	14	7
Grany Rush Apricot (LU, Netherlands)	62	30	20	12
Highland Oatmeal™ (Westons, Australia)	55	25	18	10
Highland Oatcakes (Walker's, Scotland)	57	25	15	8
LU P'tit Déjeuner Chocolat (LU, France)	42	50	34	14
LU P'tit Déjeuner Miel et Pépites Chocolat (LU, France)	45	50	35	16
LU P'tit Déjeuner Miel et Pépites Chocolat (LU, France)	52	50	35	18
LU P'tit Déjeuner Miel et Pépites Chocolat (LU, France)	49	50	35	18
mean of three studies	49	50	35	17
Maltmeal wafer (Griffin's, New Zealand)	50	25	17	9
Morning Coffee™ (Arnotts, Australia)	79	25	19	15
Nutrigrain Fruits des bois (Kellogg's, France)	57	35	23	13
Oatmeal (Canada)	54	25	17	9
Oro (Saiwa, Italy)	61	40	32	20
Oro (Saiwa, Italy)	67	40	32	21
mean of two studies	64	40	32	20
Petit LU Normand (LU, France)	51	25	19	10
Petit LU Roussillon (LU, France)	48	25	18	9

[0] indicates that the food has so little carbohydrate that the GI cannot be tested. The GL is therefore 0.
▲ indicates brand not specified

Food	GI Glucose = 100	Nominal serve size (g)	Available carb per serve	GL per serve
Prince Energie+ (LU, France)	73	25	17	13
Prince fourré chocolat (LU, France)	53			
Prince fourré chocolat (LU, France)	50			
mean of two studies	52	45	30	16
Prince Meganana Chocolate (LU, Spain)	49	50	36	18
Prince Petit Déjeuner Vanille (LU, France and Spain)	45	50	36	16
Rich Tea (Canada)	55	25	19	10
Sablé des Flandres (LU, France)	57	20	15	8
Shortbread (Arnotts, Australia)	64	25	16	10
Shredded Wheatmeal™ (Arnotts, Australia)	62	25	18	11
Snack Right Fruit Slice (97% fat-free) (Arnott's, Australia)	45	25	19	9
Thé (LU, France)	41	20	16	6
Vanilla Wafers (Christie Brown, Canada)	77	25	18	14
Véritable Petit Beurre (LU, France)	51	25	18	9

CRACKERS

Food	GI Glucose = 100	Nominal serve size (g)	Available carb per serve	GL per serve
Breton wheat crackers (Dare Foods, Canada)	67	25	14	10
Corn Thins, puffed corn cakes, gluten-free (Real Foods, Australia)	87	25	20	18
Cream Cracker (LU, Brazil)	65	25	17	11
High-calcium cracker (Danone, Malaysia)	52	25	17	9
Jatz™, plain salted cracker biscuits (Arnotts, Australia)	55	25	17	10
Puffed Crispbread (Westons, Australia)	81	25	19	15

Puffed rice cakes
Puffed rice cakes (Rice Growers, Australia)	82	25	21	17
Rice cakes, Calrose (low-amylose) (Rice Growers, Australia)	91	25	21	19
Rice cakes, Doongara (high-amylose) (Rice Growers, Australia)	61	25	21	13
mean of three studies	78	25	21	17

Rye crispbread
Rye crispbread (Canada)	63	25	16	10
Ryvita™ (Canada)	69	25	16	11
High-fibre rye crispbread (Ryvita, UK)	59	25	15	9
Rye crispbread (Ryvita, UK)	63	25	18	11
mean of four studies	64	25	16	11
Kavli™ Norwegian Crispbread (Players, Australia)	71	25	16	12
Sao™, plain square crackers (Arnotts, Australia)	70	25	17	12
Stoned Wheat Thins (Christie Brown, Canada)	67	25	17	12

[0] indicates that the food has so little carbohydrate that the GI cannot be tested. The GL is therefore 0.
▲ indicates brand not specified

Food	GI Glucose = 100	Nominal serve size (g)	Available carb per serve	GL per serve
Water cracker				
Water cracker (Canada)	63	25	18	11
Water cracker (Arnotts, Australia)	78	25	18	14
mean of two studies	71	25	18	13
Premium Soda Crackers (Christie Brown, Canada)	74	25	17	12
Vita-wheat™, original, crispbread (Arnott's, Australia)	55	25	19	10

DAIRY PRODUCTS AND ALTERNATIVES

Food	GI Glucose = 100	Nominal serve size (g)	Available carb per serve	GL per serve
Custard				
No Bake Egg Custard (Nestlé, Australia)	35	100	17	6
Custard, home made (Australia)	43	100	17	7
TRIM™, reduced-fat custard (Pauls, Australia)	37	100	15	6
mean of three studies	38	100	16	6
Ice-cream, Regular/NS ▲				
Ice-cream, NS ▲ (Canada)	36			
Ice-cream (half vanilla, half chocolate) (Italy)	57			
Ice-cream, NS ▲ (USA)	62			
Ice-cream, chocolate flavored (USA)	68			
Ice-cream (half vanilla, half chocolate) (Italy)	80			
mean of five studies	61	50	13	8
Ice-cream, reduced or low fat				
Ice-cream, vanilla, (Peter's, Australia)	50	50	6	3
Ice-cream, (1.2 % fat), Prestige Light vanilla (Norco, Australia)	47	50	10	5
Ice-cream, (1.4% fat), Prestige Light toffee (Norco, Australia)	37	50	14	5
Ice-cream, (7.1 % fat), Prestige macadamia (Norco, Australia)	39	50	12	5
Ice-cream, premium				
Ice-cream, Ultra chocolate, 15% fat (Sara Lee, Australia)	37	50	9	4
Ice-cream, French vanilla, 16% fat (Sara Lee, Australia)	38	50	9	3
Milk, full-fat				
Full-fat (Italy)	11			
Full-fat (3% fat, Sweden)	21			
Full-fat (Italy)	24			
Full-fat (Australia)	31			
Full-fat (Canada)	34			
Full-fat (USA)	40			

[0] indicates that the food has so little carbohydrate that the GI cannot be tested. The GL is therefore 0.
▲ indicates brand not specified

Food	GI Glucose = 100	Nominal serve size (g)	Available carb per serve	GL per serve
mean of five studies	27	250	12	3
Fermented cow's milk (ropy milk, Sweden)	11			
Fermented cow's milk (filmjölk, Sweden)	11			
mean of two foods	11	–	–	–
Milk, full-fat, plus bran				
Full-fat + 20g wheat bran (Italy)	25			
Full-fat + 20g wheat bran (Italy)	28			
mean of two studies	27	250	12	3
Milk, skim (Canada)	32	250	13	4
Milk, condensed, sweetened (Nestlé, Australia)	61	250	136	83
Milk, low fat, chocolate, with aspartame, Lite White™ (Australia)	24	250	15	3
Milk, low fat, chocolate, with sugar, Lite White™ (Australia)	34	250	26	9
Mousse, reduced-fat, mix with water				
Butterscotch, 1.9% fat (Nestlé, Australia)	36	50	10	4
Chocolate, 2% fat (Nestlé, Australia)	31	50	11	3
Hazelnut, 2.4% fat (Nestlé, Australia)	36	50	10	4
Mango, 1.8% fat (Nestlé, Australia)	33	50	11	4
Mixed berry, 2.2% fat (Nestlé, Australia)	36	50	10	4
Strawberry, 2.3% fat (Nestlé, Australia)	32	50	10	3
mean of six foods	34	50	10	4
Pudding				
Instant, chocolate, made from powder and milk (White Wings, Australia)	47	100	16	7
Instant, vanilla, made from powder and milk (White Wings, Australia)	40	100	16	6
mean of two foods	44	100	16	7
Yoghurt				
Yoghurt, type ▲ (Canada)	36	200	9	3
Low fat yoghurt				
Low fat, fruit, aspartame, Ski™ (Dairy Farmers, Australia)	14	200	13	2
Low fat, fruit, sugar, Ski™ (Dairy Farmers, Australia)	33	200	31	10
Low fat (0.9%), fruit, wild strawberry (Ski d'lite™, Dairy Farmers, Australia)	31	200	30	9
Non-fat yoghurt, sweetened with acesulfame K and Splenda				
Diet Vaalia™, exotic fruits (Pauls, Australia)	23	200	16	4
Diet Vaalia™, mango (Pauls, Australia)	23	200	14	3

[0] indicates that the food has so little carbohydrate that the GI cannot be tested. The GL is therefore 0.
▲ indicates brand not specified

Food	GI Glucose = 100	Nominal serve size (g)	Available carb per serve	GL per serve
Diet Vaalia™, mixed berry (Pauls, Australia)	25	200	13	3
Diet Vaalia™, strawberry (Pauls, Australia)	23	200	13	3
Diet Vaalia™, vanilla (Pauls, Australia)	23	200	13	3
mean of five foods	24	200	14	3
Reduced-fat yoghurt				
Reduced-fat, Vaalia™, apricot & mango (Pauls, Australia)	26	200	30	8
Reduced-fat, Vaalia™, French vanilla (Pauls, Australia)	26	200	10	3
Reduced-fat, Extra-Lite™, strawberry (Pauls, Australia)	28	200	33	9
mean of three foods	27	200	24	7
Yoghurt drink, reduced-fat, Vaalia™, passionfruit (Pauls, Australia)	38	200	29	11
Soy-based dairy product alternatives				
Soy milks (containing maltodextrin)				
Soy milk, full-fat, Original (So Natural, Australia)	44	250	17	8
Soy milk, full-fat, Calciforte (So Natural, Australia)	36	250	18	6
Soy milk, reduced-fat, Light (So Natural, Australia)	44	250	17	8
Soy milk drinks				
Soy smoothie drink, banana, 1% fat (So Natural, Australia)	30	250	22	7
Soy smoothie drink, chocolate hazelnut, 1% fat (So Natural, Australia)	34	250	25	8
mean of two drinks	32	250	23	7
Up & Go™, cocoa malt flavour (Sanitarium, Australia)	43	250	26	11
Up & Go™, original malt flavour (Sanitarium, Australia)	46	250	24	11
mean of two drinks	45	250	25	11
Xpress™, chocolate (So Natural, Australia)	39	250	34	13
Soy yoghurt				
Soy yoghurt, peach and mango, 2% fat, sugar (So Natural, Australia)	50	200	26	13
Tofu-based frozen dessert, chocolate (USA)	115	50	9	10

FRUIT AND FRUIT PRODUCTS

Food	GI Glucose = 100	Nominal serve size (g)	Available carb per serve	GL per serve
Apples, raw				
Apple, ▲ (Denmark)	28	120	13	4
Apple, Braeburn (New Zealand)	32	120	13	4
Apple, ▲ (Canada)	34	120	16	5
Apple, Golden Delicious (Canada)	39	120	16	6

[0] indicates that the food has so little carbohydrate that the GI cannot be tested. The GL is therefore 0.
▲ indicates brand not specified

Food	GI Glucose = 100	Nominal serve size (g)	Available carb per serve	GL per serve
Apple, ▲ (USA)	40	120	16	6
Apple, ▲ (Italy)	44	120	13	6
mean of six studies	38	120	15	6
Apple, dried (Australia)	29	60	34	10
Apple juice				
Apple juice, unsweetened, reconstituted (Berri, Australia)	39	250	25	10
Apple juice, unsweetened (USA)	40	250	29	12
Apple juice, unsweetened (Allens, Canada)	41	250	30	12
mean of three studies	40	250	28	11
Apricots				
Apricots, raw (Italy)	57	120	9	5
Apricots, canned in light syrup (Riviera, Canada)	64	120	19	12
Apricots, dried (Australia)	30	60	27	8
Apricots, dried (Wasco, Canada)	32	60	30	10
mean of two studies	31	60	28	9
Apricot fruit bar, (Mother Earth, New Zealand)	50	50	34	17
Apricot fruit spread, (Glen Ewin, Australia)	55	30	13	7
Apricot Fruity Bitz™ (Blackmores, Australia)	42	15	12	5
Banana, raw				
Banana (Canada)	46	120	25	12
Banana (Italy)	58	120	23	13
Banana (Canada)	58	120	25	15
Banana (Canada)	62	120	25	16
Banana (South Africa)	70	120	23	16
Banana, ripe (all yellow) (USA)	51	120	25	13
Banana, under-ripe (Denmark)	30	120	21	6
Banana, slightly under-ripe (yellow with green sections) (USA)	42	120	25	11
Banana, over-ripe (yellow flecked with brown) (USA)	48	120	25	12
Banana, over-ripe (Denmark)	52	120	20	11
mean of 10 studies	52	120	24	12
Banana, processed fruit fingers, Heinz Kidz™ (Australia)	61	30	20	12
Breadfruit (*Artocarpus altilis*), raw (Australia)	68	120	27	18
Cherries, raw, NS[8] (Canada)	22	120	12	3
Chico (*Zapota zapotilla coville*), raw (Philippines)	40	120	29	12
Cranberry juice cocktail (Ocean Spray, Australia)	52	250	31	16
Cranberry juice cocktail (Ocean Spray, USA)	68	250	35	24
Cranberry juice drink (Ocean Spray®, UK)	56	250	29	16

[0] indicates that the food has so little carbohydrate that the GI cannot be tested. The GL is therefore 0.
▲ indicates brand not specified

Food	GI Glucose = 100	Nominal serve size (g)	Available carb per serve	GL per serve
Custard apple, raw, flesh only (Australia)	54	120	19	10
Dates, dried (Australia)	103	60	40	42
Figs, dried, tenderised (Dessert Maid, Australia)	61	60	26	16
Fruit Cocktail, canned (Delmonte, Canada)	55	120	16	9
Grapefruit, raw (Canada)	25	120	11	3
Grapefruit juice, unsweetened (Sunpac, Canada)	48	250	20	9
Grapes, raw				
Grapes, NS ▲ (Canada)	43	120	17	7
Grapes, NS ▲ (Italy)	49	120	19	9
mean of two studies	46	120	18	8
Grapes, black, Waltham Cross (Australia)	59	120	18	11
Kiwi fruit, raw				
Kiwi fruit, Hayward (New Zealand)	47	120	12	5
Kiwi fruit (Australia)	58	120	12	7
mean of two studies	53	120	12	6
Lychee, canned in syrup and drained, Narcissus brand (China)	79	120	20	16
Mango, raw				
Mango (*Mangifera indica*) (Philippines)	41	120	20	8
Mango (*Mangifera indica*) (Australia)	51	120	15	8
Mango, ripe (*Mangifera indica*) (India)	60	120	15	9
mean of three studies	51	120	17	8
Mango, Frutia™ (Weis, Australia)	42	100	23	10
Marmalade, orange (Australia)	48	30	20	9
Oranges, raw				
Oranges, NS ▲ (Denmark)	31	120	11	3
Oranges, NS ▲ (South Africa)	33	120	10	3
Oranges, NS ▲ (Canada)	40	120	11	4
Oranges, NS ▲ (Italy)	48	120	11	5
Oranges (Sunkist, USA)	48	120	11	5
Oranges NS ▲ (Canada)	51	120	11	6
mean of six studies	42	120	11	5
Orange juice				
Orange juice (Canada)	46	250	26	12
Orange juice, reconstituted (Quelch, Australia)	53	250	18	9
Orange juice, reconstituted from frozen concentrate (USA)	57	250	26	15
mean of three studies	52	250	23	12

[0] indicates that the food has so little carbohydrate that the GI cannot be tested. The GL is therefore 0.
▲ indicates brand not specified

Food	GI Glucose = 100	Nominal serve size (g)	Available carb per serve	GL per serve
Paw paw/papaya, raw				
Paw paw (*Carica papaya*) (Australia)	56	120	8	5
Paw paw, ripe (India)	60	120	29	17
Papaya (*Carica papaya*) (Philippines)	60	120	15	9
mean of three studies	59	120	17	10
Peaches				
Peach, raw (Canada)	28	120	13	4
Peach, raw (Italy)	56	120	8	5
mean of two studies	42	120	11	5
Peach, canned in natural juice (Ardmona, Australia)	30	120	11	3
Peach, canned in natural juice (SPC, Australia)	45	120	11	5
mean of two studies	38	120	11	4
Peach, canned in heavy syrup (Letona, Australia)	58	120	15	9
Peach, canned in light syrup (Delmonte, Canada)	52	120	18	9
Peach, canned in reduced-sugar syrup (SPC, Australia)	62	120	17	11
Pears				
Pear, raw, NS ▲ (Canada)	33	120	13	4
Pear, Winter Nellis, raw (New Zealand)	34	120	12	4
Pear, Bartlett, raw (Canada)	41	120	8	3
Pear, raw NS ▲ (Italy)	42	120	11	4
mean of four studies	38	120	11	4
Pear halves, canned in reduced-sugar syrup, SPC Lite (Australia)	25	120	14	4
Pear halves, canned in natural juice (SPC, Australia)	43	120	13	5
Pear, canned in pear juice, Bartlett (Delmonte, Canada)	44	120	11	5
Pineapple				
Pineapple, raw (Australia)	66	120	10	6
Pineapple (*Ananas comosus*), raw (Philippines)	51	120	16	8
mean of two studies	59	120	13	7
Pineapple juice, unsweetened (Dole, Canada)	46	250	34	15
Plums				
Plum, raw, NS ▲ (Canada)	24	120	14	3
Plum, raw, NS ▲ (Italy)	53	120	11	6
mean of two studies	39	120	12	5
Prunes, pitted (Sunsweet, USA)	29	60	33	10
Raisins (Canada)	64	60	44	28
Rockmelon/Cantaloupe, raw (Australia)	65	120	6	4
Strawberries, fresh, raw (Australia)	40	120	3	1

[0] indicates that the food has so little carbohydrate that the GI cannot be tested. The GL is therefore 0.
▲ indicates brand not specified

Food	GI Glucose = 100	Nominal serve size (g)	Available carb per serve	GL per serve
Strawberry jam	51	30	20	10
Strawberry Real Fruit Bars (Uncle Toby's, Australia)	90	30	26	23
Sultanas	56	60	45	25
Tomato juice, no added sugar (Berri, Australia)	38	250	9	4
Tropical Fruity Bitz™, (Blackmores, Australia)	41	15	11	5
Vitari, wild berry, non-dairy, frozen dessert (Nestlé, Australia)	59	100	21	12
Watermelon, raw (Australia)	72	120	6	4
Wild Berry Fruity Bitz™ (Blackmores, Australia)	35	15	12	4

INFANT FORMULA AND WEANING FOODS

Formula

Food	GI Glucose = 100	Nominal serve size (g)	Available carb per serve	GL per serve
Infasoy™, soy-based, milk-free (Wyeth, Australia)	55	100 mL	7	4
Karicare™ formula with omega oils (Nutricia, New Zealand)	35	100 mL	7	2
Nan-1™ infant formula with iron (Nestlé, Australia)	30	100 mL	8	2
S-26™ infant formula (Wyeth, Australia)	36	100 mL	7	3

Weaning Foods

Food	GI Glucose = 100	Nominal serve size (g)	Available carb per serve	GL per serve
Farex™ baby rice (Heinz, Australia)	95	87	6	6
Robinsons First Tastes from 4 months (Nutricia, UK)				
Apple, apricot and banana cereal	56	75	13	11
Creamed porridge	59	75	9	5
Rice pudding	59	75	11	6
Heinz for Baby from 4 months (Heinz, Australia)				
Chicken and noodles with vegetables, strained	67	120	7	5
Sweetcorn and rice	65	120	15	10

LEGUMES AND NUTS

Baked Beans

Food	GI Glucose = 100	Nominal serve size (g)	Available carb per serve	GL per serve
Baked Beans, canned (Canada)	40			
Baked Beans, canned beans in tomato sauce (Libby, Canada)	56			
mean of two studies	48	150	15	7

Beans, dried, boiled

Food	GI Glucose = 100	Nominal serve size (g)	Available carb per serve	GL per serve
Beans, dried, type NS ▲ (Italy)	36	150	30	11
Beans, dried, type NS ▲ (Italy)	20	150	30	6
mean of two studies	29	150	30	9

[0] indicates that the food has so little carbohydrate that the GI cannot be tested. The GL is therefore 0.
▲ indicates brand not specified

Food	GI Glucose = 100	Nominal serve size (g)	Available carb per serve	GL per serve
Blackeyed beans/peas (Cowpeas), boiled				
Blackeyed beans (Canada)	50	150	30	15
Blackeyed beans (Canada)	33	150	30	10
mean of two studies	42	150	30	13
Butter Beans				
Butter beans (South Africa)	28	150	20	5
Butter beans, dried, cooked (South Africa)	29	150	20	6
Butter beans (Canada)	36	150	20	7
mean of three studies	31	150	20	6
Butter beans, dried, boiled + 5g sucrose (South Africa)	30	150	20	6
Butter beans, dried, boiled + 10g sucrose (South Africa)	31	150	20	6
Butter beans, dried, boiled + 15g sucrose (South Africa)	54	150	20	11
Chickpeas (Garbanzo beans, Bengal gram), boiled				
Chickpeas (*Cicer arietinum Linn*), boiled (Philippines)	10	150	30	3
Chickpeas, dried, boiled (Canada)	31	150	30	9
Chickpeas (Canada)	33	150	30	10
Chickpeas (Canada)	36	150	30	11
mean of four studies	28	150	30	8
Chickpeas, canned in brine (Lancia-Bravo, Canada)	42	150	22	9
Chickpeas, curry, canned (Canasia, Canada)	41	150	16	7
Haricot/navy beans				
Haricot/navy beans, pressure cooked (King Grains, Canada)	29	150	33	9
Haricot/navy beans, dried, boiled (Canada)	30	150	30	9
Haricot/navy beans, boiled (Canada)	31	150	30	9
Haricot/navy beans (King Grains, Canada)	39	150	30	12
Haricot/navy beans, pressure cooked (King Grains, Canada)	59	150	33	19
mean of five studies	38	150	31	12
Kidney Beans				
Kidney/white bean (*Phaseolus vulgaris* Linn), boiled (Philippines)	13	150	25	3
Kidney beans (*Phaseolus vulgaris*) (India)	19	150	25	5
Kidney beans (USA)	23	150	25	6
Kidney beans, dried, boiled (France)	23	150	25	6
Kidney beans (*Phaseolus vulgaris* L.), red, boiled (Sweden)	25	150	25	6
Kidney beans (Canada)	29	150	25	7
Kidney beans, dried, boiled (Canada)	42	150	25	10

[0] indicates that the food has so little carbohydrate that the GI cannot be tested. The GL is therefore 0.
▲ indicates brand not specified

Food	GI Glucose = 100	Nominal serve size (g)	Available carb per serve	GL per serve
Kidney beans (Canada)	46	150	25	11
mean of eight studies	28	150	25	7
Kidney beans (*Phaseolus vulgaris* L.) – autoclaved	34	150	25	8
Kidney beans, canned (Lancia-Bravo, Canada)	52	150	17	9
Kidney beans, soaked 12 h, stored moist 24 h, steamed 1 h (India)	70	150	25	17
Black bean (*Phaseolus vulgaris* Linn), cooked (Philippines)	20	150	25	5
Lentils, type NS				
Lentils, type NS ▲ (USA)	28			
Lentils, type NS ▲ (Canada)	29			
mean of two studies	29	150	18	5
Lentils, green				
Lentils, green, dried, boiled (Canada)	22	150	18	4
Lentils, green, dried, boiled (France)	30	150	18	6
Lentils, green, dried, boiled (Australia)	37	150	14	5
mean of three studies	30	150	17	5
Lentils, green, canned in brine (Lancia-Bravo Foods Ltd., Canada)	52	150	17	9
Lentils, red				
Lentils, red, dried, boiled (Canada)	18	150	18	3
Lentils, red, dried, boiled (Canada)	21	150	18	4
Lentils, red, dried, boiled (Canada)	31	150	18	6
Lentils, red, dried, boiled (Canada)	32	150	18	6
mean of four studies	26	150	18	5
Lima beans, baby, frozen (York, Canada)	32	150	30	10
Marrowfat peas				
Marrowfat peas, dried, boiled (USA)	31			
Marrowfat peas, dried, boiled (Canada)	47			
mean of two studies	39	150	19	7
Mung beans				
Mung bean (*Phaseolus areus* Roxb), boiled (Philippines)	31	150	17	5
Mung bean, fried (Australia)	53			
Mung bean, germinated (Australia)	25	150	17	4
Mung bean, pressure cooked (Australia)	42	150	17	7
Peas, dried, boiled (Australia)	22	150	9	2
Pigeon Pea (*Cajanus cajan* Linn Huth), boiled (Philippines)	22	150	20	4

[0] indicates that the food has so little carbohydrate that the GI cannot be tested. The GL is therefore 0.
▲ indicates brand not specified

Food	GI Glucose = 100	Nominal serve size (g)	Available carb per serve	GL per serve
Pinto beans				
Pinto beans, boiled (Canada)	39	150	26	10
Pinto beans, canned in brine (Lancia-Bravo, Canada)	45	150	22	10
Romano beans (Canada)	46	150	18	8
Soy beans				
Soy beans, boiled (Canada)	15	150	6	1
Soy beans, boiled (Australia)	20	150	6	1
mean of two studies	18	150	6	1
Soy beans, canned (Canada)	14	150	6	1
Split peas, yellow, boiled (Nupack, Canada)	32	150	19	6

MEAL REPLACEMENT PRODUCTS

Food	GI Glucose = 100	Nominal serve size (g)	Available carb per serve	GL per serve
Hazelnut and Apricot bar (Dietworks, Australia)	42	50	22	9
L.E.A.N™ products (Usana, USA)				
L.E.A.N Fibergy™ bar, Harvest Oat	45	50	29	13
Nutrimeal™, drink powder, Dutch Chocolate	26	250	13	3
L.E.A.N (Life long) Nutribar™, Peanut Crunch	30	40	19	6
L.E.A.N (Life long) Nutribar™, Chocolate Crunch	32	40	19	6
mean of two Nutri bars	31	40	19	6
Worldwide Sport Nutrition low-carbohydrate products (USA)				
Designer chocolate, sugar-free	14	35	22	3
Burn-it™ bars				
Chocolate deluxe	29	50	8	2
Peanut butter	23	50	6	1
Pure-protein™ bars				
Chewy choc-chip	30	80	14	4
Chocolate deluxe	38	80	13	5
Peanut butter	22	80	9	2
Strawberry shortcake	43	80	13	6
White chocolate mousse	40	80	15	6
Pure-protein™ cookies				
Choc-chip cookie dough	25	55	11	3
Coconut	42	55	9	4
Peanut butter	37	55	9	3
Ultra pure-protein™ shakes				
Cappuccino	47	250	1	1
Frosty chocolate	37	250	3	1

[0] indicates that the food has so little carbohydrate that the GI cannot be tested. The GL is therefore 0.
▲ indicates brand not specified

Food	GI Glucose = 100	Nominal serve size (g)	Available carb per serve	GL per serve
Strawberry shortcake	42	250	I	I
Vanilla ice cream	32	250	3	I

MIXED MEALS AND CONVENIENCE FOODS

Food	GI Glucose = 100	Nominal serve size (g)	Available carb per serve	GL per serve
Chicken nuggets, frozen, reheated (Australia)	46	100	16	7
Fish Fingers (Canada)	38	100	19	7
Greek lentil stew with a bread roll, home made (Australia)	40	360	37	15
Kugel (Polish dish containing egg noodles, sugar, cheese and raisins) (Israel)	65	150	48	31
Lean Cuisine™, chicken with rice (Nestlé, Australia)	36	400	68	24
Pies, beef, party size (Farmland, Australia)	45	100	27	12

Pizza

Food	GI Glucose = 100	Nominal serve size (g)	Available carb per serve	GL per serve
Pizza, cheese (Pillsbury, Canada)	60	100	27	16
Pizza, plain (Italy)	80	100	27	22
Pizza, Super Supreme, pan (Pizza Hut, Australia)	36	100	24	9
Pizza, Super Supreme, thin and crispy (Pizza Hut, Australia)	30	100	22	7
Pizza, Vegetarian Supreme, thin and crispy (Pizza Hut, Australia)	49	100	25	12
Sausages NS ▲ (Canada)	28	100	3	I
Sirloin chop with mixed vegetables and mashed potato (Australia)	66	360	53	35
Spaghetti bolognaise, home made (Australia)	52	360	48	25
Stirfried vegetables with chicken and rice, home made (Australia)	73	360	75	55

Sushi

Food	GI Glucose = 100	Nominal serve size (g)	Available carb per serve	GL per serve
Sushi, salmon (Australia)	48	100	36	17
Sushi, roasted sea algae, vinegar and rice (Japan)	55	100	37	20
Mean of two studies	52	100	37	19
White boiled rice, grilled beefburger, cheese, and butter (France)	27	440	50	14
White boiled rice, grilled beefburger, cheese and butter (France)	22	440	50	11
Mean in two groups of subjects	25	440	50	13

White bread with toppings

Food	GI Glucose = 100	Nominal serve size (g)	Available carb per serve	GL per serve
White bread, butter, regular cow's milk cheese and fresh cucumber (Sweden)	55	200	68	38

[0] indicates that the food has so little carbohydrate that the GI cannot be tested. The GL is therefore 0.
▲ indicates brand not specified

Food	GI Glucose = 100	Nominal serve size (g)	Available carb per serve	GL per serve
White bread, butter, yoghurt and pickled cucumber (Sweden)	39	200	28	11
White bread with butter (Canada)	59	100	48	29
White bread with skim milk cheese (Canada)	55	100	47	26
White bread with butter and skim milk cheese (Canada)	62	100	38	23
White/wholemeal bread with peanut butter (Canada)	51	100	44	23
White/wholemeal bread with peanut butter (Canada)	67	100	44	30
mean of two studies	59	100	44	26

NUTS

Food	GI Glucose = 100	Nominal serve size (g)	Available carb per serve	GL per serve
Almonds	[0]	50	0	0
Brazil nuts	[0]	50	0	0
Cashew nuts, salted (Coles Supermarkets, Australia)	22	50	13	3
Hazelnuts	[0]	50	0	0
Macadamia	[0]	50	0	0
Pecan	[0]	50	0	0

Peanuts

Food	GI Glucose = 100	Nominal serve size (g)	Available carb per serve	GL per serve
Peanuts, crushed (South Africa)	7	50	4	0
Peanuts (Canada)	13	50	7	1
Peanuts (Mexico)	23	50	7	2
mean of three studies	14	50	6	1
Walnuts	[0]	50	0	0

NUTRITIONAL SUPPORT PRODUCTS

Food	GI Glucose = 100	Nominal serve size (g)	Available carb per serve	GL per serve
Choice DM™, vanilla (Mead Johnson, USA)	23	237mL	24	6
Enercal Plus™ (Wyeth-Ayerst, USA)	61	237mL	40	19
Ensure™ (Abbott, Australia)	50	237mL	40	19
Ensure™, vanilla (Abbott, Australia)	48	250mL	34	16
Ensure™ bar, chocolate fudge brownie (Abbott, Australia)	43	38	20	8
Ensure Plus™, vanilla (Abbott, Australia)	40	237mL	47	19
Ensure Pudding™, vanilla (Abbott, USA)	36	113	26	9
Glucerna™, vanilla (Abbott, USA)	31	237mL	23	7
Jevity™ (Abbott, Australia)	48	237mL	36	17
Resource Diabetic™, vanilla (Novartis, USA)	34	237mL	23	8
Resource Diabetic™, chocolate (Novartis, New Zealand)	16	237mL	41	19
Resource™ thickened orange juice (Novartis, New Zealand)	47	237mL	39	21

[0] indicates that the food has so little carbohydrate that the GI cannot be tested. The GL is therefore 0.
▲ indicates brand not specified

Food	GI Glucose = 100	Nominal serve size (g)	Available carb per serve	GL per serve
Resource™ thickened orange juice (Novartis, New Zealand)	54	237mL	36	14
Resource™ fruit beverage, peach flavour (Novartis, New Zealand)	40	237mL	41	13
Sustagen™, Dutch Chocolate (Mead Johnson, Australia)	31	250mL	41	13
Sustagen™ Hospital with extra fibre (Mead Johnson, Australia)	33	250mL	44	15
Sustagen™ Instant Pudding, vanilla (Mead Johnson, Australia)	27	250	47	13
Ultracal™ with fiber (Mead Johnson, USA)	40	237 mL	29	12

PASTA and NOODLES
Capellini (Primo, Canada)	45	180	45	20
Corn pasta, gluten-free (Orgran, Australia)	78	180	42	32

Fettucine, egg
Fettucine, egg	32	180	46	15
Fettucine, egg (Mother Earth, Australia)	47	180	46	22
mean of two studies	40	180	46	18
Gluten-free pasta, maize starch, boiled (UK)	54	180	42	22
Gnocchi, NS ▲ (Latina, Australia)	68	180	48	33

Instant noodles
Instant 'two-minute' noodles, Maggi® (Australia)	46			
Instant 'two-minute' noodles, Maggi® (New Zealand)	48			
Instant noodles (Mr Noodle, Canada)	47			
mean of three studies	47	180	40	19

Linguine
Thick, durum wheat, white, fresh (Sweden)	43	180	48	21
Thick, fresh, durum wheat flour (Sweden)	48	180	48	23
mean of two studies	46	180	48	22
Thin, durum wheat (Sweden)	49	180	48	23
Thin, fresh, durum wheat flour (Sweden)	61	180	48	29
Thin, fresh, durum wheat with 39% w/w egg (Sweden)	45	180	41	18
Thin, fresh, 30% w/w egg (Sweden)	53	180	41	22
mean of four studies	52	180	45	23

Mung bean noodles
Lungkow beanthread noodles (National Cereals, China)	26	180	45	12

[0] indicates that the food has so little carbohydrate that the GI cannot be tested. The GL is therefore 0.
▲ indicates brand not specified

Food	GI Glucose = 100	Nominal serve size (g)	Available carb per serve	GL per serve
Mung bean noodles (Longkou beanthread) (Yantai, China)	39	180	45	18
mean of two studies	33			
Macaroni				
Macaroni, plain, boiled 5 min (Lancia-Bravo, Canada)	45	180	49	22
Macaroni, plain, boiled (Turkey)	48	180	49	23
mean of two studies	47	180	48	23
Macaroni and Cheese, boxed (Kraft, Canada)	64	180	51	32
Ravioli (Australia)	39	180	38	15
Rice noodles/pasta				
Rice noodles, dried, boiled (Thai World, Thailand)	61	180	39	23
Rice noodles, freshly made, boiled (Sydney, Australia)	40	180	39	15
Rice pasta, brown, boiled 16 min (Rice Growers, Australia)	92	180	38	35
Rice and maize pasta, gluten-free, Ris'O'Mais (Orgran, Australia)	76	180	49	37
Rice vermicelli, Kongmoon (China)	58	180	39	22
Spaghetti				
Spaghetti, gluten-free, canned in tomato sauce (Orgran, Australia)	68	220	27	19
Spaghetti, protein enriched, boiled 7 min (Catelli, Canada)	27	180	52	14
Spaghetti, white, boiled 5 min				
Boiled 5 min (Lancia-Bravo, Canada)	32	180	48	15
Boiled 5 min (Canada)	34	180	48	16
Boiled 5 min (Canada)	40	180	48	19
Boiled 5 min (Middle East)	44	180	48	21
mean of four studies	38	180	48	18
Spaghetti, white or type NS ▲, boiled 10-15 min				
White, durum wheat, boiled 10 min (Barilla, Italy)	58	180	48	28
White, durum wheat flour, boiled 12 min (Starhushålls, Sweden)	47	180	48	23
White, durum wheat flour, boiled 12 min (Sweden)	53	180	48	25
Boiled 15 min (Lancia-Bravo, Canada)	32	180	48	15
Boiled 15 min (Lancia-Bravo, Canada)	36	180	48	17
Boiled 15 min (Canada)	41	180	48	20
White, boiled 15 min in salted water (Unico, Canada)	44	180	48	21
mean of seven studies	44	180	48	21

[0] indicates that the food has so little carbohydrate that the GI cannot be tested. The GL is therefore 0.
▲ indicates brand not specified

Food	GI Glucose = 100	Nominal serve size (g)	Available carb per serve	GL per serve
Spaghetti, white or type NS▲, boiled 20 min				
White, durum wheat, boiled 20 min (Australia)	58	180	44	26
Durum wheat, boiled 20 min (USA)	64	180	43	27
mean of two studies	61	180	44	27
Spaghetti, white, boiled				
White (Denmark)	33	180	48	16
White, durum wheat (Catelli, Canada)	34	180	48	16
White (Australia)	38	180	44	17
White (Canada)	42	180	48	20
White (Canada)	48	180	48	23
White (Vetta, Australia)	49	180	44	22
White (Canada)	50	180	48	24
mean of seven studies	42	180	47	20
Spaghetti, white, durum wheat semolina (Panzani, France)				
Boiled for 11 min	59	180	48	28
Boiled for 16.5 min	65	180	48	31
Boiled for 22 min	46	180	48	22
mean of three cooking times	57	180	48	27
Spaghetti, wholemeal, boiled				
Wholemeal (USA)	32	180	44	14
Wholemeal (Canada)	42	180	40	17
mean of two studies	37	180	42	16
Spirali, durum wheat, white, boiled (Vetta, Australia)	43	180	44	19
Split pea and soy pasta shells, gluten-free (Orgran, Australia)	29	180	31	9
Star Pastina, white, boiled 5 minutes (Lancia-Bravo, Canada)	38	180	48	18
Tortellini, cheese (Stouffer, Canada)	50	180	21	10
Udon noodles, plain, reheated 5 min (Australia)	62	180	48	30
Vermicelli, white, boiled (Australia)	35	180	44	16
PROTEIN FOODS				
Beef	[0]	120	0	0
Cheese	[0]	120	0	0
Eggs	[0]	120	0	0
Fish	[0]	120	0	0
Lamb	[0]	120	0	0
Pork	[0]	120	0	0
Salami	[0]	120	0	0

[0] indicates that the food has so little carbohydrate that the GI cannot be tested. The GL is therefore 0.
▲ indicates brand not specified

Food	GI Glucose = 100	Nominal serve size (g)	Available carb per serve	GL per serve
Shellfish (prawns, crab, lobster etc)	[0]	120	0	0
Tuna	[0]	120	0	0
Veal	[0]	120	0	0

SNACK FOODS AND CONFECTIONERY

Food	GI	Serve	Carb	GL
Burger Rings™ (Smith's, Australia)	90	50	31	28

Chocolate, milk, plain

Food	GI	Serve	Carb	GL
Chocolate, milk, plain with sucrose (Belgium)	34	50	22	7
Chocolate, milk (Cadbury's, Australia)	49	50	30	14
Chocolate, milk, Dove® (Mars, Australia)	45	50	30	13
Chocolate, milk (Nestlé, Australia)	42	50	31	13
mean of four studies	43	50	28	12
Chocolate, milk, plain, low-sugar with maltitol (Belgium)	35	50	22	8
Chocolate, white, Milky Bar® (Nestlé, Australia)	44	50	29	13

Corn chips

Food	GI	Serve	Carb	GL
Corn chips, plain, salted (Doritos™, Australia)	42	50	25	11
Nachips™ (Old El Paso, Canada)	74	50	29	21
mean of three studies	63	50	26	17

Fruit Bars

Food	GI	Serve	Carb	GL
Apricot filled fruit bar (Mother Earth, New Zealand)	50	50	34	17
Heinz Kidz™ Fruit Fingers, banana (Heinz, Australia)	61	30	20	12
Real Fruit Bars, strawberry (Uncle Toby's, Australia)	90	30	26	23
Roll-Ups® (Uncle Toby's, Australia)	99	30	25	24

Fruity Bitz™, vitamin and mineral enriched dried fruit snacks

Food	GI	Serve	Carb	GL
Fruity Bitz™, apricot (Blackmores, Australia)	42	15	12	5
Fruity Bitz™, berry (Blackmores, Australia)	35	15	12	4
Fruity Bitz™, tropical (Blackmores, Australia)	41	15	11	5
mean of three flavours	39	15	12	4

Jelly beans

Food	GI	Serve	Carb	GL
Jelly beans, assorted colors (Australia)	80			
Jelly beans, assorted colors (Australia)	76			
mean of two studies	78	30	28	22
Kudos Whole Grain Bars, chocolate chip (USA)	62	50	32	20
Life Savers®, peppermint candy (Nestlé, Australia)	70	30	30	21
M & M's®, peanut (Australia)	33	30	17	6

Mars Bar®

Food	GI	Serve	Carb	GL
Mars Bar® (Australia)	62	60	40	25

[0] indicates that the food has so little carbohydrate that the GI cannot be tested. The GL is therefore 0.
▲ indicates brand not specified

Food	GI Glucose = 100	Nominal serve size (g)	Available carb per serve	GL per serve
Mars Bar® (USA)	68	60	40	27
mean of two studies	65	60	40	26
Muesli bar containing dried fruit (Uncle Toby's, Australia)	61	30	21	13
Nougat, Jijona (La Fama, Spain)	32	30	12	4
Nutella®, chocolate hazelnut spread (Australia)	33	20	12	4
Nuts				
Cashew nuts, salted (Coles Supermarkets, Australia)	22	50	13	3
Peanuts				
Peanuts, crushed (South Africa)	7	50	4	0
Peanuts (Canada)	13	50	7	1
Peanuts (Mexico)	23	50	7	2
mean of three studies	14	50	6	1
Popcorn				
Popcorn, plain, cooked in microwave oven (Green's, Australia)	55	20	11	6
Popcorn, plain, cooked in microwave oven (Uncle Toby's, Australia)	89	20	11	10
mean of two studies	72	20	11	8
Pop Tarts™, double choc (Kellogg's, Australia)	70	50	35	24
Potato crisps				
Potato crisps, plain, salted (Arnott's, Australia)	57	50	18	10
Potato crisps, plain, salted (Canada)	51	50	24	12
mean of two studies	54	50	21	11
Pretzels, (Parker's, Australia)	83	30	20	16
Skittles® (Australia)	70	50	45	32
Snack bars				
Snack bar, Apple Cinnamon (Con Agra, USA)	40	50	29	12
Snack bar, Peanut Butter & Choc-Chip (USA)	37	50	27	10
Snickers Bar®				
Snickers Bar® (Australia)	41	60	36	15
Snickers Bar® (USA)	68	60	34	23
mean of two studies	55	60	35	19
Twisties™ (Smith's, Australia)	74	50	29	22
Twix® Cookie Bar, caramel (USA)	44	60	39	17

[0] indicates that the food has so little carbohydrate that the GI cannot be tested. The GL is therefore 0.
▲ indicates brand not specified

Food	GI Glucose = 100	Nominal serve size (g)	Available carb per serve	GL per serve
SPORTS BARS				
Power Bar®				
Power Bar®, chocolate (USA)	58			
Power Bar®, chocolate (USA)	53			
mean of two studies	56	65	42	24
Ironman PR bar®, chocolate (USA)	39	65	26	10
SOUPS				
Black Bean (Wil-Pack, USA)	64	250	27	17
Green Pea, canned (Campbell's, Canada)	66	250	41	27
Lentil, canned (Unico, Canada)	44	250	21	9
Minestrone, Country Ladle™ (Campbell's, Australia)	39	250	18	7
Noodle soup (Turkish soup with stock and noodles)	1	250	9	0
Split Pea (Wil-Pak, USA)	60	250	27	16
Tarhana soup (Turkish soup)	20	–	–	–
Tomato soup (Canada)	38	250	17	6
SUGARS AND SUGAR ALCOHOLS				
Blue Agave cactus nectar, high-fructose				
Organic Agave Cactus Nectar, light, 90% fructose (Western Commerce, USA)	11	10	8	1
Organic Agave Cactus Nectar, light, 97% fructose (Western Commerce, USA)	10	10	8	1
Fructose				
25g portion (Canada)	11			
50g portion (Canada)	12			
50g portion	20			
50g portion	21			
50g portion (USA)	24			
25g portion, fed with oats	25			
mean of six studies	19	10	10	2
Glucose (dextrose)				
mean of 11 studies	99	10	10	10
Glucose consumed with 3 g American ginseng				
mean in two groups of subjects	78	10	10	8
Glucose consumed with gum/fibre				
15 g apple and orange fibre (FITA, Australia)	79	10	8	6
14.5 g guar gum	62	10	10	6

[0] indicates that the food has so little carbohydrate that the GI cannot be tested. The GL is therefore 0.
▲ indicates brand not specified

Food	GI Glucose = 100	Nominal serve size (g)	Available carb per serve	GL per serve
14.5 g oat gum (78% oat ß-glucan)	57	10	10	6
20 g acacia gum	85	10	10	9
Honey				
Locust honey (Romania)	32	25	21	7
Yellow box (Australia)	35	25	18	6
Stringy Bark (Australia)	44	25	21	9
Red Gum (Australia)	46	25	18	8
Iron Bark (Australia)	48	25	15	7
Yapunya (Australia)	52	25	17	9
Pure (Capilano, Australia)	58	25	21	12
Commercial Blend (Australia)	62	25	18	11
Salvation Jane (Australia)	64	25	15	10
Commercial Blend (Australia)	72	25	13	9
Honey NS ▲ (Canada)	87	25	21	18
mean of 11 types of honey	55	25	18	10
Lactose				
mean of three studies	46	10	10	5
Maltose	105	10	10	11
Sucrose				
mean of 8 studies	61	10	10	6
Sugar alcohols and alternative sweeteners				
Lactitol				
mean of two studies	2	10	10	0
Litesse				
Litesse II, (Danisco, UK)	7	10	10	1
Litesse III (Danisco, UK)	4	10	10	0
Maltitol-based sweeteners or bulking agents				
Malbit CR (87% maltitol) (Cerestar, Belgium)	30	10	10	3
Maltidex 100 (> 72% maltitol) (Cerestar, Belgium)	44	10	10	4
Malbit CH (99% maltitol) (Cerestar, Belgium)	73	10	10	7
Maltidex 200 (50% maltitol) (Cerestar, Belgium)	89	10	10	9
Xylitol				
mean of two studies	8	10	10	1
VEGETABLES				
Artichokes (Jerusalem)	[0]	80	0	0
Avocado	[0]	80	0	0

[0] indicates that the food has so little carbohydrate that the GI cannot be tested. The GL is therefore 0.
▲ indicates brand not specified

Food	GI Glucose = 100	Nominal serve size (g)	Available carb per serve	GL per serve
Beetroot (Canada)	64	80	7	5
Bokchoy	[0]	80	0	0
Broad beans (Canada)	79	80	11	9
Broccoli	[0]	80	0	0
Cabbage	[0]	80	0	0
Carrots				
Carrots, raw (Romania)	16	80	8	1
Carrots, peeled, boiled (Australia)	32	80	5	1
Carrots, peeled, boiled (Australia)	49	80	5	2
Carrots, NS ▲ (Canada)	92	80	6	5
mean of four studies	47	80	6	3
Cassava, boiled, with salt (Kenya, Africa)	46	100	27	12
Capsicum	[0]	80	0	0
Cauliflower	[0]	80	0	0
Celery	[0]	80	0	0
Corn (sweet)				
Sweet corn, 'Honey & Pearl' variety (New Zealand)	37	80	16	6
Sweet corn on the cob, boiled (Australia)	48	80	16	8
Sweet corn (Canada)	59	80	18	11
Sweet corn, boiled (USA)	60	80	18	11
Sweet corn (South Africa)	62	80	18	11
mean of five studies	54	80	17	9
Sweet corn, diet-pack, (USA)	46	80	14	7
Sweet corn, frozen (Canada)	47	80	15	7
Cucumber	[0]	80	0	0
French beans (runner beans)	[0]	80	0	0
Green peas				
Peas, frozen, boiled (Canada)	39	80	7	3
Peas, frozen, boiled (Canada)	51	80	7	4
Peas, green (*Pisum sativum*) (India)	54	80	7	4
mean of three studies	48	80	7	3
Leafy vegetables (spinach, rocket etc)	[0]	80	0	0
Lettuce	[0]	80	0	0
Parsnips	97	80	12	12
POTATO				
Baked potato				
Ontario, white, baked in skin (Canada)	60	150	30	18

[0] indicates that the food has so little carbohydrate that the GI cannot be tested. The GL is therefore 0.
▲ indicates brand not specified

Food	GI Glucose = 100	Nominal serve size (g)	Available carb per serve	GL per serve
Baked, Russet Burbank potato				
Russet, baked without fat (Canada)	56			
Russet, baked without fat, 45–60 min (USA)	78			
Russet, baked without fat (USA)	94			
Russet, baked without fat (USA)	111			
mean of four studies	85	150	30	26
Boiled potato				
Desiree (Australia)	101	150	17	17
Nardine (New Zealand)	70	150	25	18
Ontario (Canada)	58	150	27	16
Pontiac (Australia)	88	150	18	16
Prince Edward Island (Canada)	63	150	18	11
Sebago (Australia)	87	150	17	14
Type NS ▲ (Kenya)	24	150	28	7
White (Romania)	41	150	30	12
White (Canada)	54	150	27	15
Type NS ▲ (India)	76	150	34	26
Type NS ▲ refrigerated, reheated (India)	23	150	34	8
Canned potato				
Prince Edward Island (Cobi Foods, Canada)	61	150	18	11
New (Edgell's, Australia)	65	150	18	12
mean of two studies	63	150	18	11
French fries				
French fries, frozen and reheated (Cavendish Farms, Canada)	75	150	29	22
Instant mashed potato				
Instant (France)	74			
Instant (Canada)	80			
Instant (Edgell's, Australia)	86			
Instant (Carnation, Canada)	86			
Instant (Canada)	88			
Instant (USA)	97			
mean of six studies	85	150	20	17
Mashed potato				
Type NS ▲ (Canada)	67			
Type NS ▲ (South Africa)	71			
Type NS ▲ (France)	83			
Prince Edward Island, (Canada)	73	150	18	13

[0] indicates that the food has so little carbohydrate that the GI cannot be tested. The GL is therefore 0.
▲ indicates brand not specified

Food	GI Glucose = 100	Nominal serve size (g)	Available carb per serve	GL per serve
Pontiac (Australia)	91	150	20	18
mean of five studies	92	150	20	18
Microwaved potato				
Pontiac, peeled and microwaved on high for 6–7.5 min (Australia)	79	150	18	14
Type NS ▲, microwaved (USA)	82	150	33	27
New potato				
New (Canada)	47			
New (Canada)	54			
New (Canada)	70			
New (Australia)	78			
mean of four studies	62	150	21	13
Steamed potato				
Potato, peeled, steamed (India)	65	150	27	18
Potato dumplings (Italy)	52	150	45	24
Sweet potato				
Sweet potato, *Ipomoea batatas* (Australia)	44	150	25	11
Sweet potato, ▲ (Canada)	48	150	34	16
Sweet potato (Canada)	59	150	30	18
Sweet potato, kumara (New Zealand)	77	150	25	19
Sweet potato, kumara (New Zealand)	78	150	25	20
mean of five studies	61	150	28	17
Pumpkin (South Africa)	75	80	4	3
Squash	[0]	80	0	0
Swede				
Swede (rutabaga) (Canada)	72	150	10	7
Tapioca				
Tapioca boiled with milk (General Mills, Canada)	81	250	18	14
Tapioca (*Manihot utilissima*), steamed 1 h (India)	70	250	18	12
Taro				
Taro (*Colocasia esculenta*), boiled (Australia)	54			
Taro, boiled (New Zealand)	56			
mean of two studies	55	150	8	4
Tomato juice, canned, no added sugar (Berri, Australia)	38	250	9	4
Yam				
Yam, peeled, boiled (New Zealand)	25			
Yam, peeled, boiled (New Zealand)	35			

[0] indicates that the food has so little carbohydrate that the GI cannot be tested. The GL is therefore 0.
▲ indicates brand not specified

Food	GI Glucose = 100	Nominal serve size (g)	Available carb per serve	GL per serve
Yam (Canada)	51			
mean of three studies	37	150	36	13

INDIGENOUS OR ETHNIC FOODS

AFRICAN

Food	GI	Nominal	Carb	GL
Brown beans (South Africa)	24	50 (dry)	25	6
Cassava, boiled (Kenya)	46	100	27	12
Ga kenkey, prepared from fermented cornmeal (Ghana)	12	150	13	7
Gari, roasted cassava dough (*Manihot utilissima*) (Ghana)	56	100	27	15
Gram dhal (South Africa)	5	50 (dry)	29	1
Maize meal porridge (South Africa)	71	50 (dry)	36	25
Maize meal porridge (South Africa)	74	50 (dry)	40	30
Maize meal porridge (Kenya)	109	50 (dry)	38	41
M'fino/Morogo, wild greens (South Africa)	68	120	50	34
Millet flour porridge (Kenya)	107	–	–	–
Unripe plantain (*Musa paradisiaca*) (Ghana)	40	120 (raw)	34	13
Yam (*Dyscoria species*) (Ghana)	66	150	36	23

ARABIC AND TURKISH

Food	GI	Nominal	Carb	GL
Hummus (chickpea salad dip)	6	30	5	0
Kibbeh saynieh (made with lamb and burghul)	61	120	15	9
Lebanese roll (bread, hummus, falafel and tabbouli)	86	120	45	39
Majadra (Syrian, lentils and rice)	24	250	41	10
Moroccan couscous (stew of semolina, chickpeas and vegetables)	58	250	29	17
Stuffed grapevine leaves (rice and lamb stuffing, tomato sauce)	30	100	15	5
Tarhana soup (wheat flour, yoghurt, tomato, green pepper)	20	–	–	–
Turkish bread, white wheat flour	87	30	17	15
Turkish bread, whole wheat	49	30	16	8
Turkish noodle soup	1	250	9	0

ASIAN

Food	GI	Nominal	Carb	GL
Broken rice, white (Thailand)	86	150	43	37
Butter rice (warm white rice and butter) (Japan)	79	150	51	40
Curry rice (Japan)	67	150	61	41
Curry rice with cheese (Japan)	55	150	49	27
Glutinous rice (Thailand)	98	150	32	31
Glutinous rice (Japan)	86	150	65	55
mean of two studies	92	150	48	44

[0] indicates that the food has so little carbohydrate that the GI cannot be tested. The GL is therefore 0.
▲ indicates brand not specified

Food	GI Glucose = 100	Nominal serve size (g)	Available carb per serve	GL per serve
Glutinous rice ball with cut glutinous cake (mochi) (Japan)	48	75	28	14
Glutinous rice cake with dried algae (Japan)	83	75	39	32
Glutinous rice flour, instant, with roasted soybean (Japan)	65	100	41	27
Jasmine rice (Thailand)	109	150	42	46
Low-protein white rice with dried algae (Japan)	70	150	60	42
Lungkow beanthread (China)	26	180	45	12
Lychee, canned in syrup, drained (China)	79	120	20	16
Mung bean noodles, dried, boiled (China)	39	180	45	18
Non-glutaminous rice flour, as drink (Japan)	68	100	50	34
Rice cracker, plain (Sakada, Japan)	91	30	25	23
Rice gruel with dried algae (Japan)	81	250	19	15
Rice noodles, dried, boiled (Thailand)	61	180	39	23
Rice noodles, fresh, boiled (Australia)	40	180	39	15
Rice vermicelli, Kongmoon (China)	58	180	39	22
Roasted rice ball (Japan)	77	75	27	21
Salted rice ball (Japan)	80	75	26	20
Soba noodles, instant, reheated (Japan)	46	180	49	22
Stirfried vegetables, chicken and rice (Australia)	73	360	75	55
Sushi, salmon (Australia)	48	100	36	17
Sushi, roasted algae, vinegar and rice (Japan)	55	100	37	20
mean of two studies	52	100	37	19
Udon noodles, fresh (Australia)	62	180	48	30
Udon noodles, instant, with sauce and fried bean curd (Japan)	48	180	47	23
mean of two studies	55	180	48	26
White rice, dried algae and milk (Japan)	56	300	47	26
White rice with dried fish strip (okaka) (Japan)	79	150	50	40
White rice with fermented soybean (natto) (Japan)	56	150	43	24
White rice with instant miso soup (Japan)	61	150	47	29
White rice with low fat milk (Japan)	69	300	47	32
White rice and yoghurt (Japan)	59	150	32	19
White rice with pickled vinegar and cucumber (Japan)	63	150	43	27
White rice topped with raw egg and soy sauce (Japan)	72	150	36	26
White rice with roasted ground soybean (Japan)	56	150	51	29
White rice with salted dried plum (umeboshi) (Japan)	80	150	49	39
White rice with algae rolled in sheet of toasted algae (Japan)	77	150	51	39

[0] indicates that the food has so little carbohydrate that the GI cannot be tested. The GL is therefore 0.
▲ indicates brand not specified

Food	GI Glucose = 100	Nominal serve size (g)	Available carb per serve	GL per serve
ASIAN INDIAN				
Amaranth, *Amaranthus esculentum*, popped, with milk	97	30	19	18
Bajra (*Penniseteum typhoideum*) as bread	55			
Bajra (*Penniseteum typhoideum*)	49			
Bajra (*Penniseteum typhoideum*)	67			
mean of three studies	57	75 (dry)	50	29
Banana, (*Musa sapientum*), Nendra, unripe, steamed 1 h	70	120	45	31
Barley (*Hordeum vulgare*) ·	48			
Barley (*Hordeum vulgare*)	37			
mean of two studies	43	150	37	16
Bengal gram dhal, chickpea	11	150	36	4
Black gram dhal (*Phaseolus mungo*)	43	150	18	8
Chapatti				
Chapatti, wheat flour with bottle gourd and tomato curry	66	60	30	20
Chapatti, amaranth flour with bottle gourd and tomato curry	76	60	30	23
Chapatti, baisen	27	–	–	–
Chapatti, bajra	67	–	–	–
Chapatti, bajra	49	–	–	–
Chapatti, barley	37	–	–	–
Chapatti, barley	48	–	–	–
Chapatti, maize (*Zea mays*)	64	–	–	–
Chapatti, maize (*Zea mays*)	59	–	–	–
Chapatti, wheat, moth bean and bengal gram	66	60	38	25
Chapatti, popped wheat, moth bean and bengal gram	40	60	36	14
Chapatti, roller dried wheat, moth bean and bengal gram	60	60	38	23
Chapatti, wheat flour, thin, with green gram (*Phaseolus aureus*) dhal	44	200	50	22
Cheela (thin savoury pancake made from legume flour batter)				
Cheela, bengal gram (*Cicer arietinum*)	42	150	28	12
Cheela, bengal gram (*Cicer arietinum*), fermented batter	36	150	28	10
Cheela, green gram (*Phaseolus aureus*)	45	150	26	12
Cheela, green gram (*Phaseolus aureus*), fermented batter	38	150	26	10
Dhokla, leavened, fermented, steamed cake	35			
Dhokla, leavened, fermented, steamed cake	31			
mean in two groups of subjects	33	100	20	6

[0] indicates that the food has so little carbohydrate that the GI cannot be tested. The GL is therefore 0.
▲ indicates brand not specified

Food	GI Glucose = 100	Nominal serve size (g)	Available carb per serve	GL per serve
Dosai (parboiled rice, fermented and fried)	77	150	39	30
Dosai (parboiled rice, fermented and fried)	55	150	39	22
mean in two groups of subjects	66	150	39	26
Green gram, (*Phaseolus aureus*)	38	150	17	6
Green gram, with varagu (*Paspalum scorbiculatum*)	57	80 (dry)	50	29
Green gram dhal with varagu (*Paspalum scorbiculatum*)	78	78 (dry)	50	39
Horse gram (*Dolichos biflorus*)	51	150	29	15
Idli (rice + black dhal)	77	250	52	40
Idli (rice + black dhal)	60	250	52	31
mean in two groups of subjects	69	250	52	36
Jowar, bread from Jowar flour (*Sorghum vulgare*)	77	70 (dry)	50	39
Laddu (popped amaranth, foxtail millet, legume flour, fenugreek)	24			
Laddu (popped amaranth, foxtail millet, legume flour, fenugreek)	29			
mean in two groups of subjects	27	50	31	8
Lentil and cauliflower curry with rice (Australia)	60	360	51	31
Millet/Ragi, (*Eleucine coracana*), 1 h	68	150	34	23
Millet/Ragi (*Eleucine coracana*)	84	70 (dry)	50	42
Millet/Ragi (*Eleucine coracana*) flour eaten as roasted bread	104	70 (dry)	50	52
mean of two studies	94	70	50	47
Pongal (rice and roasted green gram dhal)	90			
Pongal (rice and roasted green gram dhal)	45			
mean in two groups of subjects	68	250	52	35
Poori with potato palya	82			
Poori with potato palya	57			
mean in two groups of subjects	70	150	41	28
Rajmah, *Phaseolus vulgaris*	19	150	30	6
Rice, with bottle gourd and tomato curry	69	150	38	26
Semolina				
Semolina (*Triticum aestivum*), steamed	55	67 (dry)	50	28
Semolina (*Triticum aestivum*), pre-roasted	76	67 (dry)	50	38
Semolina (*Triticum aestivum*) with black gram dhal	46	71 (dry)	50	23
Semolina (*Triticum aestivum*) with green gram dhal	62	71 (dry)	50	31
Semolina (*Triticum aestivum*) with bengal gram dhal	54	71 (dry)	50	27
Tapioca (*Manihot utilissima*), steamed 1 h	70	250	18	12
Varagu (*Paspalum scorbiculatum*)	68	76 (dry)	50	34
Upittu (roasted semolina and onions)	67			
Upittu (roasted semolina and onions)	69			

[0] indicates that the food has so little carbohydrate that the GI cannot be tested. The GL is therefore 0.
▲ indicates brand not specified

Food	GI Glucose = 100	Nominal serve size (g)	Available carb per serve	GL per serve
mean in two groups of subjects	68	150	42	28
Uppuma kedgeree (millet, legumes, fenugreek seeds)	18			
Uppuma kedgeree (millet, legumes, fenugreek seeds)	19			
mean in two groups of subjects	18	150	33	6
AUSTRALIAN ABORIGINAL				
Acacia aneura, mulga seed, roasted, wet ground to paste	8	50	17	1
Acacia coriacea, desert oak, seed bread	46	75	24	11
Araucaria bidwillii, bunya tree nut, baked 10 min	47	50	16	7
Bush honey, sugar bag	43	30	25	11
Castanospermum australe, blackbean seed	8	50	9	1
Dioscorea bulbifera, cheeky yam	34	150	36	12
Macrozamia communis, cycad palm seed	40	50	25	10
PACIFIC ISLANDER				
Breadfruit (*Artocarpus altilis*) (Australia)	68	120	27	18
Banana/plantain, green				
Green banana, boiled (New Zealand)	38	120	21	8
Sweet Potato				
Sweet potato, *Ipomoea batatas* (Australia)	44	150	25	11
Sweet potato, kumara (New Zealand)	77	150	25	19
Sweet potato, kumara (New Zealand)	78	150	25	20
mean of three studies	66	150	25	17
Taro				
Taro (*Colocasia esculenta*) peeled, boiled (Australia)	54			
Taro, peeled, boiled (New Zealand)	56			
mean of two studies	55	150	8	4
Yam				
Yam, peeled, boiled (New Zealand)	25			
Yam, peeled, boiled (New Zealand)	35			
mean of two groups of subjects	30	150	36	13
ISRAELI				
Melawach	61			
Melawach	71			
mean of two studies	66	115	53	35
Melawach + 15 g locust bean (*Ceratonia siliqua*) fibre (soluble)	31	130	53	16
Melawach + 15 g maize cob fibre (insoluble)	59	130	53	31
Melawach + 15 g lupin (*Lupinus albus*) fibre	72	130	53	38

[0] indicates that the food has so little carbohydrate that the GI cannot be tested. The GL is therefore 0.
▲ indicates brand not specified

Food	GI Glucose = 100	Nominal serve size (g)	Available carb per serve	GL per serve
PIMA INDIAN				
Acorns, stewed with venison (*Quercus emoryi*)	6	16	100	61
Cactus jam (*Stenocereus thurberi*)	91	30	20	18
Corn hominy (*Zea mays*)	40	150	30	12
Fruit Leather (*Stenocereus thurberi*)	70	30	24	17
Lima beans broth (*Phaseolus lunatus*)	36	250	32	12
Mesquite cakes (*Prosopis velutina*)	25	60	4	1
Tortilla (*Zea mays* and Olneya tesota)	38	60	25	9
White teparies broth (*Phaseolus acutifolius*)	31	250	32	10
Yellow teparies broth (*Phaseolus acutifolius*)	29	250	26	8
SOUTH AMERICAN				
Arepa, corn bread cake, made with corn flour (Mexico)	72	100	43	31
Arepa, made from ordinary dehulled dent corn flour (25% amylose)	81	100	43	3
Arepa, made from dehulled high-amylose (70%) corn flour	44	100	25	11
Black Beans	30	150	23	7
Brown Beans	38	150	25	9
Corn tortilla (Mexican)	52	50	24	12
Corn tortilla, with pinto beans and tomato sauce (Mexican)	39	100	23	9
Corn tortilla, fried, with mashed potato, tomato and lettuce (Mexican)	78	100	15	11
Nopal (prickly pear cactus)	7	100	6	0
Pinto beans, boiled in salted water	14	150	25	4
Wheat tortilla (Mexican)	30	50	26	8
Wheat tortilla with pinto beans and tomato sauce (Mexican)	28	100	18	5

✳ indicates that the food has so little carbohydrate that the GI cannot be tested. The GL is therefore 0.
▲ indicates brand not specified

FURTHER READING: SOURCES AND REFERENCES

Tables of GI Values

Foster-Powell K, Holt SHA, Brand-Miller JC (2002). 'International table of glycemic index and glycemic load values: 2002', *American Journal of Clinical Nutrition* 76:5–56.

GI Recommendations

American Diabetes Association (2001). 'Nutrition recommendations and principles for people with diabetes mellitus', *Diabetes Care* 24(S1).

The Diabetes and Nutrition Study Group (DNSG) of the European Association for the Study of Diabetes (EASD) (2000). 'Recommendations for the nutritional management of patients with diabetes mellitus', *European Journal of Clinical Nutrition* 54:353–355.

Dietitians Association of Australia review paper (1997). 'Glycaemic index in diabetes management', *Australian Journal of Nutrition and Dietetics* 54(2):57–63.

Food and Agriculture Organisation/World Health Organisation (1998). 'Carbohydrates in Human Nutrition, Report of a Joint FAO/WHO Expert Consultation', Rome, 14–18 April 1997. FAO Food and Nutrition Paper 66.

National Health and Medical Research Council (1999). 'Dietary Guidelines for Older Australians', *Ausinfo*, Canberra.

Position Statement by the Canadian Diabetes Association (1999). 'Guidelines for the nutritional management of diabetes mellitus in the new millenium', *Canadian Journal of Diabetes Care* 23(3):56–69.

GI and Health—General

Frost G and Dornhorst A (2000). 'The relevance of the glycaemic index to our understanding of dietary carbohydrates', *Diabetic Medicine* 17:336–45.

Jenkins DJA, Kendall CWC, Augustin LSA et al (2002). 'Glycemic index: overview of implications in health and disease', *American Journal of Clinical Nutrition* 76:266S–273S.

Ludwig DS (2002). 'The glycemic index. Physiological mechanisms relating to obesity, diabetes, and cardiovascular disease', *Journal of the American Medical Association* 287:2414–2423.

Ludwig DS, Eckel RH (2002). 'The glycemic index at 20y', *American Journal of Clinical Nutrition* 76:264S–265S.

Pi-Sunyer FX (2002). 'Glycemic index and disease', *American Journal of Clinical Nutrition* 76:290S–298S.

GI and Diabetes

Buyken AE, Toeller M, Heitkamp G, Karamanos B, Rottiers R, Muggeo M, Fuller JH and the EURODIAB IDDM Complications Study Group (2001). 'Glycemic index in the diet of European outpatients with type 1 diabetes: relations to glycated hemoglobin and serum lipids', *American Journal of Clinical Nutrition* 73:574–81.

Giacco R, Parillo M, Rivellese AA, Lasorella G, Giacco A, D'episcopo L, Riccardi G (2000). 'Long-term dietary treatment with increased amounts of fibre-rich low-glycemic index natural foods improves blood glucose control and reduces the number of hypoglycemic events in type 1 diabetic patients', *Diabetes Care* 23:1461–6.

Gilbertson HR, Brand-Miller JC, Thorburn AW, Evans S, Chondros P, Werther GA (2001). 'The effect of flexible low glycemic index dietary advice versus measured carbohydrate exchange diets on glycemic control in children with type 1 diabetes', *Diabetes Care* 24:1137–43.

Salmeron J, Ascherio A, Rimm EB et al (1997). 'Dietary fiber, glycemic load, and risk of NIDDM in men', *Diabetes Care* 20:545–50.

Salmeron J, Manson JE, Stampfer MF, Colditz GA, Wing AL, Willett WC (1997). 'Dietary fiber, glycemic load, and risk of non-insulin-dependent diabetes mellitus in women', *Journal of the American Medical Association* 277:472–477.

Willett W, Manson J, Liu S (2002). 'Glycemic index, glycemic load, and risk of type 2 diabetes', *American Journal of Clinical Nutrition* 76:274S–280S.

GI and Obesity

Agus MSD, Swain JF, Larson CL, Eckert EA, Ludwig DS (2000). 'Dietary composition and physiologic adaptations to energy restriction', *American Journal of Clinical Nutrition* 71:901–7.

Brand-Miller JC, Holt SHA, Pawlak DB, McMillan J (2002). 'Glycemic index and obesity', *American Journal of Clinical Nutrition* 76:281S–285S.

Ludwig DS (2000). 'Dietary glycemic index and obesity', *Journal of Nutrition* 130:280S–83S.

Ludwig DS, Majzoub JA, Al-Zahrani A, Dallal GE, Blanco I, Roberts SB (1999). 'High glycemic index foods, overeating, and obesity', *Pediatrics* 103(3).

Spieth LE, Harnish JD, Lenders CM, Raezer LB, Pereira MA, Hangen J, Ludwig DS (2000). 'A low-glycemic index diet in the treatment of pediatric obesity', *Archives of Pediatric and Adolescent Medicine* 154:947–51.

GI and Heart Disease

Dumesnil JG, Turgeon J, Tremblay A et al (2001). 'Effect of a low-glycaemic index-low-fat-high protein diet on the atherogenic metabolic risk profile of abdominally obese men', *British Journal of Nutrition* 86:557–568.

Ford ES, Liu S (2001). 'Glycemic index and serum high-density-lipoprotein cholesterol concentration among US adults', *Archives of Internal Medicine* 161:572–6.

Frost G, Leeds A, Dore D, Madeiros S, Brading S, Dornhorst A (1999). 'Glycaemic index as a determinant of serum HDL-cholesterol concentration', *Lancet* 353:1045–48.

Leeds AR (2002). 'Glycemic index and heart disease', *American Journal of Clinical Nutrition* 76:286S–289S.

Liu S, Manson JE, Buring JE, Stampfer MJ, Willett WC, Ridker PM (2002). 'Relation between a diet with a high glycemic load and plasma concentrations of high-sensitivity C-reactive protein in middle-aged women', *American Journal of Clinical Nutrition* 75:492–498.

Liu S, Manson JE, Stampfer MJ, Holmes MD, Hu FB, Hankinson SE, Willett WC (2001). 'Dietary glycemic load assessed by food-frequency questionnaire in relation to plasma high-density-lipoprotein cholesterol and fasting plasma triacylglycerols in postmenopausal women', *American Journal of Clinical Nutrition* 73:560–6.

Liu S, Willett WC, Stampfer MJ, Hu FB, Franz M, Sampson L, Hennekens CH, Manson JE (2000). 'A prospective study of dietary glycemic load, carbohydrate intake and risk of coronary heart disease in US women', *American Journal of Clinical Nutrition* 71:1455–61.

GI and Colon Cancer

Bruce WR, Wolever TMS, Giacca A (2000). 'Mechanisms linking diet and colorectal cancer: the possible role of insulin resistance', *Nutrition and Cancer* 37:19–26.

Franceschi S, Dal Maso L, Augustin L, Negri E, Parpinel M, Boyle P, Jenkins DJA, La Vecchia C (2001). 'Dietary glycemic load and colorectal cancer risk', *Annals of Oncology* 12:1–6.

INDEX

RECIPE INDEX